## Praise for Kathy Lynn Emerson's *Historical Mysteries*

"An enjoyable, tightly plotted gem of a novel which will keep the reader guessing until the very last page."
— *I Love a Mystery*
(on *Face Down Beside St. Anne's Well*)

"Emerson vividly portrays daily life in an age that most readers know only from high school history books."
— *Bangor* [Maine] *Daily News*
(on *Fatal as a Fallen Woman*)

"Emerson's plot is deft and complex; she is at the top of her form here and leaves us with a breathless ending and lovely possibilities for future installments."
— *Booklist*
(on *Face Down Below the Banqueting House*)

"A thoroughly satisfying historical mystery… I can't wait for the next one."
— *Cozies, Capers & Crimes*
(on *Deadlier Than the Pen*)

"Expertly written and plotted stories…offer a feast for history buffs."
— *Ellery Queen's Mystery Magazine*
(on *Murders and Other Confusions*)

"Exploiting the chaos for its criminal possibilities, Emerson poses enduringly hard questions about women and worth in this exemplary historical mystery."
— *Kirkus Reviews* (starred)
(on *Face Down Below the Wych Elm*)

"A solid bet for historical mystery fans."
— *Publishers Weekly*
(on *Face Down Among the Winchester Geese*)

How To Write Killer
Historical Mysteries

ALSO BY KATHY LYNN EMERSON

LADY APPLETON MYSTERIES
  *Face Down In the Marrow-Bone Pie*
  *Face Down Upon an Herbal*
  *Face Down Among the Winchester Geese*
  *Face Down Beneath the Eleanor Cross*
  *Face Down Under the Wych Elm*
  *Face Down Before Rebel Hooves*
  *Face Down Across the Western Sea*
  *Face Down Below the Banqueting House*
  *Face Down Beside St. Anne's Well*
  *Face Down O'er the Border*

  *Murders and Other Confusions* (short stories)

DIANA SPAULDING MYSTERIES
  *Deadlier Than the Pen*
  *Fatal as a Fallen Woman*
  *No Mortal Reason*

NONFICTION
  *Writer's Guide to Everyday Life in Renaissance England*
  *Wives and Daughters: The Women of Sixteenth-Century England*

Kathy Lynn Emerson

# How To Write Killer Historical Mysteries

## The Art & Adventure of
## Sleuthing Through the Past

2008 · Perseverance Press / John Daniel & Company
Palo Alto / McKinleyville, California

A PERSEVERANCE PRESS BOOK
Published by John Daniel & Company
A division of Daniel & Daniel, Publishers, Inc.
Post Office Box 2790
McKinleyville, California 95519
www.danielpublishing.com/perseverance

Distributed by SCB Distributors (800) 729-6423
For information concerning quantity discounts for educational institutions, writing groups, conferences,
    etc., call 1–800–662–8351

Book design by Eric Larson, Studio E Books, Santa Barbara, www.studio-e-books.com

Cover painting by Linda Weatherly S.

10 9 8 7 6 5 4 3 2 1

LIBRARY OF CONGRESS CATALOGING-IN-PUBLICATION DATA
Emerson, Kathy Lynn.  How to write killer historical mysteries : the art and adventure of sleuthing through
the past / by Kathy Lynn Emerson.
     p. cm.
  ISBN-13: 978-1-880284-92-6 (pbk. : alk. paper)
  ISBN-10: 1-880284-92-8 (pbk. : alk. paper)
1. Detective and mystery stories—Authorship.  2. Historical fiction—Authorship.  I. Title.
  PN3377.5.D4E44 2008
  808.3'81—dc22
                    2007029250

# Contents

## 3. Researching the Historical Mystery—Primary Sources

## 4. Further Research—Secondary Sources

## 5. Creating a Believable Historical Detective

## 11. Case Study—Face Down Upon an Herbal

## 12. Historical Mystery Short Stories

## 13. Selling Your Historical Mystery Novel

## 14. Getting the Word out to Historical Mystery Readers

# Preface

THIS book is my personal take on how to write historical mysteries, based on over thirty years in print as a writer of fiction and nonfiction and the publication of fourteen historical mysteries in two different series, a collection of historical mystery short stories, three novels of historical romantic suspense, and three contemporary mysteries. My experience is the core of the book; the remainder of the text consists of contributions from my fellow historical mystery writers—advice, opinions, anecdotes, and suggestions for research—and input from assorted editors, booksellers, reviewers, and historical mystery fans. I owe a great debt to all of them for their generosity.

I have included a number of Internet addresses (URLs) in the text. These were accurate and the websites were active as of early 2007, but I make no guarantees beyond that. Information about libraries, book sales, and promotion applies to the situation in the U.S. in 2007 and may or may not apply elsewhere or in later years.

You will notice that there is a considerable number of references to historical mysteries I have written. This is not gratuitous self-promotion. In fact, I made an effort to use examples from the books of other historical mystery writers whenever possible. However, it only made sense to illustrate certain points with examples from the books I know best. When it was necessary to give away significant plot details, or even reveal whodunit, to make a point, I chose to spoil the suspense in one of my own novels rather than compromise the reader's enjoyment of someone else's mystery.

Quotations from novels and published interviews are identified and acknowledged in the text, as are comments, anecdotes, and tips from writers solicited specifically for this work. You will find more detailed citations for my published and online sources in the bibliography at the end of this volume. Lists of historical mystery titles written by contributing authors are included in the Sampling of Historical Mysteries that follows Chapter Fourteen.

Whether you are an old hand at writing historical mysteries, or a neophyte who has only dreamed about delving into the past, or a reader and fan of the genre, I hope you will find inspiration and entertainment here.

*How To Write Killer
Historical Mysteries*

# CHAPTER 1

# Historical Mysteries— An Introduction to the Genre

BECAUSE you are reading this book, you have probably already given some thought to the idea of writing historical mysteries. You may have progressed beyond just thinking about it. If not, now is the time to take up pencil and paper or sit down at your computer keyboard and get serious. *How To Write Killer Historical Mysteries* offers practical advice on the entire process, along with tips from some of the hardest-working writers in the genre.

Chapters Two through Twelve deal with the how-to aspects of writing a historical mystery, and Chapters Thirteen and Fourteen tell how to sell and publicize it. Before moving on to the nuts and bolts, however, a few definitions are in order. The historical mystery genre contains immense variety. In addition, several other types of fiction actually make use of elements of the historical mystery.

## What Are Historical Mysteries?

Historical mystery fiction is a subgenre of mystery fiction that makes special demands on the writer. It is not just fiction, not just mystery, and not just historical. To be successful, historical mysteries must blend all three elements.

### Fiction

Initially, I didn't think I'd need to define fiction. The difference between fiction (stories made up by the author) and nonfiction (true accounts) seems pretty straightforward…on the surface. However, the categories of docudramas, books "based on a true story," and at least some memoirs, make the waters murkier.

Historical mysteries are fiction, written to entertain. Yes, the writer does research in order to get the historical background right. Real historical figures may appear. Real events may play a significant role in the plot. But the writer's goal in a work of fiction is to suspend disbelief. The reader should believe, while reading, that the events in the work of fiction *might* have happened. If the story is a mystery based on a real murder, the reader should believe events could have fallen out the way the writer says they did. But neither the writer nor the reader should come away from the experience thinking this was a factually accurate account of what really happened.

### *Mystery*

Historical mysteries have to be mysteries, but what are mysteries? The definition I used when I began my writing career came from that classic college text, Thrall, Hibbard, and Holman's *A Handbook to Literature*: "works of prose fiction in which the element of mystery or terror plays a controlling part." Included were detective stories, gothic novels, suspense novels, spy stories, crime stories, and woman-in-jeopardy stories. For many people, however, only novels of detection are true mysteries. Thrillers, novels of suspense, capers, and the like are considered related but separate types of fiction. According to *A Handbook to Literature*, a detective story is "a novel or short story in which a crime, usually a murder—the identity of the perpetrator unknown—is solved by a detective through a logical assembling and interpretation of palpable evidence, known as clues," but the editor adds that "in practice much variation occurs."

More recent definitions are no more satisfactory, although bibliographer Jill H. Vassilakos has come up with one I rather like. She defines a mystery as "a book in which a crime is suspected and the action of the plot is driven by an attempt to identify the perpetrator." She devised this definition in order to exclude quest novels and put the focus on crime.

There is a difference, too, between a novel containing a mystery or mystery elements and a mystery novel. Take Dorothy Dunnett's six-volume masterpiece, known collectively as The Lymond Chronicles, for example. These novels have a mystery at their core, solved in the last few pages of the last book, but neither separately nor collectively are they historical mysteries. In a mystery novel the focus must stay on the mystery aspect.

**Cozy and Hard-Boiled** The terms *cozy* and *hard-boiled* are often used to distinguish between two radically different types of mystery novel. No one really agrees on what either means and they do not work well in defining historical mysteries. That said, you may find it helpful in the planning stages, and again at the marketing stage, to understand what they seem to mean to most people.

The annual meeting of cozy-mystery fans, Malice Domestic, calls itself "a convention of fans and authors who gather…to celebrate the traditional mystery." By that they mean books and short stories typified by the works of Agatha Christie. This subgenre has "no excessive gore, gratuitous violence, or explicit sex," and is made up of mysteries that often, but not always, feature an amateur sleuth, a confined setting, and characters who know one another.

If the cozy descends from the work of Agatha Christie, the hard-boiled detective is the child of early twentieth-century private-eye novels, exemplified by Dashiell Hammett and Raymond Chandler. Hard-boiled mystery fiction, sometimes called *noir*, usually features a professional detective, either a private eye or someone employed in law enforcement. In contrast to cozies, these novels don't hesitate to provide all the gruesome details (aka "gritty reality") of the crime scene. There may also be scenes of graphic sex and/or violence.

As generalizations, the terms *cozy* and *hard-boiled* are useful—it is good to know where on the spectrum your writing falls—but they can also create perception problems. I consider my novels to be historical cozies, but while the word *cozy* is a recommendation to some readers, others regard it as a pejorative term.

Asked in a 2003 magazine interview if cozies are still as popular as they once were, veteran historical mystery writer Elizabeth Peters replied that "cozies are timeless." In her opinion, the genre has always been popular and will continue to be, but is "critically overshadowed by so-called realistic books."

Some reviewers do seem to have a bias against cozies, even when they manage to overcome their feelings long enough to lavish praise on a specific book. Dick Adler's comments in the Chicago *Tribune* are an example: "Part of the problem is that many cozies tend to veer toward the corner of Coy and Cute—a place I'd normally walk a mile to avoid. Giving the lead character an arcane hobby or occupation doesn't make up for a distinct shortage of narrative skill or basic literary ability."

Which historical mysteries are definitely *not* cozies? I asked this question of the CrimeThruTime Internet group at Yahoo.com (henceforth referred to as CTT) and although most were not sure the term *hard-boiled* was any more appropriate than *cozy*, they did come up with a number of examples. Walter Mosley's Easy Rawlins series, set in the U.S. in the 1940s and '50s, led the list, followed by David Liss's *Conspiracy of Paper* and *A Spectacle of Corruption*, which take place in 1720s London. Other suggestions were Arturo Perez-Reverte's series set in early seventeenth-century Spain, Oakley Hall's *Ambrose Bierce and the Death of Kings* set in 1890s San Francisco, David Wishart's Roman series, Bill Pronzini's Carpenter and Quincannon series set in the American West in the 1890s, Maureen Jennings's 1890s Toronto-based series featuring police detective William Murdoch, and Kris Nelscott's Smokey Dalton series set in the 1960s.

Keep in mind that the boundaries are flexible. Some historical mystery series move freely back and forth across the hard-boiled line. Anne Perry's William Monk series is not particularly cozy (although *The Face of a Stranger* and *Defend and Betray* were both nominated for Malice Domestic's Agatha Award). Her Thomas and Charlotte Pitt series, decidedly cozy in the early volumes, becomes much darker in later novels. Novels such as those in Steven Saylor's *Roma Sub Rosa* series and P.F. Chisholm's Sir Robert Carey series, set in the 1590s, also straddle the line.

The term *soft-boiled* has been bandied about to describe novels that aren't entirely cozies but aren't quite hard-boiled either. It has the same problems the other terms do—it doesn't quite fit historical mysteries. The best advice I can give is to be aware of these labels but avoid being confined by them as much as possible. Write the sort of mystery you'd like to read.

***Stand-Alones and Series*** One further mystery definition needs to be taken into account early in the writing process. When mysteries are published they tend to be classified as either *stand-alones* or part of a series. Sometimes a stand-alone later becomes a series, but if you are *planning* to write a series, then you need to think in those terms from the beginning. Since you will be proposing your novel to an editor as the first book in a series, you need to know where that series is going.

The stand-alone, once in a great while, turns into a blockbuster. Among historical mysteries, Umberto Eco's *The Name of the Rose* (1327 Italy), Caleb Carr's *The Alienist* (1896 New York City), and Elizabeth Kostova's *The Historian* (1970s/1930s Europe) are big books in more than one sense. If you look at most of what is published as historical mystery in the U.S., however, it is obvious that big, single-title, bestselling books are not typical of the genre. In fact, most historical mysteries are much shorter. And an overwhelming number of historical mysteries are series books. When a writer creates a successful sleuth, both publishers and readers want to see more of that character. After Caleb Carr's success with *The Alienist*, even he wrote a sequel.

### Historical

Historical mysteries are set in the past. That means a book that takes place entirely in the present day, even though it solves a mystery from the past, is not a historical mystery. Josephine Tey's *The Daughter of Time*, though a classic, is not a historical mystery. Detective Alan Grant, recovering from an accident in a hospital, becomes intrigued by a portrait of Richard III and sets out to prove him innocent of murdering his nephews in the fifteenth century, but there are no scenes taking place in that earlier era. Grant studies old records and portraits, uses a research assistant, and reasons out a solution to the crime.

Mysteries with dual timelines, sometimes called present/past mysteries, come closer to qualifying as historical mysteries. These usually feature characters in the present but take the reader into one or more past times for a significant portion of the novel. Katherine Neville did this in *The Eight*. The story moves back and forth between 1972 (contemporary, since it was first published in 1988) and 1790. In general, present/past novels are not classed as historicals, but the portions set in the past certainly require the same skills and techniques to create as more traditional historical mysteries.

### How Close to "Now" Can Historicals Be Set?

How far back in time must a work of fiction take place in order to be considered historical? Whether a given novel or short story is historical or not depends in part on the publication date. Mysteries that were contemporary when they were written but are, for us, set in a bygone era—novels by Agatha Christie and her contemporaries, and the original Sherlock Holmes stories, for example—are not historical mysteries. Christie wrote only one historical mystery novel, *Death Comes as the End*, set in Ancient Egypt.

Mysteries written today and set in Christie's heyday or that of Sir Arthur Conan Doyle *are* historicals. If you want a specific date—*x* years ago is historical; more recent than that is not—there are several available. Most definitions of historical mysteries assign an arbitrary cut-off date. *Murder in Retrospect: A Selective Guide to Historical Mystery Fiction* excludes any mystery by a contemporary writer set later than World War II. Guidelines for novels nominated for the Bruce Alexander History Mystery Award state that they must be set more than fifty years before their publication date.

A poll for members of CTT offered nine choices in defining what makes a mystery "historical." When tallied in early 2007, 35% of the votes went to "when a writer makes a specific effort to recreate a time period" and 17% to "any era prior to the one it is written in." In third place, with 15% of the votes, was "fifty years or more before its original publishing date."

A definition most readers can live with classifies a mystery as historical if it takes place in a time that is clearly distinct from our own. Given technological advances during the last few decades, this could include any date before computers and cell phones came into general use. Kim Malo, who maintains the CTT website and moderates the Yahoo.com group, makes a case for calling a novel historical set as late as 1975. "Technological, social, and political changes have made that a past that truly *is* another country. Just think of how much...didn't exist then or was extremely rare." And she goes on to ask, "How many people today have never seen or heard an LP?"

Is the milieu in which the mystery is set significantly different from the time in which it was created? That's really the key question for the writer. Whether you are setting your mystery in Roman Britain or in Viet Nam in the 1960s, the following chapters will show you how to take the germ of an idea and turn it into a historical mystery. If you already know what you want to write about and are anxious to get started, feel free at this point to skip ahead to Chapter Two. The definitions below are intended to give readers who are less certain a sense of just how far-reaching the boundaries of historical mystery can be.

## Specialized Areas

This book is designed to teach the reader how to write historical mystery fiction. For most people that means novels intended for an adult audience. There are also short stories, for which see Chapter Twelve. In addition, there are mysteries written with a younger reader in mind, and plays and screenplays.

### Historical Mysteries for Young Readers

The vast majority of historical mysteries are written for an adult audience, although many of them are read by teenagers and reviewed in *School Library Journal* as if they were YA (Young Adult) novels. The genre also includes historical mysteries written specifically for children and for young adults. The Edgar Award (from Mystery Writers of America) for Best Juvenile Mystery went to Cynthia Voight in 1984 for *The Callender Papers*, a novel set in nineteenth-century Massachusetts; to Barbara Brooks Wallace in 1994 for *The Twin in the Tavern*, set in Victorian times; and to Elizabeth McDavid Jones in 2000 for *The Night Flyers*, set in 1918. Jones's *Ghost Light on Graveyard Shoal* was an Agatha finalist in 2004. MWA also awards an Edgar for Best Young Adult Mystery.

Several other juvenile and YA historical mysteries have also been nominated for mystery awards. Edgar nominations went to Avi's *The Man Who Was Poe*, Patricia Finney's *Assassin*, Charlie Higson's *Young Bond, Book One: Silverfin*, D. James Smith's *The Boys of San Joaquin*, and Kathleen Ernst's *Trouble at Fort Lapointe*. Ernst's *Betrayal at Cross Creek* and *Whistler in the Dark* were nominated for the Agatha, as were Elise Weston's *The Coast Watcher* and Sarah Masters Buckley's *The Curse of Ravenscroft*. All the Ernst books and several other nominated titles were published under the banner of the American Girl History Mysteries. These are set in a variety of time periods.

A list of historical mysteries for young people can be found online at http://members.tripod.com/BrerFox/Kids_YA/historicalmystery.html

### Historical Mystery Plays and Screenplays

Since plays and screenplays do occasionally fit the three-part definition of *fiction*, *mystery*, and *historical*, I include them here as a category but I will not be discussing how to write them. Although those who wish to write for stage or screen may find some of the material in the following chapters useful, scriptwriting is a specialized area beyond the scope of this book.

Not many historical mysteries *are* written directly for stage or screen. Although Shakespeare's *Hamlet* is sometimes cited as being a mystery as well as a revenge tragedy, I don't believe it can properly be termed historical. For all intents and purposes, Shakespeare's "Denmark" was contemporaneous with late sixteenth-century England. Most other examples that spring readily to mind, such as Ellis Peters's Cadfael mysteries on PBS's *Mystery!*, have been adapted from novels. An outstanding exception is *Gosford Park*, which won its writer, Julian Fellowes, an Academy Award for Best Original Screenplay.

## Variations

Three separate types of cross-genre novel make use of the same skills and techniques one needs in order to write historical mysteries.

### Historical Romantic Suspense

By a variety of names—"Woman in Jeopardy" was popular for quite a while—this type of fiction has been around for a long time. It combines mystery, romance, and historical settings.

I wrote a few of these myself back in the 1990s, all set in the sixteenth century. *Winter Tapestry*, *Unquiet Hearts*, and *The Green Rose* are murder mysteries as well as romance novels. In fact, *Winter Tapestry* was the prototype for my Face Down series. Initially I attempted to sell it as a mystery and was busily collecting rejection slips when an editor suggested that if I added 30,000 words and beefed up the romance elements, she could buy it as a historical romance. I did, she did, and I continued to write historical romantic suspense until I could no longer resist the urge to try my hand at historical mystery again. "Cordell Allington" from *Winter Tapestry* became an older, less happily married "Susanna Appleton" in *Face Down In the Marrow-Bone Pie*.

Some of the best examples of historical romantic suspense written today are by Amanda Quick, who also writes contemporary romantic suspense under her real name, Jayne Ann Krentz. Three of the Quick novels, set in nineteenth-century England, regularly turn up on historical mystery lists, since they feature a sleuthing couple, Lavinia Lake and Tobias March, and can thus be classed as a series. Others of Quick's novels contain just as much mystery but are shelved as romance.

Quick considers romantic suspense "a genre unto itself" and feels it should have its own section in bookstores, but she is a realist. "That is not the case," she says, "and it is highly unlikely that it will ever be the case. Authors, publishers, and bookstore people are, therefore, faced with a dilemma. You either put the books in the romance section or you put them in the mystery section. Now, here are the facts of bookselling life: the romance genre is bigger than the mystery genre. It has more readers and it sells more books. In addition, romance readers are far more likely to read a book with suspense in it than mystery readers are to wander over to the romance section."

If you are planning to write historical mysteries with a strong romance element, keep this caveat in mind as you read the chapters that follow. At some point you will have to choose whether to emphasize mystery or romance in marketing your manuscript. Romance Writers of America makes a point of keeping track of the percentage of the market romance sales command. Statistics compiled from Ipsos Book Trends, Book Industry Study Group, American Booksellers Association reports, and tallies in Ingram's catalogue of all book releases indicate that Romance Fiction comprised 39.3% of all popular fiction sales in 2004. Mystery/Detective/Suspense fiction accounted for 29.6%. Science Fiction/Fantasy sales were 6.4%, while General Fiction came in at 12.9% of all popular fiction sold in the United States in that year.

Modern historical romantic suspense descends from the romantic suspense novels, misnamed "gothics," of the 1960s and 1970s. Many have contemporary settings, but among the bestsellers of that era were a number of historicals by Victoria Holt and Phyllis A. Whitney. The first Barbara Michaels novel, *The Master of Blacktower* (1853 Scotland), is classic historical romantic suspense. In a *Publishers Weekly* interview with Michaels, who also writes historical mystery as Elizabeth Peters, the interviewer, summarizing both the Michaels and the Peters books, calls them "novels featuring female protagonists who survive danger and solve mysteries with wit, good humor and, usually, good fortune in romance."

Until the 1990s, historical romantic suspense novels were never sexually explicit. Today they often contain long, detailed love scenes—what many mystery readers would consider graphic sex—although it is still rare for one to include much violence. Some pre-1990 novels also featured paranormal elements. Today's gothic is not prudish about either sex or violence and the focus in many of them is again on the supernatural.

### Paranormal Historical Mysteries

Paranormal historical mysteries come in endless variety. What some readers call "woo-woo" elements include the use of vampires, ghosts, werewolves, witches, wizards, immortals, and time travelers as characters. Many of these books, the ones with minimal sex and violence, regularly turn up on YA reading lists, even though they were written with an adult audience in mind. This isn't too surprising. Even before the advent of Harry Potter, children liked to read about magic and things that go bump in the night.

Vampires aren't hard to find in mystery fiction, although they are somewhat more scarce in the historical variety. Jack Fleming, P.N. Elrod's vampire sleuth, operates a nightclub in 1930s Chicago. The first of Barbara Hambly's two books featuring Oxford professor James Asher, *Those Who Hunt the Night*, is set in 1907 in England. Asher is called upon to find out who is killing London's vampires, assisted by a vampire who has been "living" there since the days of Elizabeth I. *An Ancient Evil* by P.C. Doherty deals with a demon who drinks blood and is loose in medieval Oxford.

More recent is *The Historian*, in which the underlying motivation for the characters is to find out the truth about Dracula. Elizabeth Kostova's novel, although perhaps more quest than mystery, uses the present/past structure, telling part of the story through events that occur in 1972 and part in letters from earlier dates. In most books, simply including the contents of old letters would not be enough to take the reader into a past time, but here the letters are long narratives that create a novel within the novel.

Under the name Ann Dukthas, P.C. Doherty wrote four mysteries featuring Nicholas Segalla, starting with *A Time for the Death of a King* (1994), which investigates a crime from 1567. Segalla has lived in many time periods, and the other books in the series take him ahead to 1815 and 1899 and back to 1558.

Alanna Knight has written several mysteries featuring Tam Eildor, a time traveler from the twenty-third century, who solves mysteries in various eras. In the first, *The Dagger in the Crown* set in 1566, Tam has amnesia and doesn't know why he is able to predict the future. Other books in this series are set in 1660 and 1811.

I have mentioned present/past mysteries. Many of them also fall into the paranormal category by virtue of employing supernatural means to transport readers to the past. Time travel can work in this way; so can ghosts and reincarnation.

A variant on the ghost element creates an interesting and unique sleuthing team in Charles Todd's Inspector Ian Rutledge (a victim of shell shock during World War I) and Corporal Hamish MacLeod. Rutledge returns to Scotland Yard in 1919 with a voice in his head, that of Hamish, a dead soldier.

There are far too many examples of paranormal elements in historical mysteries to mention all of them here, but one more does deserve to be singled out. Sharan Newman ordinarily bases her Catherine LeVendeur mysteries, set in twelfth-century France, firmly in the real world. In *The Witch in the Well* she departed from this practice by introducing several supernatural scenes, all of them essential to the solution of the mystery. The book won the Bruce Alexander History Mystery Award in 2005.

### Alternate History Mysteries

Distinct from paranormal historical mysteries are alternate history mysteries. It has been suggested that all paranormal mysteries could be considered alternate history. And that historical mysteries in which the sleuth is a real person also belong in this subgenre. The true definition is somewhat different: alternate history mysteries are those historical mysteries in which the detecting is done in a world different from our own *because some historical event has been altered.*

Randall Garrett's Lord Darcy mysteries, set in an England made great by Richard the Lionheart's long, prosperous reign, are alternate history and mysteries and they certainly have a historical *feel* to them, but they are *not* historical mysteries. The novels and short stories take place in an alternate *present* where the Plantagenets still rule and magic really works. Those that are dated are set in the same year Garrett wrote them.

The best examples I've found of true alternate history *historical* mysteries are the books by Robert Barnard writing as Bernard Bastable. In these, Mozart does not die young. Instead he lives to a ripe old age, thus enabling him to solve mysteries in England during the early nineteenth century.

## Enough with the Definitions, Already!

I could go on giving definitions and examples, but if you bought this book because you want to write your own historical mystery, you don't need any more. You've been reading historical mysteries, probably for years now. You know what you like and what drives you crazy in other people's books. You're looking for practical advice on how to craft your own entry into the genre.

Chapter Two awaits.

# 2 *When, Where, Who, What, and What Do You Call It?*

IF YOU'RE considering writing historical mysteries, you've probably already given some thought to the when, the where, and the who. You may know what crime your sleuth will solve. You may even have a title picked out. If you don't, now is the time to move from vague to specific in all these areas.

## When

Since these are historical novels, the "when" comes first for most people. If you want to write a book that historical mystery fans will enjoy, you must know and love the era in which your story is set. It isn't enough to dress the characters in period costumes and toss in a few details of everyday life. Readers want to be transported to the world your characters inhabit. Even if your plot has no connection to the political, military, or religious controversies of your chosen time period, your characters don't live in a vacuum. To give an extreme example—if you are toying with an idea for a murder mystery set during the French Revolution but don't want to deal with mob violence and executions by guillotine, consider a different setting!

### Popular Pasts

What are the most popular periods for historical mysteries? A poll taken at CrimeThruTime gave participants nineteen choices, from "Ancient Egypt" to "1960s and more modern." This is a small sampling of readers, only a few hundred, but it will perhaps give some indication of reader preferences. The favorites were "Medieval" with 12% of the votes, "Ancient Roman/Roman Empire" with 9%, "Victorian" with 8%, and "Ancient Egypt" and "Renaissance" tied at 7% each.

Booksellers see similar trends. Robin Agnew of Aunt Agatha's Mystery Bookshop (Ann Arbor, Michigan) ranks them this way: Victorian, Renaissance/Medieval, Civil War ("oddly, these are mostly male readers"), and World War I ("thanks to Winspear, Todd, Airth"). She adds: "I personally enjoy Revolutionary War series, but these don't seem to go as well as some others." Jim Huang of The Mystery Company (Carmel, Indiana) lists "the obvious: medieval, Victorian, Elizabethan, Regency—basically most all English history—plus Ancient Rome." Deb Andolino, whose brick-and-mortar store in South Carolina, Aliens and Alibis, has now, sadly, closed (she's still on the Web), listed her customers' favorite time periods as the Victorian era, Ancient Rome, and "the Beau Brummel age," but added that "World War I is getting more popular." Dean James, former manager of Murder by the Book in Houston, listed "medieval, Victorian, Regency, and the ancient world, not necessarily in that order" and adds that "American historical mysteries are harder to sell. There have been several attempts at series set in colonial and post-colonial America, for example, and while some of the books were outstanding (like Margaret Lawrence's wonderful *Hearts and Bones*), readers seem less interested in American history."

Popular pasts are popular for a reason. However, if there are already series and stand-alones set in the period you're most interested in, it is probably a good idea to avoid the same years those authors have chosen to write about. You don't need to read all those novels. In fact, you probably shouldn't. But skim a sampling to get an idea of style, plot, characters, and so forth. And in particular, look at exactly *when* the books are set. If you are determined to enter an already crowded field, try not to make things any harder on yourself than you have to.

Then again, there's no way to second-guess which period is about to become popular. In 1993, when I started writing the first Face Down mystery, there were already several mystery series set in the sixteenth century. One, by Michael Clynes (one of the many P.C. Doherty pseudonyms), was set during the reign of Henry VIII. Three, by Edward Marston, Leonard Tourney, and P.F. Chisholm, were set toward the end of the Elizabethan era. The middle of the century did not appear to be in use, so I set my story in 1559, the first year of Elizabeth Tudor's reign.

Little did I know that in the same month my *Face Down In the Marrow-Bone Pie* came out in the U.S., the first book in Fiona Buckley's Elizabethan mystery series would appear in the U.K., with U.S. publication following a few months later. It is also set in 1559. A couple of years later, Karen Harper's series featuring Queen Elizabeth as the detective debuted, also set at the beginning of her reign. In the years since, possibly because of the popularity of *Shakespeare in Love* and several movie and television biographies of Elizabeth I, even more mystery series set in sixteenth-century England have appeared—Iris Collier's Lord Nicholas Peverell series and C.J. Sansom's Matthew Shardlake series (both set in the reign of Henry VIII); Judith Cook's Simon Forman series, John Pilkington's Thomas Finbow series, Martin Stephen's Henry Gresham series, and Peter Tonkin's Tom Musgrave series (all Elizabethan); and Shakespeare-related series from Leonard Tourney, Philip Gooden, and Simon Hawke. Also, Audrey Peterson's *Murder in Stratford* features Shakespeare's wife, Anne Hathaway, as sleuth.

Steven Saylor had a similar experience, which he recounts in an essay in *Mystery Readers Journal*: "When I started *Roman Blood*, I thought I was working on a fairly lonely patch of literary ground." By the time the book was published, however, six others, two of which would become mystery series, were also out: Colleen McCullough's *First Man in Rome*, Lindsey Davis's *Silver Pigs*, John Maddox Roberts's *SPQR*, Joan O'Hagan's *A Roman Death*, Ray Faraday Nelson's *Dogheaded Death*, and Ron Burns's *Roman Nights*. Saylor goes on to observe that "it's clear that none of the writers involved took inspiration from the others—it was just a curious coincidence that we all experienced a similar brain wave at roughly the same time."

This is not to say, of course, that you should simply select a period based on anyone else's likes and dislikes. You're the one who will be spending thousands of hours in the era you choose. You're the one who has to remain enthusiastic about it.

### Why That When?

There are as many reasons for choosing a "when" as there are time periods. Lauren Haney had been reading about Ancient Egypt for many years and "didn't have to think twice about where to set the Lieutenant Bak stories. Though the written history of Ancient Egypt spanned nearly 3000 years, narrowing that down to a specific time was equally easy. I'd long ago focused my interest on the early 18th Dynasty, especially the dual reign of Queen Hatshepsut and King Thutmose III and the following decades when he served as sole ruler of Egypt. I considered setting the stories during his reign (after Hatshepsut 'vanished from history,' as Egyptologists say); however, he was a warrior king. I didn't want Lieutenant Bak constantly marching off to war. I wanted my stories to be about the land and people of the Nile valley rather than ancient warfare. Therefore I set the stories midway in Hatshepsut's twenty-one-year dual reign with her nephew."

Patricia Wynn, who previously wrote about Regency England, chose the preceding early-Georgian era for her Blue Satan mystery series featuring a nobleman turned highwayman. The era has plenty of potential for murder and intrigue, thanks to the Jacobite rebellion and the schemes of the Pretender, but that was not why Wynn selected it. Rather, she was influenced by fond memories of her mother reading Alfred Noyes's poem "The Highwayman" to her when she was a child. She always knew she wanted the hero of her mysteries to be a highwayman but it wasn't until she started doing research on actual highwaymen in England that she discovered the period of their operation was the reign of George I.

Peter Lovesey, in the essay "Have You Tried Murder?" reveals that he "chanced on Victorian London almost accidentally. I was mainly interested in sport. It just happened that the sports event I used as background for *Wobble to Death* occurred in 1879." Lovesey expanded on this in an interview with Mystery Readers International (MRI): "People say you should write about what you know, so I wrote *Wobble to Death*, a whodunit using a Victorian long distance running race as the setting. The history of athletics had long been an interest of mine, and I'd published a nonfiction book on running the previous year." As it turned out, "the Victorian era had all I wanted: the hypocrisy, the die-hard institutions, the over-the-top characters, the brilliant entertainments, and the sense that life inside was comfortable and warm while the streets seethed with criminality and vice."

Carola Dunn jokes that she chose the 1920s for her Daisy Dalrymple mysteries on the same basis she selected the Regency period for her romances—comfortable clothing. But there is a practical reason behind that statement. Think about it—you're going to be telling a story from the point of view of people living in a certain era. In essence, you are going to be wearing what they wear.

Dunn set her series in the 1920s because "it was a period of flowering freedom for women." She continues,

> Apart from the social changes—forced by WWI—that allowed women to take a variety of jobs previously considered male territory, two particular aspects attracted me: the changes in transportation that made it possible for women to travel freely, and the clothes that allowed them to move freely in a different sense.
>
> For centuries, with brief relief during the Regency, women, or at least ladies, wore incredibly restrictive clothing. Georgian hoops forced them to turn sideways to go through a door; Victorian crinolines made them—in the words of Wilkie Collins— "take up the room of three men;" Edwardian fashions forced their bodies into the infamous "Grecian Bend;" all with corsets so restrictive it's no wonder girls fainted right, left, and center. The Great War started the change. By the 'Twenties, we can

recognize the beginnings of modern fashion. Any woman today could wear a '20s jersey "costume" by Coco Chanel without feeling as if she was wearing fancy dress. The hip-level waist returns periodically, and the current mania for thinness echoes the "no bosom, no bottom" boyish look. Though women still didn't normally wear trousers except for riding (astride, not sidesaddle!), sports clothes allowed those so inclined to play tennis and golf without getting entangled in ankle-length skirts. Daisy's figure will never comply with the fashionable ideal, but the clothes she wears in no way impede her movement. It seems to me this is a great advantage for an amateur sleuth!

### Narrowing Down the "When"

Once you decide you want to set your novel in a certain era, you need to narrow down the "when" still further. Pick a single year.

Dale Furutani got the idea for his Samurai Mystery Trilogy while visiting a seventeenth-century Japanese farmhouse in Yokohama. "I was sipping a steaming cup of green tea and marveling at floorboards worn glass smooth by centuries of bare feet crossing them," he recalls.

> It occurred to me that in fiction about ancient Japan, the people who lived in that farmhouse were often just stage props to some greater pageantry, such as the fight to become the Shogun. Yet they also had stories to tell, and I decided to tell at least some of them through the vehicle of a mystery trilogy.
>
> Having chosen the actors, my next decision was to select the time of the action. To most Japanese, the year 1603 has a familiarity to it like the year 1776 has to Americans. That is the year Ieyasu Tokugawa declared himself to be Shogun of Japan, and it marked a turning point in Japanese history. For the next 250 years, Japanese culture, politics, and the social order were regulated by the oppressive hand of the Tokugawa Shogunate. This period has been covered by many works of fiction and nonfiction, but I was interested in the hinge of history; that brief period when an entire nation was in the midst of a pervasive and profound change, before the Tokugawa Shogunate had extended its tentacles into every aspect of Japanese life.

Given the pacing a mystery novel demands, it is a good idea to continue to narrow your time frame to a limited period within the year you have chosen. If the investigation of the crime stretches out over too long a period, your story is likely to suffer.

Even if you don't share this information with your readers, it will help you in your plotting to know the actual date on which your story begins. You can find calendars for any year online or in an almanac. The dates of important historical events are easy to come by. As you read about your historical period, keep track of these. One may well trigger some significant action in your novel. In *Deadlier than the Pen*, the first of my Diana Spaulding Mysteries, I make considerable use of the Blizzard of 1888, which blew in on March 13, immobilizing New York City and most of New England for the best part of a week.

## Where

In discussing the "when," I've already touched on the "where." They often go together. Sixteenth-century England. Seventeenth-century Japan. Ancient Egypt under Hatshepsut. But the "where," like the "when," needs to be narrowed down.

In Lauren Haney's case, there was a good reason to get away from certain areas: "Most novels written about Ancient Egypt focus on royalty and nobility and are set in and around the palace. The elite classes represented a tiny percentage of the population, so those books paint a very unrealistic picture of Egypt as a whole. I decided to exile Lieutenant Bak to the southern frontier so I would not be tempted to make him walk the corridors of power." She adds that "after the first few books, the temptation faded away, and I could send him anywhere, including the capital, with barely a thought of the upper echelons of society."

As with the "when," consider what other mysteries are set in the same place. Weigh the popularity of a given location against the risk of being lost in a crowd. Since so many Victorian-era novels are set in England, Carole Nelson Douglas decided early on to set her Irene Adler mysteries elsewhere. *Good Night, Mr. Holmes* begins and ends in London but takes what Douglas calls "an adventurous detour." Subsequent mysteries solved by the American opera singer, the only woman ever to outwit Sherlock Holmes, start in Paris and take her to Monaco, Prague, Transylvania, and New York City.

When asked why she didn't keep the Adler series close to Holmes in London, Douglas replies that "Sir Arthur Conan Doyle wouldn't let me. 'A Scandal in Bohemia' opens with Irene Adler dead. Or so Watson says. The story ends with Irene fleeing London. To take up her tale, I had to send her somewhere. Paris seemed convenient. A presumed 'dead' woman couldn't gallivant back to London unless in disguise, so I gave her Continental cases. Watson often reported Holmes working solo for Europe's reigning families, so that kept the Irene/Sherlock rivalry going."

### Use a Real Place or Make One Up?

Whatever country you choose as a setting for your historical mystery, you'll need to decide on specific locations. Whether you use an urban setting or a rural one makes a tremendous difference, as does the decision to use a real place or invent one.

In her Silver Rush series featuring saloonkeeper Inez Stannert as sleuth, Ann Parker uses a real place, Leadville, Colorado, as her principal setting. As she recalls, it was "Leadville's rich and rowdy past that prompted me to try my hand at writing fiction, long before I'd ever visited the town.

> There are certainly pluses to inventing a town in which to wreak fictional murder and mayhem. You can name the streets to suit yourself. You can set it up in the mountains, down in the valleys, by a river, or in the desert. No one will write you to assert that you got your fictional town's geography and history "all wrong." For me, though, the pluses of working with an existing location and its history proved irresistible. Even if I were to create a fictional town, I would simply be hauling all the trappings of Leadville into it. I loved the names of streets and geographical landmarks: Stillborn Alley (behind the red light district), Carbonate Hill, California Gulch, Stray Horse Gulch, Mosquito Pass—history and real-life stories lurked behind every name.

Specific incidents in Leadville's history also called to Parker.

> There was the railroad war (complete with guns, barricades, and Bat Masterson) between the Denver & Rio Grande and the Atchison, Topeka, & Santa Fe over which would build the first line into this silver-rich region. Add to that the fact that, in 1880, the first train to town brought none other than Ulysses S. Grant and his entourage. How could I resist working these bits of real history into a story? And how could I pretend that it happened somewhere else? By the time I finished toting up all I wanted to steal from Leadville, I realized that what I *really* wanted was the town itself. It would have been a sham to put a different name to it.

Parker makes a pilgrimage to Leadville once or twice a year to look for telling details. She has walked through the graveyard, looking at the names on gravestones, and taken a tour through the opera house, built in 1879, and touched the original upholstery on the chairs. She has walked the streets—some of which are still boardwalks, just as in the 1880s—at different times of day. "As I strolled," she says, "I focused on those details that stay true over time. What is the light like? The sky at night? How cold is the air when you breathe and how does it feel on your face? What about the sound of footsteps on the boardwalks? I took copious notes and photographs. Those timeless sights and sensations helped bring the past alive when I sat down to write about it at home."

Even when you choose to use a real place, of course, there will be times when you must make something up. For *Iron Ties*, Parker wanted to use a particular gulch she'd discovered during her wanderings through the region. Unfortunately, although the spot is only a short drive from Leadville today, it would not be as easy to reach in 1880. "I needed a gulch," she recalls, "and it had to be less than a half-day's ride from town. I checked and rechecked all the appropriate areas closer in, feeling more desperate as time went on. This was too far, that was too close, this didn't have the right geological configuration. Finally, I gave up and invented Disappointment Gulch."

Parker's decision to use a real city for her setting has a lot to recommend it, but often it is impossible to find out much about the history of a particular place. Sometimes what is known is contradictory. For the Face Down and Diana Spaulding series I use a combination of real and fictional settings. For cities, I research what London or Denver or New York was like at that time and present it as faithfully as possible. For rural areas, however, I prefer to combine bits and pieces of real places to create something that suits my plot and characters. In the Face Down books, Lady Appleton's home, the fictional Leigh Abbey, is located in an extremely rural area of Kent. No detailed records exist concerning what was there in the sixteenth century. That gives me leave to make things up.

## Who

Choosing a sleuth takes into consideration both the "when" and the "where," since characters have to function believably in their historical milieu. Once again, it may be helpful to take a look at what's already out there in published books. Certain occupations work better than others for historical sleuths.

If you are writing about a time period when some kind of official police force existed, a male sleuth can be a member of that body. Or not. If not, you need a good reason for your protagonist to become involved in solving crimes. The amateur detective is an odd creature, especially in a historical mystery. The average person does not want to get involved in solving a crime, nor does the average person have the skills necessary to solve a mystery. This doesn't mean that an amateur can't appear in a historical mystery...just that you have to give the matter a great deal of careful thought.

Private investigators, by a variety of titles—Steven Saylor's "Gordianus the Finder," Lynda S. Robinson's "Eyes and Ears of Pharaoh," Laura Joh Rowland's "Most Honorable Investigator of Events, Situations, and People"—crop up in historical mysteries set in many eras. In *real* life, until the late nineteenth century, they all seem to have been men. The same is true of most agents sent to investigate crimes by a ruler or some other government official, although there are historical records of women employed as spies.

### Female Sleuths

If your detective is a woman, you need to think long and hard about how believable her actions will be, given the historical time and place you've chosen. That's not to say you can't use a female sleuth, simply that in writing about some eras you'll need to put a lot of effort into making it work. If you push your protagonist too far outside what was considered acceptable behavior for a woman, she won't be able to do much investigating. Not only will no one cooperate with her, she may end up in jail or be run out of town or at least be ostracized when she tries.

Roberta Gellis had been setting her romances in the twelfth and early-thirteenth centuries for ten years when she ventured into the historical mystery genre. She knew she wanted to use a medieval setting, but "the protagonist was a more difficult problem. In medieval times common people did not have the freedom of movement that they have today. One had to 'belong' somewhere. In particular a female...would be tied to duties in her household, with her husband and children. Moreover murder after murder in the same castle, village, or town, in which the lady was somehow involved, might put a serious strain on the reader's suspension of disbelief. Not to mention that the above-mentioned husband might have strong objections to his wife's detective activities."

Reluctant to add to the number of "holy ladies and gentlemen mixed up in murder," Gellis wanted "a lady without a husband or household and not bound to the Church, who was free to do what she liked and settled into circumstances that provided a large and varied human traffic." Because she intended to write a series, Gellis knew she'd also need murder victims who were "rich or powerful or both."

Given those requirements, the identity of her ideal sleuth was obvious.

Gellis made her "the madam of a very expensive and very elegant whore-house." Since she wanted her protagonist to have the speech and manners of a lady, she created "a background of life-threatening abuse from which she had escaped. Because I wanted my heroine to be vulnerable, but not completely at the mercy of anyone who wished to denounce her, I gave her two powerful protectors. And thus was born Magdalene la Bâtarde."

### Occupations for Amateur Sleuths

There are a number of logical occupations for amateur detectives in historical mysteries, chief among them physicians (Caroline Roe's Isaac of Gerona and C.L. Grace's Kathryn Swinbrooke), herbalists (Ellis Peters's Brother Cadfael and my own Susanna, Lady Appleton), nurses or former nurses (Anne Perry's Hester Latterley and Jacqueline Winspear's Maisie Dobbs), and midwives (Victoria Thompson's Sarah Brandt and Margaret Lawrence's Hannah Trevor).

Servants are in an ideal position to hear things, and historical detectives sometimes go undercover as maids, valets, secretaries, and the like in order to investigate crimes. In Anne Perry's mysteries, both Charlotte Pitt and her sister Emily have done this. Jeanne M. Dams's Hilda Johansson is a young Swedish emigrée whose real job *is* that of a housemaid, and Patricia Wynn's Hester Kean is a waiting gentlewoman, which means she can go out into society with her employer.

A writer is sufficiently snoopy for the role of sleuth…and likely to end up in interesting places. My own Diana Spaulding works for a nineteenth-century scandal sheet, Carola Dunn's Daisy Dalrymple writes about stately homes for a posh magazine, and Robin Paige's Kate Ardleigh is the author of "penny dreadfuls."

Professions that allow for travel are always useful for detecting, especially if they put characters in contact with more than one level of society. Edward Marston's Domesday Book series sends his sleuths on the road in 1086 to survey the population in a variety of areas in England for the Domesday Book. Entertainers of all sorts also have an excuse to move around. Daniel Stashower's trilogy of mysteries features magician Harry Houdini. Carole Nelson Douglas's Irene Adler is an opera singer. And Alan Gordon's sleuth is a professional fool.

For Gordon, the "who" came before the "when" or the "where." "Most historical novelists come with backgrounds in history," he comments. "Their love for a particular time has led them to imagine it and bring it alive for the rest of us, drawing upon their vast knowledge while cribbing on their Ph.D. dissertations." Gordon instead took an honors seminar in

Shakespeare and it was because of this course that Feste the Fool exists today. After one of the weekly four-hour-long sessions, when Gordon was admittedly "punchy," he "proposed that the various fools in the plays were one and the same. He just kept moving from gig to gig and changing his name, ultimately dying in Elsinore. Out of this came an image of Feste, from *Twelfth Night*, sitting in a tavern and being told of the death of the Duke of Orsino. This image stuck in my head for years." The eventual result was *Thirteenth Night* and the creation of the fictional Fool's Guild.

### Amateur–Professional Teams

While amateurs with crime-solving skills abound in historical mystery fiction, professionals, from police detectives to village constables to spies, have an easier time of it. This is why an amateur detective is so often paired with a professional of some sort, sometimes in a romantic relationship, frequently in an antagonistic one. It may be to your advantage to invent a sleuthing couple or a sleuthing team instead of a single detective brilliant enough to unravel mystery after mystery all alone.

### Vital Statistics

Whoever your sleuth is, consider his or her vital statistics before you start to write. Think about age in particular. How many books do you hope to write in the series? How far apart will the action be in fictional time? How long did most people live in that historical period? I chose to make Susanna Appleton the same age as Queen Elizabeth. Assuming she could live as long as the queen did, that gives me the entire reign to play with.

### Name That Sleuth

Last but not least, name your sleuth. You may already have done this. Even if you have, give it a bit more thought. You want a name you can live with, perhaps for years. And make sure it is a name that was in use during the historical period and in the place you've chosen to write about. The female given name Erin, for example, is modern. It won't work for medieval Ireland.

Speaking of medieval Ireland, Peter Tremayne's first choice for a name for his sleuth was Sister Buan, quite accurate for seventh-century Ireland but unfortunately one that his editor thought might strike modern readers as odd-sounding. Tremayne's second choice was Fidelma.

If you want to see what names are already in use for characters in historical mystery novels, there are several places online that list mystery series and their sleuths, including www.crimethrutime.com. Reference books like Willetta L. Heising's *Detecting Men* and *Detecting Women* also provide lists of detectives' names.

## What

You know the overall "what"—a mystery. But what crime has been committed? It doesn't have to be murder, although it usually is. After all, with a murder there is more at stake.

Do you need to know whodunit before you begin? Not necessarily. And even if you do, you may change your mind if you come up with a better solution while you are writing. You do, however, need to think about the central plot—the solving of the crime—and the possible methods and motives.

The era in which your story is set affects all aspects of the crime. Some methods of murder have always been around—beating, stabbing, poisoning, shooting with an arrow, causing a fatal fall. Others came into being with advances in technology—shooting with a gun, for example. Some poisons are only found in certain places unexplored in earlier eras and cannot be used until they were introduced into the country where your novel is set.

You may find that the means of murder changes as you read more about the historical period you've selected. Keep this factor fluid. It is helpful to know who the victim is, who the killer is, and what the motive is before you begin, but sometimes, even when you think you have it all figured out, you discover a better method of killing someone or a better villain in the course of writing the book.

## What Do You Call It?

The best titles clue readers in to two facts—that the book is historical and that it is a mystery. I had my first title, *Face Down In the Marrow-Bone Pie*, before I started writing, but it was not until after the book sold that I realized I'd also stumbled upon a perfect way to let readers know these books were part of a series—begin all the titles with the words *Face Down*.

Variations of repeated-words titles abound. Margaret Frazer's medieval mysteries are *The Novice's Tale*, *The Servant's Tale*, *The Outlaw's Tale*, and so on. Stephanie Barron's mysteries featuring Jane Austen as sleuth are *Jane and the Unpleasantness at Scargrave Manor*, *Jane and the Man of the Cloth*, *Jane and the Wandering Eye*, and so forth. Although these could be titles of mysteries set in modern times, they all have a hint of the past about them.

In my other series, the Diana Spaulding Mysteries, each title contains a "death" word—*Deadlier Than the Pen*, *Fatal as a Fallen Woman*, *No Mortal Reason*, and *Lethal Legend*. A similar pattern is followed in Lindsey Davis's early Falco novels: *The Silver Pigs*, *Shadows in Bronze*, *Venus in Copper*. Although not specific to Roman times, they all have a certain historical flavor. Karen Harper uses archaic spellings to signal that the books are set in the age of Elizabeth—*The Poyson Garden*, *The Tidal Poole*, *The Twylight Tower*, and so on. The titles in Jill Churchill's Grace and Favor series, set in the 1930s, and Ed Gorman's Sam McCain mysteries, set in the 1950s, are all contemporary songs.

A cautionary tale comes from Laurie R. King in an "At Home" interview with MRI. Her original title for *The Beekeeper's Apprentice* was instead the subtitle of the book on beekeeping written by Sir Arthur Conan Doyle's fictional character, Sherlock Holmes: "With some Observations upon the Segregation of the Queen." It was appropriate to both the plot and the characters, but had one problem, as King's editor reminded her: "segregation" is a word with decidedly negative connotations.

The best title in the world can confuse readers if it is attached to more than one book. There is no copyright on titles, so good ones tend to crop up again and again. Sometimes two or more books with the same title are published at the same time, to the shock and dismay of all parties. There isn't much you can do to prevent that unfortunate situation, but you can do an Internet search to make sure there are no other books with your title already in print. If there are, it doesn't mean you have to change your title, but you should at least consider doing so. When I was trying to decide between *Lethal Legend* and *Lethal Legacy* for the fourth book in the Diana Spaulding Mysteries, I searched for both titles using Google and on Amazon.com. Not only did other novels turn up under "lethal legacy," so did books on the potential for ecological disaster. To avoid confusion, I decided to go with *Lethal Legend*.

## The Basic Decisions

Whatever decisions you've reached as you've read this chapter, remember that you will be living with those choices for a long time. It's important for any writer to write about what s/he loves. Which era, which country, which historical figures have you always found most fascinating? Your selection of "when," "where," "who," and "what," as well as what title to use, should be guided by what excites you. If you are enthusiastic about your choices, then everything about writing your historical mystery will be easier.

# 3 Researching the Historical Mystery—Primary Sources

TRADITIONALLY, research is categorized into primary and secondary sources. Primary sources include materials such as diaries and letters, newspaper accounts, and parish records—things written *at the time*. Portraits and maps also fall into this category. So do visits to living history centers, participation in re-enactments, and trips to locations you use in your historical mystery. Secondary sources, among other things, are books written about the subject *at a later date*—textbooks, histories, biographies— and documentaries. I'll go into more detail about secondary sources in the next chapter.

First, though, a few words on why research is so important to the writer of historical mysteries.

## What Do You Owe Your Readers?

You're writing fiction, but that doesn't mean your historical mystery can be inaccurate. Chances are good that many of the readers who pick up a book set in a particular historical period already know something about that era. That's why they selected this book in the first place from among the many available to them, and why they'll be upset if they encounter inaccuracies in the text. The research stage of any historical mystery project is crucial, no matter what audience you have in mind. In fact, if you are writing your historical mystery for children or young adults, you have an even greater obligation to be accurate.

Although their goal is to entertain, historical mysteries cannot play fast and loose with history. Yes, a certain amount of latitude is covered by "poetic license," but go too far in that direction and you risk alienating the very people you hope will buy your books. Avid readers of historical mysteries have been known to throw a volume across the room in disgust if they find too many careless mistakes or if they feel the writer has taken too many liberties with history.

Anachronisms in historical mysteries are particularly annoying to readers. Chapter Ten is devoted to this subject. Feel free to skip ahead and read it now, or continue here for a discussion of the nuts and bolts of doing research.

## Painless Research

The old adage "write about what you know" is particularly true in dealing with historical fiction. You get to "know" the era in which your book is set by turning yourself into an expert on its history.

Even though you won't use more than a fraction of what you discover, you cannot stint on research, if for no other reason than this: when you know a lot, you can pick and choose which details best suit your story. And you can always save the leftovers for another project.

If you hated doing term papers in high school or college, you may be dreading this part of the writing process. Cheer up. This isn't an assignment, it's a project you've chosen for yourself and that makes all the difference. Many writers find they enjoy digging for tidbits of information so much that they have trouble moving on to actually writing the book. Why? Because this kind of research has a great deal in common with solving a mystery.

If you do no research before you start to write your historical mystery, you are likely to have a great many gaps in your manuscript—notes to yourself to look up what people wore or what they ate or how they managed to get from point A to point B. That's why a certain amount of research should be done before you begin writing. However, once you feel comfortable with what you know about the historical period you've chosen, it's time to get to work on your novel. There will be more research— it's an ongoing part of the process—but in many cases you won't know which bit of information you need until you need it.

## Hie Thee to the Library!

There is no need to study original manuscripts in order to write a work of fiction, although you certainly may if you want to. For most people, however, spending time on a trip to England in the Public Records Office searching for some elusive detail, for example, would probably be more frustrating than productive. Unless you are qualified to read the handwriting and interpret the language of the period you're interested in—and I assure you, I cannot do that for the Elizabethan period, and don't want to—then you're better off leaving it to the experts.

Published books can be either primary or secondary sources, depending on their content. Modern editions—translated and annotated—of books written during the time your mystery is set are available for most historical periods.

For sixteenth-century England, for example, useful primary sources in modern editions include the *Itinerary* of John Leland, a survey of England in the 1540s; William Harrison's *The Description of England* (1587); Gervaise Markham's *The English Housewife* (1615); and John Stow's *A Survey of London* (1598). There are also later compilations of previously unpublished materials, such as Henry Machyn's *Diary* for the years 1550–1563 and Muriel St. Clare Byrne's six-volume *The Lisle Letters*.

My advice to every fiction writer concerning research has always been this: Find a college or university library in your area. Meet and make friends with the reference librarian. If you are not a student or faculty member, ask about a courtesy card to allow you to borrow books and request inter-library loans. If you live in a large city, you'll also want to make use of your public library. Even in small towns, public libraries have access to inter-library loans, although the process may take a little longer. No matter what else you do for research, you will benefit from the resources libraries provide.

### Photographs and Contemporary Illustrations

Photographs, of course, are not available for time periods in the distant past, but there are contemporary illustrations you can study—portraits, sketches, even maps, which were sometimes drawn in great detail, including tiny reproductions of houses and people. From the advent of printing, notorious crimes were written up in pamphlets illustrated with woodcuts. They're crude, but they contain clues to the way things were.

Travel books are another source of visual aids, especially in the nineteenth century. Many books published then are still available in the original and others have been reprinted. Railroads also published books to promote travel, illustrating them lavishly and including information on each town along the way.

Photograph collections are maintained by some libraries and many local historical societies. Some have even been published in book form. Check the real towns and counties near the area where your book is set. See what they have available and how accessible the collections are. You may even be able to access the archives online. Taking a look at contemporary illustrations, especially photographs, is well worth your time. There's a lot of truth in the old saying that a picture is worth a thousand words.

### Newspapers and Magazines

Newspapers and magazines provide a wealth of information. The library at a branch of the University of Maine near my home has a complete collection of the *New York Times* on microfilm. Although that newspaper doesn't cover every news story, it includes some reports from every state and around the world. Just as important, it contains ads, telling me what was available to buy and how much it cost. As P.N. Elrod puts it, "A few days in a library's basement spinning through the microfiche or flipping fragile pages is almost as good as a time machine."

Even small libraries may have newspapers on microfilm or microfiche, at least for their local area. If you cannot find such resources in your town's library, try the local historical society. Larger libraries will also have collections of magazines.

Unfortunately, libraries do not generally use inter-library loan for periodicals or microfilm, although they may agree to make copies of specific pages for you. In the future, old issues may become available on the Internet. Some are already, although at present most require a subscription and the majority don't go back very far. Old newspapers and magazines may also turn up for sale on eBay. I found a Maine almanac for 1888 that has proved invaluable for things like the time of sunrise and sunset and high tide, and for lists of county officials for that year.

Some time ago, I needed to know what the weather was like in Denver for certain dates in 1888. The weather wasn't a factor in the story but if there had been a major storm on one of those dates I didn't want to ignore it. For some times and places there are extant diaries with a wealth of such information. By 1888, the U.S. Weather Service was in operation and daily weather reports appeared in some newspapers. On an earlier trip to Denver I had visited the public library and copied several pages from local newspapers for future use, but I hadn't been looking for specific dates or for weather reports. Since I live in Maine, this wasn't something I'd travel back to Colorado for. Instead, my local inter-library-loan librarian requested the information I needed from a colleague at the Denver Public Library and the librarian there looked up the dates I needed and made printouts from the microfilm to mail to me. It turned out there were very few mentions of the weather, which was all to the good for my fictional purposes. Sometimes negative results are the ones you want.

### Historical "Truth"

One warning: early newspapers were not exactly unbiased in their reporting. This is true of other primary sources as well. Memoirs and letters are particularly suspect. Writers have always slanted the accounts they've left behind to make themselves look better and to reflect their own opinions — or those of the people paying them to record events for posterity. Sir Thomas More's *History of King Richard III* (1513) is a case in point. More might have lost his head much sooner if he hadn't written what Henry VIII wanted to read about his predecessors.

It is unwise to leap to *any* firm conclusions based on records left by our ancestors. Let's say you've found a book that reprints a series of laws dealing with criminal offenses, passed in the time and place you're writing about. They were in effect, but did everyone obey them? Were they enforced? Did people living at the time, concerned with their own survival, away from the city or the court, even know they existed, let alone what they said? English law in the sixteenth century specified hanging as the punishment for a variety of crimes, including the theft of anything valued at a shilling or more. In case after case, this sentence was not carried out. Felons were branded instead, or acquitted in spite of overwhelming evidence of guilt. Then, as now, nothing is cut and dried. Historical "truths" can be interpreted in a variety of ways. You will need to use common sense to apply the realities of everyday life in a bygone age to the "facts" of history.

## A Note on Dates

Something else to keep in mind when doing research is that not every country used the same system of dating. In England, dates on *official* documents, at least those from the fifteenth and sixteenth centuries, tend to be recorded in terms of the monarch's reign. Those years start with the day the king or queen ascended the throne. Thus, "ii Elizabeth" is the second year of the reign of Elizabeth I of England, which began on November 17, 1559 and ended November 16, 1560.

The Julian calendar was used to date everything else, as it was all over Europe until 1582. In that year, in order to ensure that church holidays occurred in the proper season, Pope Gregory XIII issued a decree that dropped ten days from the calendar. Protestant countries, including England and all her colonies, naturally ignored this new Gregorian calendar. Thus, when you read reports about the Spanish Armada in 1588, those written by English witnesses are dated ten days earlier than those written by Spaniards, and the events described take place on different days of the week.

To add to the confusion, in the Elizabethan era the new year was still considered to begin on Lady Day, March 25, even though January 1 was already *called* New Year's Day. This is why you will see double dating (February 2, 1588/9) for the early part of some years. The English continued to use the old Julian calendar until 1752, when the date jumped from September 2 to September 14, dropping twelve days to bring the date into alignment with the Gregorian calendar.

For those characters who do not read or write and have little idea what a calendar is, and even for some who do, years can also be distinguished in terms of momentous events. Earthquakes, comets, battles—all can be used to mark the passage of time. An Elizabethan speaking in 1590 might well refer to something happening "in the Armada year" rather than say 1588. Be wary, though—this method of dating can only be used *after* the event!

If you are using a calendar unfamiliar to most of your readers, it may be a good idea to include an author's note. Chinese, Roman, Jewish, Islamic, and Aztec calendars, even the Republican Calendar used in France from 1793 to 1809, all take some explaining.

Sharan Newman begins the first chapter of the first novel in her Catherine LeVendeur series, *Death Comes as Epiphany*, with the dateline "Feast of St. Thecla, Saturday, September 23, 1139." In later books in the series, after Catherine's Jewish heritage is revealed, datelines are even more complex. One from early in *The Difficult Saint* reads: "Sunday, pridie kalends April (March 31), 1146; 15 Nisan, 4906. Easter Sunday, the first day of Passover."

Is it necessary to have a dateline? Of course not. In some cases it may be to your advantage not to be too specific. But whether you choose to share the exact date with your readers or not, you will need to create some kind of time line for your own use. If you map out the plot of your story in terms of days of the week, it will help you to avoid contradicting yourself as you write.

## Interviewing People As Research

For more recent historical periods, it is still possible to consult primary sources—real people—in person. Hal Glatzer, whose Katy Green mysteries are set in the Swing Era of the 1930s, does part of his research by having "conversations with many women friends, especially in the Art Deco Society, and with my mother. They have helped me set the stage and frame Katy's character so that she is a believable product of her time."

Kerry Greenwood's Phryne Fisher series is set in Australia (where Greenwood lives) in 1928. "I write about 1928," Greenwood says, "because I did a Legal History thesis-length essay on the 1928 wharf strike.

Everyone else was doing "My father the Judge" and my dad was a wharfie, so I thought, why not? So when it came to writing a detective story I thought I knew 1928 pretty well. As it happened, I didn't.

The trouble with the recent past is that it is another country, not so foreign as say, Ancient Greece, but not contemporary, so it needs constant checking: how did one light a stove? Matches? What sort of matches?...Since there were stocking mending kits, they must have been mended, but how did you mend stockings? What does Art Silk feel like? How often did Phryne wash her hair and what did she wash it with? How about the Ladies' Travelling Necessities, which sound like disposable sanitary pads? How, in fact, did one maintain oneself, when such a lot of familiar things hadn't been invented (not to mention things like films and radio and popular culture, a minefield and easily got entirely wrong).

These things are not in newspapers, my primary source, but they are in memoirs and in people's heads. I went and hunted down every old lady still in possession of her senses and relentlessly listened to everything she could tell me about being a young woman in the '20s. I drank buckets of tea and ate bushels of scones and absorbed 1920s womanhood through the pores. The really nice thing about this sort of research is that old people like to feel that their memories are valued, and the ruthless author is actually spreading a little cheer as well as garnering irreplaceable information.

Carolyn Haines, whose stand-alone title, *Penumbra*, is set in 1952 Mississippi, went about her historical research in the same way she researches a contemporary novel. "I honestly didn't think it was a historical book—or didn't think of it in those terms. I was born in 1953, and it seemed that my small town was a decade behind larger cities when I was growing up. I loved the lack of asphalt—the lack of population—the sense of another world. I drew a lot on my own heritage. I've been very lucky because so many people from the '50s are still alive and can pull up recollections. Even in the '70s, the rural areas of George County were still much like the '50s. So I had my own memories to pull from, too."

At the time she responded to my questions, Haines had just finished *Blood Nimbus*, set in 1944 New Iberia, Louisiana, and added, "In my imagination, I can go back to a place less cluttered with 'progress.' I think that's why I like to write about the past."

## History on the Small Screen—the Ultimate Painless Research

If you are unable to travel to the place where you've set your mystery, check into the resources available on video and on the Web. Are these primary sources? The visual parts are. Most commentary should be considered a secondary source.

### Videotapes and DVDs

My own library of videotapes (accumulated in the years before DVDs, since I've been at this a long while) includes programs on underwater archaeology, architecture at Plimoth Plantation, scenic tours of English villages, Hadrian's Wall, "Robin Hood Country," a segment on priest holes, several shows on castles, a piece on llamas, and a biography of Suleyman the Magnificent. Some I've found useful. I'm hanging on to others with the idea that someday I may need the inspiration they can provide.

PBS, The Learning Channel, The History Channel, and other networks sell copies of their programs through catalogs and online stores. In addition to documentaries and docudramas, PBS programming in recent years has included a number of "reality shows" featuring modern families living in houses or communities from other centuries. Interested in England in 1900? The American frontier? Colonial America? Each was the basis of a mini-series. A slightly different production sent twenty-first-century men and women to a Regency House Party. While I would not rely on any television program for complete historical accuracy—check what you learn against more traditional sources—this sort of thing can provide useful insights into life in another era.

### Websites

Using the Internet for research is a natural these days, but let the buyer beware. You need no credentials to post information online. What your search engine turns up may be as well researched as anything in a library…or pure fantasy on the writer's part.

What you *can* usually trust are photographs and video clips provided by the towns, cities, counties, and states you are using for your settings. Granted, they are going to show only the attractive side of the area, but the places are real. Similarly historic sites and museums with websites may offer glimpses of their collections, and in the case of buildings, a look at furnishings and architecture.

Among the most useful sites on the Internet are those that reproduce primary sources. Some are free; others require membership. Family history sites such as Genealogy.com and Ancestry.com make their libraries available, scanned page by scanned page, for a subscription fee, allowing you to search, among other things, old newspapers, old public records, and books published in the nineteenth century. Larger public libraries may offer free access to one or more of these resources.

Facts related to the natural world are also available on the Internet. It is possible to find out, for example, for any given year and location, what constellations were visible in the night sky, the phase of the moon, and the times of high tide. You may not be able to discover if it was raining on a certain date, but if a full moon plays a role in your plot, spend some time at www.fourmilab.ch/cgi-bin/uncgi/Yoursky.

## Hands-on Research

Even better than watching historical recreations on the small screen is actually experiencing some of what you want to write about. Go to museums that have restored buildings from the period in which you are interested, and above all, visit living history centers. The latter attempt to create an environment that closely resembles what a particular place was like at a specific time in the past.

At Plimoth Plantation in Plymouth, Massachusetts, re-enactors take on the roles of real settlers and do not step out of them as long as they are in costume. They "live" in the reconstructed village and speak in the accents of seventeenth-century England, even to their individual counties of origin. They work with the tools of the period, thatching roofs, firing muskets, growing crops, and raising livestock.

Each living history center is a little different but all endeavor to give visitors an accurate picture of life in the past. As varied as Colonial Williamsburg in Virginia; King's Landing in New Brunswick, Canada; Washburn-Norlands in Livermore, Maine; and the Littleton Historical Museum near Denver, living history centers provide writers with a wonderful source of material—a firsthand look at how things were.

So do re-enactment groups. From the Society for Creative Anachronism to the folks who recreate Civil War battles, these are people who love their chosen period of history. No, the armor isn't exactly like it was in medieval times. Some accommodations are made for comfort and for financial reasons, but don't overlook what these organizations provide. If you want to experience the past you're writing about, this is one way to do it.

Kathleen Ernst is a historical mystery writer who has been able to take full advantage of hands-on experiences. She worked for more than ten years at Old World Wisconsin, an outdoor ethnic museum near Milwaukee that features a crossroads village and ten working farmsteads ranging in date from 1845 through 1915. She "learned how to warp a loom, how to milk cows, how to make rennet and lye soap, wine and sauerbraten, hops yeast, and Finnish egg coffee," and was then able to give many of these skills to her characters.

For Ernst, hands-on experience with living history sites and events also provided "the specific sensory details that bring a scene to life.

> I know what hog intestines smell like when they're being prepared for sausage casing, how flax fibers feel between my fingers as they twine into linen thread, what threshing machines sound like when they rattle to life in the middle of a newly shorn wheat field. And because I have a novelist's imagination, my experiences at the site provided compelling insight into the lives of people long gone. Standing on a brick kitchen floor until my knees ached, having to fetch draft horses that broke through fences, wanting to weep when cabbage moths or drought destroyed crops I had carefully nurtured, cutting oats with a sickle so slick with sweat it was hard to grasp—this kind of experience provided new perspectives of the women who peopled both the restored homes I worked in and the pages of my novels.

Ernst points out that "even sites only tangentially related to your time and place might provide some useful sensory experiences," and recommends asking re-enactors and interpreters "questions that go beyond process and facts, and get to the experiences of the people they portray. Ask if you can hold their musket, or try your hand at tamping cabbage into sauerkraut, or whatever else is going on." On your own, you can "be creative about finding ways to experience bits of life. Sew (or order) a wool frockcoat, or a corset and period-appropriate dress. Learn how to tat lace or carve shingles with a drawknife. Grow heirloom vegetables. Ask a farmer to show you how to pluck chickens. Make a firepit in the backyard, and try baking bannocks or cooking stew or frying flatbread. Get your hands dirty. You, and your readers, will be glad you did."

Another historical mystery writer who advocates hands-on experience is Barbara Hambly. She knew from a very early age that she wanted to write historical fiction and went out of her way "to do and learn things for that purpose: horseback riding, fencing, and hand-to-hand combat (karate, in my case). I was never very good at any of them, but at least I know how it feels to square off against somebody a lot bigger than you who'll hurt you." She's "fed, brushed, and saddled a horse, which probably most people in the nineteenth century did without even thinking about it. I never learned to ride sidesaddle, which I'd still like to try, though I've talked to people who've done it; one day I'd like to learn to drive as well as ride horses."

Friends took Hambly out to the desert with an assortment of muskets and pistols so that she could experience black-powder shooting. They took her through the loading procedure, and although she "couldn't hit a thing," she "learned the difference in the kick between a black-powder load and a modern smokeless powder…and observed the little lag-time it takes for the spark to jump to the powder in the pan."

## On-site Research

Barbara Hambly also travels to do research. For *Traveling with the Dead*, Hambly went to Vienna. It was a good thing she did, for she discovered "that the chase through the back alleys of the old city would have to be rewritten because there *are* no back alleys in old Vienna—though there are some darn narrow little streets. On the same journey, I found that the quality of the light in Istanbul is like nowhere else: a very light, dry, glittery quality that always seems golden. I saw that the gold backgrounds of Byzantine mosaics, that always look so flat and drab in photographs and prints, look that way because of the floodlight quality of flash photography. The mosaics themselves were designed to be viewed by candlelight, and random tiles within them are angled slightly, to sparkle sharply in the wavering glow of flame."

Closer to home, for her Benjamin January series, Hambly has spent considerable time in New Orleans, where she "learned the burnt-sweet smell of refining sugar, and how it permeates the thick fog that blankets that city in winter." As in Vienna, "There are no alleys in the oldest part of New Orleans, either. Carriages came in from the street and were stored in the courtyard." For *Dead Water*, she "went upriver on a steamboat…and learned how cold the wind blows down the Mississippi."

Perhaps you can see yourself doing the same thing, or spending a few weeks "on location" elsewhere in the U.S. But what if you are living there and want to set your mystery in another country? Must you travel to the scene of the crime?

Sharan Newman has long been an advocate of on-site research, which she calls "absolutely essential. No matter how much you read, there are things you're not going to find out." When she first visited the site of the Paraclete in France (the convent where her sleuth, Catherine LeVendeur, is a postulant at the start of *Death Comes as Epiphany*), Newman was particularly struck by the quality of the mud—"thick and greenish." In addition, because the river keeps changing course, there is swampy land all around. Those are details not commonly reported in guidebooks and yet they would have a bearing on the way her characters go about their daily lives.

In *Strong as Death*, Catherine and her husband, Edgar, go on a pilgrimage to Compostela. As Newman recalls, "I would have had people taking carts. It wasn't till I saw the road that I realized there *were* no roads. They were paths and you couldn't get two or three people abreast in a lot of places." Since nothing with wheels could have managed the trip, she immediately abandoned the idea of using carts. The same research trip produced another surprise. Between the Pyrenees and Compostela the landscape changes in ways that books are unlikely to reveal. As Newman came over a hill into Galicia in April, she felt as if she had stepped from Spain into Scotland—"There was heather on the hills."

For some places, of course, there is nothing close to the original setting left, but even then there are ways to step back into the past. Newman suggests that someone looking for the feel of medieval London, for example, visit one of a number of small English villages whose buildings date back to that era.

Lauren Haney had a research experience that illustrates one of the clear disadvantages of not being able to see a location firsthand. When she decided to set one of her Lieutenant Bak mysteries at the turquoise mines at Serabit el-Khadim in Sinai, she searched through the books she had at home, bought and read others, and tried without much success to research the area on the Internet.

"I thought I knew Serabit el-Khadim fairly well," she says.

> One of my best reference books contained a relief map, but the elevation numbers were too small to read. From several vaguely worded texts, I assumed the mines were located in a deep valley and, without legible elevations, the relief map could be interpreted that way. Then I traveled to Sinai to visit Serabit el-Khadim. Imagine my surprise when I found myself making a three-hour climb up the side of a tall plateau in order to reach the mines! If I had not visited the site, if I'd depended upon books alone, the novel would have contained an unforgivable and very obvious error. No matter how much you know, no matter how much research you do, there's no substitute for seeing the site for yourself.

I agree with that…in principle. In an ideal world in which all writers receive huge advances, every one of us would probably opt to spend as much time as necessary living on the spot, absorbing every detail of our surroundings. In the real world, this isn't always possible.

I'd have loved to travel to England before I started the Face Down series, but whenever I had enough money to go, I didn't have the time. When I might have been able to leave home for several weeks at a stretch, I couldn't afford the expense. As a result, until after the publication of the sixth book in the series, the only time I had been to Europe was as a college student in the spring of 1968. My memories of that trip have more to do with student riots in Leeds and Paris than with sixteenth-century architecture or the geography of any particular English county.

The official reason for my return to England in the summer of 2001 was to visit as many sixteenth-century country manor houses as I could find. I was planning *Face Down Below the Banqueting House* at that point and for the first time meant to set an entire book in Lady Appleton's home. I'd never done more than give brief glimpses of a couple of rooms in earlier books. Now I had to come up with a floor plan and lots of descriptive details.

There aren't too many locales that have remained completely unchanged since the sixteenth century. I visited over a dozen houses extant then, and all had been improved upon. Cothele in Cornwall is still as it was in the seventeenth century, but most of the rest had additions that were made much later.

A problem I hadn't expected, though I should have, came from seeing so much in such a short period of time. I had only a little over two weeks to visit all the places on my list. Soon all those houses started to run together in my mind. The detailed notes I made, the ones that made perfect sense on the scene, were less easy to interpret after I got home. Furthermore, most historic homes won't let visitors touch things or take photographs or shoot video indoors. It is possible to make photography arrangements ahead of time at some of the locations, but not always.

Outdoor footage has its own value, particularly for reminding the writer not to put in hills where none exist. That sort of geography doesn't change. A camcorder proved far more useful for research purposes than my still camera, allowing me to shoot 360 degrees from the center of the inner courtyard of a manor house or straight ahead as I walked down a path through a garden. In two weeks, I filled eight one-hour tapes.

The first of the houses I visited in my "search for Leigh Abbey," Haddon Hall in Derbyshire, has an excellent guidebook with floor plans and offers many postcards. Not all houses do as well with these aspects. But I have trouble imagining spatial relationships: distances, height, size. And if you look at professional pictures, you notice that they almost never include people, which can be a guide to size. The stills I took in the courtyard give me a sense of this.

Official pictures of the so-called Great Room do not show that one side gallery is supported only in the center and by a single rough-hewn post. There is no entry into this gallery. It sags visibly. I don't know if the post was there originally, but seeing it firsthand prompted an idea about a musician's gallery rigged to collapse in a murder plot.

But how *do* you tell what was really there more than 400 years ago and what has been added since? The guides at National Trust and English Heritage properties are well versed in history and eager to be helpful, but sometimes they don't know either. In the case of one Tudor palace, what is now a mellow shade of red brick was painted bright red with accents in white and black in the sixteenth century. I got that detail out of a book by an expert on Tudor palaces. I'd never have known from visiting the place, nor would I have known to ask. Similarly, although I could see that extant sixteenth-century black-and-white townhouses sag, I am not enough of an expert to know if they did so even in the sixteenth century. Those built in medieval times may well have.

Even more misleading is present-day landscaping. Although Tudor houses would have had gardens, the gardens I saw were, for the most part, Victorian or later. Except for the occasional small section given over to a knot garden or a maze, they aren't at all as they would have been in the period I was interested in. There are also many plants in them that an Elizabethan would not recognize.

A word of advice: if you don't know what questions to ask when you visit, or if you even suspect you may have questions later, introduce yourself to one of the guides, or better yet the estate manager if there is one on the premises, and get an address to which you can send questions. I had bookmarks with me listing all the titles in my Face Down series, and discovered that most of the volunteers who serve as guides in these houses are avid readers. They are also familiar with areas of the houses that are not open to the public and could tell me, for example, that the ceilings in the garrets at Speke Hall are high enough to allow a person to stand upright.

In some cases, replicas give a more accurate representation than originals, if they are built after careful research. Barrington Court is filled with furniture made and displayed for sale by Stuart Interiors. These replicas *can* be touched, and signs clearly date each object. The New Globe Theatre in London, built just a few years ago, is already weathered, but it's the sort of weathering the original would also have experienced after a few years. I also boarded replicas of two ships, the *Matthew*, modeled after John Cabot's ship from the 1490s, and the *Golden Hinde*, modeled after the ship in which Francis Drake sailed around the world in 1577–1580. Formal pictures cannot convey the size of these. I already owned a six-hour documentary on the *Matthew*, but now I have video of myself on board. I know where the lintel would crack me in the forehead and when the ropes on deck would trip me. Much more vivid, I assure you.

Visiting jails and dungeons may also be helpful in writing a crime novel. I found one in London—actually a museum at the site of the original Clink—and one in Lancaster Castle. It doesn't hurt to get a feel for what it would be like to be locked up, and if you can examine such things as shackles, weapons, and torture devices, so much the better. Many American museums offer a similar experience, including the chance to put your own head and hands in the stocks.

If you are going to use herbs in your book, whether for cooking or poisoning, take advantage of the opportunity to visit real herb gardens. Modern ones will still have some of the classic herbs, but there are a number of places that have made an attempt to recreate medieval gardens. The Cloisters in New York City is an excellent one. I use herbs in my books all the time but I am not an expert. In fact, I have trouble telling one plant from another. I can rely on herbals to tell me what a plant looks, smells, feels, and tastes like, but it never hurts to go out and actually look at one growing in a garden. Many of the poisonous herbs and flowers, such as foxglove, are not hard to find.

But to return to England—what about topography? Does that stay the same? Not always, and that can be a good thing, leaving the writer free to imagine what once was there. What was decidedly rural in the sixteenth century—the site of my fictional Appleton Manor—is now part of Greater Manchester. Not only is the entire area covered by a modern city, but the canal system put in during the nineteenth century has completely changed the course of the rivers.

In Kent, however, although it is a well-populated county, an amazing amount is unchanged. Narrow country lanes lead to Barfrestone, the village at the geographical location ("halfway between Canterbury and Dover") that I blithely assigned to Leigh Abbey in the first book in the Face Down series. The present-day village consists of a Norman church, a pub, and a few houses. The surrounding land is gently rolling and wooded.

The video I brought back was extremely useful when it came to writing scenes set there.

If you cannot visit the location of your novel, should you abandon the idea of writing a historical mystery set there? Of course not. Yes, it is an advantage to be on-site, but you *can* find a great deal of material in books or on the Internet. You may also be able to contact someone who lives in the area or has spent some time there. Find out as much as you can. Try to avoid elaborating on details if you're uncertain about them. However — you *are* a writer. The ability to imagine is a requirement of your profession. You can visit sixteenth-century England, or any other time and place, and become an expert on it, *without* leaving home. Best of all, you can write a historical mystery that will take your readers there with you.

Some research using primary sources, whether it be reading old newspapers, visiting another country, or attending the re-enactment of a Civil War battle, is essential to creating believable historical mystery fiction. Consulting secondary sources, however, is just as important. Chapter Four will tell you what these are and how to make the best use of them.

# CHAPTER 4

# Further Research–Secondary Sources

SECONDARY sources include books and documentaries produced by people who have studied the primary sources, or other secondary sources, and compiled that information in a way that is easily accessible to the public. Some are aimed at a scholarly audience. Others are written for the general reader. My own *Writer's Guide to Everyday Life in Renaissance England* and similar volumes on the daily life of a particular era are secondary sources referring the reader to, mostly, other secondary sources. They are a good place to start your research, but they are only a starting point.

## Books, Books, and More Books!

If you are writing fiction, as opposed to doing a scholarly study on some specific subject, then secondary sources and a sprinkling of published primary sources may provide sufficient information for your purpose.

From the moment you get the idea for a story and know its setting, start reading about the place and the period. Keep good notes and find a way to organize them. If you need a specific detail as you are writing, you don't want to spend hours searching through your books and file folders to locate it.

Scholarly tomes may yield only a few paragraphs of information, but if it is exactly what you need, it is worth the time it takes to find. There are books out there on all kinds of things, from records of lawsuits and trials to handbooks on the superstitions surrounding common herbs. To cite the sixteenth century, between historians studying the reigns of the Tudors and scholars interested in Shakespeare and his fellow dramatists, there are few areas of everyday life that have not been examined in detail.

Inasmuch as any writer whose books are still in print must have mixed feelings about the sale of used books, for which no royalties are paid, I do think used book and antiquarian book stores are an invaluable resource for research. For most books, out-of-print doesn't mean unavailable.

Through Internet sources like ABE Books, Alibris, Hamilton Book, Scholar's Bookshelf, and others, you can find new or used copies of almost any volume you need. Whether you want to pay as much as the seller is asking is another matter.

That brings us back to the library. Many libraries now have online card catalogs, which means you can do preliminary research on your computer at home. The URSUS system in Maine is fairly typical and includes not only the holdings of all branches of the state university system but also those of one of the larger public libraries in the state and the state library. To see what I'm talking about, go to http://130.111.64.3/search. Look for similar systems in your own state.

Once you find a book you want online, you may be able to borrow it directly. If not, copy the bibliographical information (author, title, publisher, place and date of publication) and take this to your local library. No matter how small it is, any public library in the U.S. can borrow a book from another U.S. library through the inter-library-loan system. Occasionally, there is a charge but much of the time inter-library loans are free.

As I mentioned in the last chapter, if you can get to a large city or the local branch of your state university, by all means do make a trip to the library there. It may well be that they have someone on staff who does nothing but inter-library loans. In addition, there are several useful secondary sources that libraries do not loan, multi-volume reference books that you will find in the reference rooms of most of the larger libraries.

The *Oxford English Dictionary* is the most complete dictionary of English words. It gives details on the earliest recorded use of each word in print in English. That doesn't mean the word was not used before the date given, only that it did not appear in print in English before that date. I'll be talking more about the *OED* and how to spot an anachronistic word in Chapter Ten.

The *Dictionary of National Biography* (for Great Britain) and the *Dictionary of American Biography* are essential resources if you're using any historical figures as characters. If your library has an older set of these volumes, be aware that some entries were written in the early 1900s and more recent research has been done on their subjects. Even in outdated versions, however, these capsule biographies can keep you from making silly mistakes. If you present someone as an adult when in fact that person would still be in swaddling clothes, and your readers realize that—and many of them will, because historical mystery readers also tend to read nonfiction—then you will lose credibility, and worse, may lose sales. The *DNB* and *DAB* entries are also useful in providing the names of the subject's friends, relatives, and associates, allowing you to find their biographies, which in turn may contain more information on the individual in whom you are interested.

### And Still More Books

What sort of books should you look for next if you have only a vague idea of what was going on in the period you want to write about? In addition to books that address "Everyday life in..." search out specialized encyclopedias, dictionaries, and atlases. For Ancient Egypt, for example, there are Donald B. Redford's *The Oxford Encyclopedia of Ancient Egypt* (three volumes) and Ian Shaw and Paul Nicholson's *The Dictionary of Ancient Egypt*. Further examples: S. Ireland's *Roman Britain, a Sourcebook* and John Julius Norwich's books on Byzantium provide information on those locales. Mary Fitton's translation of Maurice Andrieux's *Daily Life in Venice in the Time of Casanova* gives information on the eighteenth century. Donald A. Low's *The Regency Underworld* does the same for the early nineteenth century.

Atlases are available for most locations and some contain more text than maps. They range from John Baines and Jaromir Malek's *Cultural Atlas of Ancient Egypt* to the *National Trust Historical Atlas of Britain: Prehistoric to Medieval*, edited by Nigel Saul, and Jeremy Black's *Historical Atlas of Britain: The End of the Middle Ages to the Georgian Era*.

After books giving general information, the most useful secondary sources for the fiction writer are biographies and social histories, including accounts of real crimes. They are much more likely to have details that will enable you to create fictional plotlines than books that focus on political, religious, or military history. Look also for books that emphasize the roles women played in the past. These tend to be rich in domestic details. Depending on your plot and setting, you will also need to venture into specific areas—art, music, architecture, and so on.

Ancient Egypt? Try T.G.H. James's *Pharaoh's People* and Paul T. Nicholson and Ian Shaw's *Ancient Egyptian Materials and Technology*. Roman Britain? *Life and Letters on the Roman Frontier* by Alan K. Bowman and Andrew Dalby and Sally Grainger's *The Classical Cookbook*. Peter Thornton's *The Italian Renaissance Interior 1400–1600* is packed with domestic details, as is Mark Girouard's *Life in the English Country House*. Looking for information on and photographs of New York City at the end of the nineteenth century? Try Grace Mayer's *Once Upon a City*. For the late nineteenth-century American West, there are C. Robert Haywood's *Victorian West: Class & Culture in Kansas Cattle Towns* and Carol Padgett, ed., *Keeping Hearth and Home in Old Colorado: A Practical Primer for Daily Living*.

[My thanks to Carrie Bebris, Jane Finnis, Roberta Gellis, Alan Gordon, Lauren Haney, Beverle Graves Myers, Ann Parker, and Mary Reed and Eric Mayer for the foregoing suggestions.] Many historical mystery writers include bibliographies at their websites. Some put one at the end of each novel.

Since we are writing mysteries, books on crime in past eras are particularly useful. There are plenty of them, from dry, scholarly accounts to books that read almost like novels. They are as varied as Beatrice White's *Cast of Ravens: The Strange Case of Sir Thomas Overbury*, John W. Weatherford's *Crime and Punishment in the England of Shakespeare and Milton*, and Susannah Fullerton's *Jane Austen & Crime*. Read those relating to your period to glean details of how the criminal justice system worked then.

### An Aside on Poisons

If you plan to poison someone in your book, you will need to do specialized research in two distinct areas. First, you'll need to find out what people knew *then* about the poison you want to use, including the folklore associated with it. What they believed may have been completely wrong, but that doesn't mean you can change it. As the author of the story, however, you also have the responsibility to find out what we know *now* about that same poison. Why? So that you can be accurate in what you describe. Even though your detective may have no understanding of reaction time, side effects, or statistical odds for survival, you need to have that information at your fingertips and make sure your chosen poison affects the victim as it really would.

Where do you find information on poisons? If you go to a writers' conference that features a program by Luci Zahray, "the poison lady," make sure to attend. In addition, this is one time the Internet is useful. Not only can you find scientific information there, you may also be able to locate a chemist or physician willing to answer specific questions. D.P. Lyle, M.D. (author of *Forensics for Dummies* and other books for mystery writers) has a very helpful website at http://www.dplylemd.com.

In the realm of books, most herbals will tell you something about poisonous plants. Two older books that may also prove useful are C.J.S. Thompson's *Poisons and Poisoners*, published in 1931, and John Mann's *Murder, Magic, and Medicine* (1992). *Deadly Doses, A Writer's Guide to Poisons* by Serita Deborah Stevens with Anne Klarner is a good starting point to help you select a poison but needs to be supplemented by more in-depth research once you've chosen it.

### Evaluating a Secondary Source

Secondary sources are readily available, but are they reliable? Sadly, not always. Sometimes secondary sources simply rehash the contents of older works, which means that they may be repeating misinformation. If the first person to transcribe or translate a document got it wrong, that mistake may be repeated in multiple sources over the years, until another scholar goes back to the original and catches it.

In addition, nonfiction or not, books tend to be written with an agenda in mind. Academics are not unbiased. History is constantly being rewritten. The author's pet theory or bias may color which historical facts are emphasized in the text. Take any controversial moment in history and you will find radically opposed arguments in print about what really happened and why. In reaction to years of neglect by scholars of the distaff side of history, the 1980s saw a proliferation of books with a radical feminist, revisionist slant. Some aren't any more accurate than the books that ignored women's roles completely, but they have increased the amount of information on domestic life that is readily available.

How do you evaluate a secondary source? First check the publication date. Then take a look at the bibliography and footnotes if any. Be wary if no primary sources (documents, letters, newspapers, and so on) are listed. If there is no bibliography at all, be *very* suspicious of the contents. Also see what you can learn about the author's expertise in the field. It isn't necessary to have a Ph.D. to be a good researcher, but there should be something motivating the writer to delve into the past. An enthusiastic amateur scholar obsessed with tracking down an ancestor, for example, may prove to be a wonderful source of accurate information. An academic in a rush to publish something in order to keep his job may be somewhat careless about checking facts.

Since I'm going to be negative, I will use one of my own nonfiction titles as an example of a reference book to be wary of. *Wives and Daughters: The Women of Sixteenth-Century England* was written because I had accumulated a great deal of research in order to write historical novels. None of these early fiction attempts sold but I hate to waste anything. So, in 1979, I started trying to sell a sort of Who's Who of Tudor women. The proposal was rejected by just about every publisher ("too scholarly" for a general audience, "not scholarly enough" for university presses) but finally found a home with a small independent scholarly press. This was my first book sale. I knew nothing about contracts and did not have an agent and ended up signing away far more than I should have. Why do I mention this? Because the book is still available in a print-on-demand edition and in libraries and I have no control over it. I can't update it or correct it.

So, let me evaluate *Wives and Daughters*. The copyright date is 1984. Right off the bat, that indicates that the material is more than twenty years out of date. Does this matter? In many cases, no. But since this is a collection of mini-biographies of 570 sixteenth-century Englishwomen, at least a few of them are now inaccurate. Previously undiscovered documents—or simply information I was unaware of when I was writing the entries in 1980 (yes, it took four years for the manuscript to reach book form)—mean my book must be considered unreliable.

There are no footnotes, although there are references within some entries. There's a good reason for this. Most of the entries were compiled from a sentence here, a footnote there in histories and biographies about sixteenth-century England. Footnotes would have doubled the size of the volume and not have been particularly useful.

Look at the bibliography and you find it runs only seven pages and contains no book published later than 1981 (and only one that late). Again, this should be a clear warning not to rely exclusively on the contents. One of the entries may be a good starting point for a character in your historical mystery, but you'll need to seek out more recent works that may have more information about her. For example, a 2001 biography of John Dee (Benjamin Woolley's *The Queen's Conjurer*) contains much more information about Jane Fromond, Dee's wife, than I was able to find in 1980.

Common sense is the best guide to knowing when it is safe to use someone else's research. If you question a "fact," find more than one source for it. The more you read about your chosen historical period, the better you will become at spotting someone else's sloppy research. A red flag will go up when you find an error. If you do find a glaring mistake, then the entire book should be considered suspect.

One reputable scholar, in his book's chapter on food, makes the statement that Henry VIII banned all stews. Thus, this writer concludes, it was forbidden to eat this particular dish during the sixteenth century. In fact, the "stews" legislated against were whorehouses. That isn't a mistake you want to repeat in your historical mystery...unless you're going for a laugh.

And yet, you are writing fiction. You are trolling for details that will make that fiction come alive. You are not writing a dissertation. Sometimes it is possible to find inspiration in a source that *isn't* all that accurate.

I researched brothels for *Face Down Among the Winchester Geese*, in which several scenes are set in the stews of Southwark. One of the books I consulted deals exclusively with these brothels, but it contains several mistakes in historical fact. Calling Mary Boleyn (Anne's sister) the long-time mistress of Henry VII when she was really the short-term mistress of Henry VIII was the red flag in this case. That and other errors made all the material in the book suspect.

And yet, it contains wonderful, evocative details, things I *wanted* to be true. The author maintains, for instance, that pictures of individual prostitutes were hung on the walls of some brothels in order to allow customers to make their selection. As I plotted my book, I wondered whether or not I could trust this "fact." The sixteenth century was a time when only the wealthy could afford to commission portraits. But was there some way I could use this detail anyway? If I did, for myself and for my readers, I knew I'd have to have a reason why it *could* be true. I decided that an impoverished artist might have traded his work for favors. Did any real brothel in Elizabethan times have such portraits? I don't know. But for the reason I gave my readers, mine could.

In looking at secondary sources, don't neglect lavishly illustrated books, including children's books. The latter often focus on the smaller details that interest young people…and everyone else. Evaluate them the same way you would any other book, but do take a look at them. David Macauley's *Castle* and *Cathedral* are particularly good examples of what I mean. For adults, a book like *The Treasure Houses of Britain: Five Hundred Years of Private Patronage and Art Collecting*, edited by Mary Yakush and Frances Smyth, is a gold mine of inspiration. So are AA (U.K.) and AAA travel guides and publications of the National Geographic Society.

## Online Research

The Internet provides another source of information, but one has to be even more be careful in evaluating the reliability of material found there. As I said in the previous chapter, anyone can put up a website on any subject. The text may have been written by an expert in the field, or by the PR person hired to produce the webpage, or by a high school kid doing a project. Sometimes you can't tell. Many websites are, to be kind, misleading. Not even online encyclopedias can be trusted. Wikipedia, which will often appear first when you use a search engine, allows anyone to post and does not verify the information in the entries.

That is not to say the Internet can't be useful. There are accurate sites. There are discussion groups on the most arcane subjects. You can track down experts on almost anything, most of whom are delighted to answer questions by e-mail. Just be careful. Find out if your source is reliable *before* you use the information in your novel.

## Sources to Avoid (and a Few Exceptions to the Rule)

Although films made on location may show you the terrain, and in some cases, the costumes and settings may be painstakingly recreated, in general movies and television shows are not accurate. Getting the details right plays a distant second fiddle to story, even in those movies that claim to have done their homework. As a student of the Elizabethan era, I shudder at the film *Elizabeth* (with Cate Blanchett), delight in television's more recent *Elizabeth I* (Helen Mirren), and enjoy the old PBS *Elizabeth R* (Glenda Jackson). *Shakespeare in Love* is somewhat free with historical fact but does a good job of capturing the "feel" of the era.

Most people who know anything about medieval life and/or the real William Wallace have strong negative reactions to *Braveheart*. A list of "Fallacies about the Middle Ages" posted at medieval historian/mystery writer Sharan Newman's website includes the *"jus primae noctis,"* the idea that the lord of the manor had the right of "first night" with any bride. That's just one misconception that *Braveheart* perpetrates. Similar examples from other historical periods are not hard to find. The basic rule of thumb is this: Don't trust everything you see on television or at the movies.

On the other hand, for Terence Faherty, whose Scott Elliott private eye series is set in Hollywood in the 1940s and later, movies are a prime research tool. He studies the backgrounds of movies made in the era he's writing about, just as he might study newsreels from that period, looking for telling details. In fact, as Faherty related to mystery fans when he appeared on a panel at the Malice Domestic fan convention, his series was inspired by his love of old movies. In *Kill Me Again*, the first entry, moviemakers are filming a sequel to *Casablanca*. Faherty's sleuth works for "Hollywood Security." Subsequent books in the series use other real movies as starting points. But they are only starting points. Faherty then outlines in great detail in advance of writing, a practice he finds useful for uncovering which topics he needs to research in more traditional ways.

Relying on other people's novels for information is also, generally, a bad idea. Read other people's fiction to see how the novels and short stories are structured, but *do not use historical novels for historical research*. In fact, it is probably not wise to read historical novels set in the same period you are writing about at all. You have no way of telling how much other writers have invented and the last thing you want is to have another writer's fictional creation sneak into your work.

Author Georgette Heyer, whose knowledge of Regency England was extensive, found one phrase that became a favorite of hers—"to make a cake of oneself"—in a privately printed memoir unavailable to the general public. Later writers, imitating her to the point of plagiarism, could only have borrowed the expression from Heyer's novels. At least one of these imitators also accepted as fact that spangles on the Prince Regent's coat (in *Regency Buck*) were behind his rift with Beau Brummell, a detail that Heyer made up. Even if you are absolutely sure another fiction writer's research is thorough, *do your own!*

Naturally, there are exceptions. There are *always* exceptions. For her award-winning short story "Too Many Cooks," Marcia Talley reread Dorothy Dunnett's novel about the historical Macbeth, *King Hereafter*. She did not, however, rely on that as her only source of information. She also read period writings.

Carola Dunn, who writes about the 1920s, reads mystery stories written in the 1920s and 1930s as part of her research. She finds "novels written during the period much more useful to get a feel for how people thought and lived, and details of daily life, than any history book." Dunn's other favorite sources, however, are nonfiction. In particular, she consults a 1912 *Nelson's Encyclopedia*: "This has lots of info about things that aren't in modern American encyclopedias because they aren't of much interest to modern Americans and there's too much newer stuff current editions have to cover." *The Blue Guide to London 1933* "is a little past the date my series has reached but is nonetheless useful because London didn't change that much during the five or six intervening years. It has information about the postal system, the cost of meals in various grades of restaurants, etc." Period newspapers, particularly local papers, provide articles about local people and also ads, both commercial and classified. In addition, she has a 1950s AA Road Atlas to show "routes the way they were before motorways."

## Consulting an Expert

When it comes to tracking down particularly elusive details, it may be useful to consult an expert. This has already been mentioned in connection with poisons.

Ph.D. candidates have to do original research for their dissertations. That means a great many scholars have expertise in very narrow areas of history. You can find one though an Internet search or the recommendations of other writers.

In writing *Face Down O'er the Border*, I needed information on the law in sixteenth-century Scotland. I knew it was different from that in England, but not precisely how, and I was not having much luck finding books on the subject. I asked Candace Robb, who has set several historical mysteries in Scotland, if she had any suggestions. She referred me to a professor at the University of Guelph. By lucky chance, this expert's current research project dealt with exactly the time and place in which I was interested. The information she provided changed the way I intended to have events play out in my historical mystery. I had to come up with a new series of plot twists. The result is accurate. It is also much more interesting.

## Making History Work for You

Steven Saylor, in an interview printed in *Murder: Past Tense* in 2002, talked about a problem he encountered in writing *A Murder on the Appian Way*. There was a period of forty days when nothing happened in the real-life trial at the core of his story. Rather than change history by shortening this gap, Saylor chose to have his sleuth, Gordianus, kidnapped and held prisoner for that forty-day period. Kidnapping witnesses was something the man on trial was known to do. Saylor made an inconvenient historical fact work for him.

Dale Furutani, whose Samurai Trilogy is set in Japan in 1603, wanted in *Kill the Shogun* to have his sleuth, Kaze, hide in a Kabuki theater. The makeup and costumes, Furutani thought, would help Kaze conceal his identity. Unfortunately, research revealed that Kabuki was a relatively new art form in 1603, and worse, as Furutani revealed in an online interview in 2000 with Ron Miller, Kabuki was "considered a rather scandalous form of entertainment since it featured dancing girls who often aroused the male customers, then serviced them later, backstage.... Rather than abandon the idea, Furutani decided to run with it. As a result, we see Kaze accidentally helping 'change the nature' of Kabuki during his brief time as a member of the performing company."

### But It Really Happened That Way!

A slightly different problem comes up when you know "what really happened" but the truth is so preposterous that no one will believe it. My *Deadlier than the Pen* contains an anecdote about a runaway camel in the heart of the theater district in Manhattan. The story comes straight out of an issue of the *New York Times* from 1888, but one editor who read (and rejected) an early version of the book felt that scene should be cut because it was too far-fetched. Do you risk disbelief or stick to the truth? In the case of the camel, I was stubborn enough to keep trying to figure out a way to use it until I felt I succeeded...or at least until I'd written it in a way that wouldn't be deleted by the editor who finally published the book.

Possibly this was a mistake. As Steven Steinbock, review editor for *The*

*Strand Magazine*, points out, "There are many anecdotes about exasperated authors, after being told to cut a particular chunk of text because of its implausibility, insisting to their editors, 'But it's true, that's the way it happened.' The truth is that truth often really is stranger than fiction. Fiction, ironic as it seems, demands a lot more logic than fact does."

## The Thin Line between Research and Plagiarism

Plagiarism is a complex subject, made more confusing by the number of lawsuits filed in the hope of a large financial settlement. From Faye Kellerman's claim in 1999 that *Shakespeare in Love* infringed on the copyright of her dark and brooding historical mystery novel, *The Quality of Mercy*, to the 2006 lawsuit against Dan Brown over the ideas in *The Da Vinci Code*, many claims of plagiarism have been made but few have been proven. If you want details of a genuine case of plagiarism, you can find them online by using the search string "Nora Roberts" + "Janet Dailey." Roberts, whose work was plagiarized by Dailey, donated the settlement she received to charity.

Sadly, we live in a society where high schools and colleges frequently fail to teach students what plagiarism is, let alone that it is morally and legally wrong. Plagiarism happens when one writer copies or closely imitates the work of another writer and tries to pass off the result as his or her own creation. This doesn't necessarily mean copying word-for-word. It can also apply to copying details of a plot, even if the character names and actual words are different.

Copyright infringement occurs when the copied material comes from a work covered by the current copyright law. Those who plagiarize may be sued under this law. Copyright infringement also includes the use, in a story or book or magazine or fanzine, without permission, of any characters or setting created by another writer. And it prohibits quoting from another writer's work without crediting the source, or if the quote is longer than "fair use" allows, without getting permission from the author.

All this seems straightforward enough...until you get down to specifics. Is there such a thing as "accidental" plagiarism? Can you "internalize" passages from another's work and really believe they are your own? And is this a valid excuse, even if it is true? Not if you are talking about more than one stray passage.

How do you avoid being accused of plagiarism? To start with, when you do research, be extremely careful in your note-taking. If you are recording someone's exact words, put them in quotes. Better yet, if it is information you know you will use in your novel, purchase your own copy of the source or make a photocopy of the entire page in question. Then you will know what the original words were and where they came from.

But wait. What about clichés? What about proverbs? What about catchphrases? To take a contemporary example, are writers of fiction supposed to stop and give credit to the source every time a character quips, "Where's the beef?" or "Have it your way"? And for writers of historical fiction, must we avoid ever repeating the exact words someone else previously used to describe a building or a person? There are only so many ways to say some things, especially if you want to avoid words that weren't yet in use at the time of your novel.

The solution for writers of nonfiction is to use quotation marks and footnotes. This does not work in fiction. Remember, please, that I am not talking now about wholesale borrowing from someone else's writing. That is clearly wrong. But writers of historical mysteries often face a choice between accuracy—occasionally inserting a few "real" passages into the text—and changing every word of every source, even if that means using anachronistic language.

In *Face Down Upon an Herbal*, two of my characters are talking about a favorite Christmas food. I wanted to get the details right, so I relied upon William Harrison's *Description of England*, written in 1587. Given that date, this is not a copyright issue. The book is in the public domain. But does the fact that I took eighteen words from the following description, and put it in the mouth of one of my characters, constitute plagiarism?

This is Harrison's account of the making of brawn:

> It is made commonly of the fore part of a tame boar, set up for the purpose by the space of a whole year or two, especially in gentlemen's houses (for the husbandmen and farmers never frank them for their own use above three or four months, or half a year at the most), in which time he is dieted with oats and peason, and lodged on the bare planks of an uneasy cote till his fat be hardened sufficiently for their purpose; afterward he is killed, scalded, and cut out, and then of his former parts is our brawn made; the rest is nothing so fat, and therefore it beareth the name of souse only and is commonly reserved for the serving-man.... The neck pieces, being cut off round, are called collars of brawn, the shoulders are named shields; only the ribs retain the former denomination, so that these aforesaid pieces deserve the name of brawn.

In my use of this information in fiction, this became: "'Brawn is the forepart of a tame boar,' he explained. 'In Lancashire, in rich gentlemen's houses, the beast is fed on oats and peas for a year or more and lodged on the bare planks of an uneasy cote till his fat be hardened sufficiently for the purpose. Some are slaughtered in the autumn, but most are saved for Christmas. The neck pieces are called collars of brawn, the shoulders shields.'"

Should I have changed "lodged on the bare planks of an uneasy cote till his fat be hardened sufficiently for the(ir) purpose" to something else? What, exactly, *could* I have changed it to and still kept the flavor of the language? What other words would have been as evocative or as accurate in describing the process? Then, too, the character's familiarity with Lancashire ways, and ways of saying things, played a key role in the solution of the mystery.

At a copyright workshop a librarian friend of mine attended in 2000, a lawyer with the Indiana University/Purdue University Copyright Management Center offered the opinion that phrases of description—the example he gave was of a historic and well-known building—are allowed, since there are only so many ways to write that description. Would this ruling apply to the "uneasy cote" if Harrison's work were still protected by copyright law? I think so, but would Harrison, living in these litigious times, agree?

It is probably inevitable that, in the creation of a *historical* mystery novel, bits and pieces of dozens, perhaps hundreds of sources, find their way into the text. A few borrowed words here and there, selected to give the flavor of the times to your creation, do not constitute either plagiarism or copyright infringement...unless they all come from the same source. As Malcolm Gladwell points out in "Something Borrowed," an essay in *The New Yorker*, "Under copyright law, what matters is not that you copied someone else's work. What matters is *what* you copied, and *how much* you copied. Intellectual-property doctrine isn't a straightforward application of the ethical principle 'Thou shalt not steal.'... There are certain situations where you *can* steal."

The best suggestion I can make is always to be aware of your sources. If you do choose to copy even a few words verbatim, do so for a specific, well-thought-out reason. And become very familiar with what plagiarism and copyright infringement are. The website at http://www.copyright .iupui.edu is a good place to start.

Also, and I cannot stress this too strongly, be very careful about what you absorb from reading other people's historical novels. Fiction is a work of creation, the "child" of the author. To take from it, even inadvertently, is to violate both the work and the creator. Although Georgette Heyer, a very private person, never brought suit for copyright infringement, there is no question but that she was plagiarized. On two occasions she went so far as to draw up detailed lists of the borrowings. In a letter to a legal advisor, Heyer wrote that one imitator knew "rather less about the period than the average schoolchild." To add insult to injury, some fans attributed this plagiarist's work to Heyer herself, suggesting that she was "publishing shoddy work under a pseudonym."

Ideas, like titles, cannot be copyrighted. This is why, to use a non-mystery example, *West Side Story* isn't generally considered to be a case of "stealing" Shakespeare's plot in *Romeo and Juliet*.

In most cases, the inspiration for a historical mystery comes from a multitude of sources, not just one. But if the core of your novel was inspired by a particular account in one scholar's book, something you haven't seen anywhere else, or by a specific real crime and the contemporary accounts of it, then you would probably do well to acknowledge your source in an author's note. If you were inspired by someone else's novel or a movie, be very, very careful how much detail from that source survives in the final draft of your creation.

## Writing What You Know

I am often asked if it is necessary for a writer to have a good background in history before attempting to write historical mystery fiction. It doesn't hurt, but it isn't essential. What is essential is to develop a "feel" for the era you are writing about.

The fiction writer's fascination with a particular historical period is more important than any formal training. You need to be willing to read, or at least skim and take notes on, enough books about your setting to avoid bloopers. You need to learn what "everyone knows" and which of these facts are really fallacies. If you are enthusiastic about the subject, research shouldn't be a hardship, and once you have a firm grasp of what life was like in your era, you can make intelligent decisions about what is right for your book.

We're storytellers, not scholars. The scholars have already done the hard part. We get to take advantage of that, picking and choosing what works for our plots and characters. We make ourselves experts on a particular time and place and then we write historical mysteries that will take our readers into that fictional past.

Their guide on the journey is usually the sleuth, which leads me to the next topic of discussion — how to create a believable historical detective.

# 5 Creating a Believable Historical Detective

CREATING believable characters is essential in historical mysteries. Your sleuth has to have the special skills necessary to solve crimes and yet be part of his or her world. The supporting cast has to be carefully thought out as well. They should all be products of their time and place. That means the beliefs they hold may not be politically correct in this day and age. Your challenge will be to present them as they would have been, warts and all, and still make them accessible and sympathetic to modern-day readers.

## Selecting Point of View

Your selection of a point of view to write in will affect how readers see your protagonist. First-person narration by your sleuth is more immediate. It requires you to become your character. And it is often used for humorous effect, or to make readers more sympathetic toward a protagonist who has a few character flaws. Author Lindsey Davis (character Marcus Didius Falco), Marilyn Todd (Claudia Seferius), Fiona Buckley (Ursula Blanchard), Elizabeth Peters (Amelia Peabody Emerson), Rhys Bowen (Molly Murphy), P.N. Elrod (Jack Fleming), and many others have created exceptionally memorable characters using first-person point of view.

First-person narration by a secondary character (a "Watson") is another alternative. You lose access to the sleuth's thoughts, but gain the advantage of describing the detective from the outside. Then again, Steven Saylor wrote the first sixty pages of *Roman Blood* using Cicero as narrator, then "realized that to spend twenty-four hours a day with him was going to be an ordeal. And having him as the sympathetic narrator wouldn't have worked for the whole series." Writing in the point of view of a secondary character will be discussed at greater length in Chapter Six.

I chose to use third-person narration with multiple viewpoint characters in the Face Down series, set in sixteenth-century England, in part because I felt it would be too difficult to make the language used by a first-person narrator convincing. I also wanted to be able to delve into the thoughts of more than one character. When you use your sleuth as the only narrator, whether in first person or third person, you are limited to what that individual can discover. You can only go where he or she can go, see what he or she can see. The sleuth has to be exceptionally clever, or extremely lucky, to solve case after case. Adding scenes in another character's point of view, perhaps several other characters' points of view, gives the reader information the sleuth may not have and broadens the reader's exposure to life in another time and place.

Chances are that either first-person or third-person narration will feel more natural to you, but if you aren't certain which will work best, experiment with both. Writing in first person is a good way to get to know your sleuth, even if you eventually rewrite those scenes in third person. You also have the option of using both first- and third-person narration in the same novel.

Another possibility, although not precisely a point-of-view decision, is to write in present tense. Jenny White's highly praised *The Sultan's Seal* is written partly this way and partly from the point of view of a first-person narrator speaking in the more usual past tense. The novel begins: "A dozen lamps flicker across the water, moving up the strait in silence, the oarsmen invisible. A dry scuffling noise drifts from shore." For some readers, this as-it-is-happening style of narration pulls them immediately into the scene. Others have a hard time getting past it and into the story.

## The Sleuth

You made some preliminary decisions about your detective's sex, age, occupation, and name while reading Chapter One. Now is the time to look more closely at your choices and decide if some tinkering is called for. Certainly you need to think long and hard about every aspect of this character's life.

### Character Traits

In some ways creating the central character for a historical mystery is easier than creating secondary characters. There are certain parameters within the plot. The hero or heroine has a definite relationship to other characters. It is also easier to tell if the protagonist is getting "out of character" because you come to know him or her so much better than any of the others.

Readers are supposed to like, or at least tolerate, your detective, and believe him or her — or them, since a sleuthing couple is also an option —

capable of solving the crime. As creator, you start out with some idea beforehand about a physical description, job or social position, living conditions, likes and dislikes, personal problems and relationships, and so forth. There also has to be some reason why this person is called upon to solve a murder.

A curious nature, a strong moral character, a sense of right and wrong, and a belief that those who commit crimes—particularly murder—should be punished for what they have done, along with a certain degree of stubbornness, are among the traits of a successful detective. It also helps if the sleuth is the sort of person who notices details, especially those that are "wrong" for some reason.

One of the reasons Troy Soos chose to make his professional baseball-player sleuth, Mickey Rawlings, a utility infielder rather than a star was because someone whose job depends on seizing every chance to make a difference in a game has to be more observant than most people. The same skill that makes Mickey useful to his team also allows him to excel as a detective.

A useful trait for any sleuth, although one not crucial to solving the mystery, is some quality that enables him or her to avoid becoming a victim. Is your sleuth a crack shot, or good with a knife, or a fast runner? In order to have Lady Appleton escape the villains in *Face Down Under the Wych Elm* by leaping overboard and swimming to shore, I had to make sure I explained, early in the book, how she had learned to swim. That skill was fairly unusual in the sixteenth century, even for men.

Characters in law enforcement aside, it isn't always easy to find a good reason for someone to get involved in investigating a crime. In a series, the amateur detective needs a reason that will last from book to book. Some of the most common professions and skills for amateur sleuths have already been mentioned in Chapter Two. Now consider what other factors may come into play, both as incentives to solve crime and as deterrents.

In writing her eighteenth-century waiting woman, Hester Kean, Patricia Wynn has to "struggle to think of ways she can free herself to detect because although strong in mind and educated by a vicar father, she is totally financially dependent on her lady's lord." On the other hand, Hester has a useful attribute for a sleuth—she *has* been educated. Wynn observes, concerning her setting in the reign of George I, that "education in a female was often only for the dependent classes who needed something to barter for their support," a possible reason, she suggests, why so many of the protagonists in early novels of historical romantic suspense were governesses.

### Mindset

Jane Finnis, writing about Roman Britain, finds the hardest part of imagining life two thousand years ago not "reconstructing their material world but recreating the character's mindset. I can envisage a society that predated the invention of printing, electricity, powered transport, and the many other wonders of our world today. But to get inside the heads of people, even the most brilliant people, who predated worldwide Christianity, or Islam, or Darwin, or Freud—that's the real challenge."

In some earlier eras, everyone would have believed in the supernatural, especially demons, witches, and acts of God. You need to think about how this might complicate a case of murder, and how your detective (clever enough to make the connection, for example, between the victim eating banewort berries and his sudden death) might be viewed. Although modern readers tend to have extensive knowledge of how murders are solved today, thanks to the proliferation of crime and forensic dramas on television, that would not have been the case in the past. Someone trying to prove a witch innocent would probably end up being accused of witchcraft herself. And in spite of being an expert on poisonous herbs, my Lady Appleton has no way to do a chemical analysis or an autopsy. She would think the latter an abomination. She would not balk, however, at feeding a suspected poison to an animal to see if it would die.

### Backstory

Backstory is important, even if none of it ever appears in print. Not only do you need to know what your sleuth does and doesn't know (knowledge gained by education and life experience) but it is also a good idea to know the background of your sleuth's relationships with other characters, especially those you may use again in future mysteries.

A sleuth has special skills that make the solution of the murder possible. These are found in your character's fictional history. Inventing one will also allow you to come to logical conclusions about how that character, having been raised in a particular historical period in a particular way, would realistically react to any given situation.

A frequent criticism of historical detectives is that they are too modern in their thinking. Chapter Ten, on anachronisms, will get into this issue in more detail, but suffice it to say that you need to be aware of the social, political, and religious restrictions that apply to your character and how he or she reacts to them.

Not everything you know about your sleuth will be shared with readers. If you're writing a series, it may be wise not to be too specific. Each book in a mystery series has to have continuity with the previous stories. Make a character extremely complex and you put yourself at greater risk of forgetting, in Book Five, some point you established in Book One. You don't want to create a cardboard detective—that's why you have to know so much—but be wary of telling all too soon.

Keeping your sleuth's character fresh in book after book can be a challenge. It is far too easy to start repeating yourself. However, one of the advantages of writing fiction is that you can jump ahead as far as you like between books. That means there can be major changes in the sleuth's life from one novel to the next, changes reflected by differences in the way s/he looks at what happens next.

One of the easiest ways to keep a character fresh is to give him or her a disruptive personal life. In the Face Down series, Lady Appleton is constantly growing and changing and getting more deeply involved in the lives of the people who are important to her. Each book centers around a murder mystery but also has a subplot that involves the development of relationships with friends, enemies, relatives, and lovers.

## Should Your Sleuth Have a Sex Life?

The decision about how much "reality" to put in a historical mystery is entirely up to the writer. Graphic sex, graphic violence, graphic description of the squalor of a past time—these are all areas about which readers have strong likes and dislikes. I'll talk more about the last two in later chapters, but sex, particularly if it involves the sleuth, falls under the heading of "character development."

If you describe a sexual encounter in any detail it risks being labeled gratuitous unless it advances the plot in a way nothing else could, or it is essential to reveal something about the participants. Margaret Frazer had an experience that illustrates how historical mystery fans are likely to respond to scenes involving sex.

"When I started telling people that I was doing a second series with the player Joliffe as the main character," she recalls, "half the time the response I got was along the lines of: 'Oh, good! You can have more sex in those books!' In the first one, there wasn't any place to put an occasion for carnal intercourse, but when plotting the second one I decided to be more cooperative."

The result wasn't quite what she expected. A reader accused her of writing "filth in order to increase sales," and sent her own copy of *A Play of Dux Moraud* to Frazer's editor "so the grandchildren wouldn't chance on it around the house."

"I didn't put in the sex to increase sales," Frazer writes, "though if that happens, great! Sex is integral to the plot on a number of levels. The central plot centers on the corruptive, destructive power of sex when it's only used as a weapon.... Descriptions of ugly wounds are used in all but the most cozy of cozy mysteries," Frazer adds. "Nasty, ugly, hurtful, deadly things done to the body are acceptable reading, but pleasure (suitable to the story) isn't? I have trouble accepting that severely skewed standard."

I.J. Parker, who writes the Sugawara Akitada series, set in eleventh-century Japan, agrees. "In *Dragon Scroll*, the first novel, Akitada is young and unmarried. How would you expect him to feel about sex? Later he is a married man, but his sidekick is always available for 'a roll in the hay' in the interests of detection. Sexual practices are, in any case, part and parcel of the historical setting, and readers of historical novels ought to be interested. We ought to be honest about our characters and the time and place we write about."

But there are other issues, too, as Rhys Bowen points out. "In the first draft of my first Molly Murphy book, I had quite a steamy sex scene between Molly and Daniel, because I felt we'd been building up to it throughout the book, but my editor made me take it out. She thought it made the book too romancey and she wanted it to be taken seriously. When I finally did let Molly have a sexual encounter in *In Like Flynn*, I was suitably restrained. Personally I am highly uncomfortable reading explicit sex, just as I am reading explicit violence."

When Troy Soos had Mickey Rawlings and Margie Turner "live in a state of light housekeeping," some readers objected, but living together was not that uncommon in the 1920s, especially when both parties—an actress and a baseball player—were not from the "better part of society."

Beverle Graves Myers usually takes her characters to the bedroom door and stops the scene there, "but at least one reviewer has suggested that I am too hesitant to 'embrace the city (Venice) dedicated to masquerade and pleasure' and that my protagonist (Tito Amato) is a bit aloof. I take that to mean, among other things, that he would like to see more sex in the books."

And what do readers think? Here are a few responses to that question from CrimeThruTime. Reader Diana Sandberg wrote:

> I am interested in knowing about characters' emotional lives. I am considerably less interested in the physical details, though I recognize that there is inevitably some overlap, and that's fine. I would just point out that there is always a great deal left out of any tale—one doesn't get a bite-by-bite description of meals, a

chapter on each night's sleep, or a thorough depiction of trips to the outhouse, either. Though all of these things can be personally significant, I don't see that they are at all necessary to a story except in a general description.... I am interested in reading about people, and how they solve problems, both personal/emotional problems and criminal investigation problems. Graphic sex and graphic violence are both just voyeurism.

Alan J. Bishop, editor of "Criminal History" (www.criminal-history.co.uk), feels that "explicit (or even semi-) sex scenes in novels should follow the rule concerning swearing—only go as far or include when it makes sense. While some characters are celibate, most are not. An author shouldn't be so explicit that it detracts from the essential plot. It comes back to the level of realism and incidental detail that the author (and readers) wish to be presented with.... Not all readers will share the same 'detail tolerance' as the writer. It's a tricky balance."

Lois H. Ward, who calls herself "just a reader," estimates she has read over 6000 mysteries in the last sixty-two years. She is "constantly astounded that so many editors feel that readers still don't have any idea what goes on 'behind closed doors' and are determined to edify them on the subject, rather than getting on with a well-written story."

What if your detective is homosexual? Diana Gabaldon's *Lord John and the Private Matter*, set in 1757, is a good example of integrating into a detective story the difficulties a sleuth might face because of his sexual orientation, particularly the problem of keeping his sexual preference secret. In many times and places homosexuality wasn't only illegal, it was punishable by death. Be prepared to do a great deal of specialized research into the social and legal aspects of homosexuality in the historical period you've chosen.

If your sleuth is a lesbian, research may be even more of a challenge. For some eras, you'll find scholars making the remarkable statement that lesbianism did not exist! It has something to do, I presume, with the fact that during much of our past both church leaders and historians were exclusively male.

At the time of writing, there are several historical mystery series in print which feature male sleuths who have been castrated. Beverle Graves Myers chose to make Tito Amato a castrato because she is "a huge fan of baroque opera." Her sleuth is "one of thousands of boys who were gelded to preserve their pure, silvery soprano voices into adulthood. Europe was mad for Italian opera, and the *castrati* were the divas, or 'American Idols,' of the eighteenth century."

Myers feels that "Tito turned out to be a good choice for the protagonist of a historical mystery series. This Venetian singer is very much a man of his time, and as an entertainer he comes in contact with people of all classes. The poor stand shoulder-to-shoulder to watch his operas, while the rich are entertained while they socialize, dine, and play cards in luxurious boxes. Thus, Tito has access to interrogating all types of people to solve the crimes that come his way. Behind the theater curtain, he is part of a subculture that bubbles with ambition, competition, and intrigue. Fertile ground for murder all around."

In addition, "Tito's status as a eunuch gives him a unique perspective. While not effeminate, he is obviously different. The hormonal changes make him beardless, tall, long-limbed, with a high speaking voice. Many who applaud him at the opera house wouldn't want to sit next to him in a tavern. Especially in countries outside of Italy, he and his fellow *castrati* are often the object of scorn in print and to their faces. Tito feels the injustice of his situation keenly. Being castrated as a boy, with no say in the matter, makes him sensitive to injustice of all sorts. He is particularly enraged by the Venetian authorities' tendency to turn a blind eye to crimes of the wealthy while eagerly pinning crimes on the poor, the Jews, and other outcasts of society."

Mary Reed and Eric Mayer also chose to use a castrated character as sleuth, but for a very different reason. "We needed our detective to be a confidante of Emperor Justinian. This narrowed the list of candidates considerably and one sixth-century occupation in particular leapt out at us: Lord Chamberlains were close advisors to the emperors and were relied on to carry out a wide variety of tasks. A little detecting would probably not be beyond them. We gave our Lord Chamberlain the name John which was then, as now, a popular choice and one that wouldn't grate on modern sensibilities. However, it was a little bland. We knew that Lord Chamberlains had often been eunuchs, which was true of many of those involved in administrating the Eastern Roman Empire. Justinian's real life advisor Narses had been a eunuch." From that research came both their sleuth's name and his sexual identity: John the Eunuch.

## Using Real People

If you have chosen to use a real historical figure as your sleuth, some of the character development is already done, but don't make the mistake of thinking you've chosen the easy route. There are both advantages and disadvantages to this choice. One advantage is that a great deal is known about some historical figures. That is also the disadvantage. There are serious pitfalls involved in having real people solve crimes. The most obvious is that if they are known to have been elsewhere at the time, you need to present a very convincing reason to put them where you want them.

Karen Harper, whose protagonist is Queen Elizabeth I of England, knew that in the week after the queen's coronation, Elizabeth took to her bed with a bad cold...just at the time Harper wanted *The Tidal Poole* to be set. Her solution was to have the fictional Elizabeth fake her illness, a ploy to give herself time to solve the crime in secret. That is how Harper adapts historical fact without ignoring recorded history.

"You need to do your homework," Harper says, "much more than someone who has a fictional sleuth working in a historical era. You must be true to that character. Queen Elizabeth I as a shy, quiet person? No way. George Washington as a self-serving, dishonorable man—perish the thought and perish your series."

Harper sees many advantages to using a real person as a detective. "Readers love to get into the hearts and heads of actual historical people." In addition, "using an actual person for the main character gives you an in-depth, dynamic character to work with, one who is probably already fascinating and bright." Harper's queen "comes with the dysfunctional family from hell, which adds great depth to her character. I could not have created this multi-dimensional character if I had been forced to."

Also in the plus column are the numerous plot ideas available in the life of a real person. In *The Twylight Tower*, Queen Elizabeth investigates a real case. Harper read the conclusions of earlier writers, then came up with her own solution to the crime. In addition, the "hook for the book" of the queen as sleuth garnered extra press coverage from *People Magazine* for *The Poyson Garden* and prompted the inclusion of books in the series on reading lists at summer Shakespeare Festivals.

Most historical mystery writers will agree that the biggest problem with using real people is that for some readers (and reviewers), these stories will never be believable. Whether it is Elliot Roosevelt writing mysteries in which his mother, First Lady Eleanor Roosevelt, is the sleuth, or Rosemary Stevens writing about Beau Brummell, or Daniel Stashower about Harry Houdini, a segment of historical mystery fans will be unable to suspend disbelief long enough to enjoy the story.

That didn't stop Peter Heck from choosing Mark Twain as his detective. He writes on his website that "the idea for the series grew pretty naturally out of having the 1910 edition of Twain's complete works in my parents' library as I was growing up.... Mr. Clemens (as my narrator calls him) had exactly the right combination of mental qualities that make a good detective." In this case, the character also provided an abundance of source material. "Twain's self-portrayals make his best nonfiction as much fun as his fiction. Also, he was a world traveler, and he mingled with all classes and types of people—so I could believably introduce him into almost any situation."

Stephanie Barron also discovered a situation ideal for turning a real person into a detective when she came upon the fact that no one knows what author Jane Austen was really doing between May 1801 and September 1804. After Austen's death, her older sister Cassandra burned letters from this period and cut out parts of others with a pair of scissors. Barron's premise is that Austen spent those years solving mysteries and that her unconventional behavior was the reason Cassandra was later driven to destroy all records of that time.

## Creating a Sleuth from Another Author's Character

Taking a fictional character created by someone else and making him or her your sleuth is an option only if the original work is in the public domain. For all others, copyright law prevents the use of someone else's characters without the permission of the original author or his/her estate.

In other words, don't do this unless you are certain you won't be sued.

Quite a number of historical mystery writers *do* use fictional characters originally created by other writers. Alan Gordon's sleuth, Feste, came from William Shakespeare's *Twelfth Night*. Themed short-story anthologies have featured an assortment of characters from both Shakespeare and Dickens. And Carrie Bebris saw potential sleuths in two of Jane Austen's characters and created the Mr. & Mrs. Darcy series. She writes on her website that "the Darcys are natural protagonists for a mystery series. Though they would never think of themselves as 'detectives,' Elizabeth and Darcy make a great team when it comes to solving problems and piercing the armor of people they encounter. Elizabeth is a sharp observer of human nature...who relies on her instincts. Darcy...is a deductive reasoner and a man who knows how to move about in the world." Bebris sees them as "a dynamic, resourceful investigative couple in the tradition of *The Thin Man's* Nick and Nora Charles."

Characters from the Sherlock Holmes canon are also fair game for other writers. There have been innumerable pastiches and several series. Carole Nelson Douglas's sleuth is Irene Adler from "A Scandal in Bohemia." Martin Davies uses Holmes's landlady, Mrs. Hudson, as the detective. John Gardner uses Professor Moriarty, as does Michael Kurland. M.J. Trow's books feature Inspector Lestrade. Lora Roberts uses Holmes as a lesser character and lets the housekeeper at his leased manor house do the sleuthing in *The Affair of the Incognito Tenant*. Several series featuring Holmes himself have been written and there are at least two children's mystery series that feature the Baker Street Irregulars as characters. And of course, in Laurie R. King's series about Mary Russell, the American Mary marries a much older Sherlock Holmes, after which they solve cases together.

According to an interview with King in *Deadly Women*, the idea for Mary Russell came from watching a television production of one of the Holmes stories. King was struck by the fact that "this much vaunted man was only using skills possessed by any woman who has a child over the age of two, and many women who were not mothers at all. Call it common sense or feminine intuition, when it is found in a male it is considered extraordinary."

## Sleuthing Couples

Does the use of a pair of sleuths (as distinct from a sleuth and a sidekick or support staff) make the writer's job easier? Are two heads better than one? In my Diana Spaulding Mysteries, although Diana alone gets credit in the subtitle, she is actually half of a sleuthing couple. I emphasize this by using a dual point of view, a technique that lends itself extremely well to writing about a pair of sleuths.

One advantage of two sleuths is that one can often go where the other cannot. Leonard Tourney's characters Matthew and Joan Stock bring different qualities to the table in sixteenth-century England. He's the constable; his wife has an ear to the ground for local gossip and a bit of psychic ability. In Anne Perry's series about Thomas and Charlotte Pitt, although Charlotte cannot go wandering through Whitechapel, Thomas, a policeman, can. Thomas isn't welcome in the drawing rooms of London, but Charlotte is. In addition, by officially assigning Pitt to a murder investigation, Perry gives both characters access to essential information about the crime, details that would not ordinarily be shared with the general public.

Sleuthing couples, even when they don't get along, above all need abilities that complement each other. Diana Spaulding is a journalist, which not only brings her into contact with crime but also allows her more freedom than most women enjoyed in America in 1888. Ben Northcote is a physician and a coroner, and that specialized knowledge augments Diana's skills.

One of Candace Robb's two medieval series carries the subtitle "The Owen Archer Mysteries" but in fact it has always been about a sleuthing couple. As Robb recalls, "In the beginning a couple were brought together over a murder investigation involving the woman's dying husband, and by the end of the book the couple were together. Thus had I inaugurated the Owen Archer and Lucie Wilton Mysteries. My editor called it 'An Owen Archer Mystery,' and when I corrected *him* he corrected *me*, saying that I would give away the ending of *The Apothecary Rose* if I added Lucie's name to the series."

Robb accepted the decision, but by the third book had decided that "despite what the publishers called it, the series starred both Owen and Lucie, and in that book I gave Lucie a more central role in the investigation—at the request of the prioress of the convent sheltering the woman under investigation. Since then, except for one instance, although Owen is the one known in York as a sleuth, Lucie is as integral a part of a team as she can be, considering her responsibilities. I realized early on that I'd tied Lucie both to her apothecary and to her children; but Owen depends on her knowledge of poisons and her keen mind." Robb's fans seem to like having Lucie play a key role in the stories. Her absence from *A Gift of Sanctuary* was noticed "and not too happily!"

Not every couple in historical mystery fiction share the detecting equally, even the ones readers commonly think of as a team. In Elizabeth Peters's Amelia Peabody series, at least before Ramses and Nefret grow up, it is clearly Amelia who tells the stories and she who does most of the detecting. Her husband, while acknowledged as her partner in all things, generally plays a supporting role. Amelia is the one determined to find the killer and see justice done.

If you do decide to use a sleuthing couple, you have the option of varying the balance from book to book. The couple can work together as equal partners or one sleuth can take on the dominant role while the other, although remaining a key player in plot and subplots, essentially functions as a sidekick.

Sidekicks, along with other secondary characters, make up the rest of the cast in a historical mystery. Without them, the sleuth would have little to do…and no one to talk to about his or her brilliant deductions.

# 6 Creating Believable Secondary Characters

JUST AS your sleuth needs to fit into the historical setting, so do all the other characters. Sidekicks, suspects, and villains alike have to belong to their milieu. The creation of believable secondary characters—whether imagined or actual—is crucial to the success of any historical mystery.

## Sidekicks

No matter how brilliant your detective is, he or she can benefit from having other characters to help with the sleuthing. This may vary from one assistant to a band of loyal retainers.

If you write about a sleuthing couple, you may not need a sidekick. Otherwise, most detectives have at least one. The professional sleuth's most frequent sidekick is a professional subordinate—an officer of lower rank, a secretary, or a clerk. If the detective is an amateur, particularly a woman, then servants make convenient sidekicks.

The significant other is a frequent choice as a sidekick, and may, depending upon the sleuth, vary from book to book in a series. In an interview with Recorded Books, Troy Soos admits to trying out girlfriends for Mickey Rawlings in three successive books before settling on the one he liked best, Margie Turner, to reuse in later volumes. Margie, with her theatrical connections, proves particularly useful in *Murder in Ebbets Field*, but simply by being a woman, she is able to go places in 1920s American society that Mickey can't.

Whatever character you use in the role of sidekick, create a backstory, just as you did for the sleuth. You may even end up using the sidekick's problems as a subplot.

### Comic Sidekicks

Sidekicks can also be used to provide comic relief. Murder is hardly a laughing matter, but unless you are aiming for unrelenting darkness, an occasional light moment is a good idea. When I wrote the first book in the

Face Down series I didn't realize that Jennet, Lady Appleton's tiring maid (i.e. attiring maid, and in later books her housekeeper and confidante) would generate chuckles. After the book was published and people commented favorably on my use of humor, I realized it was an element I wanted to keep.

It is not easy to create. What one reader finds amusing, another may not. Humor that comes naturally, out of character, is usually the most successful kind. I've written and discarded many scenes in which my attempts to provide comic relief from the grim realities of investigating a murder slipped over into farce or melodrama. Characters with eccentricities or obsessions lend themselves to humor, but they need to be handled judiciously. Overdo it and readers will find them unbelievable.

With Jennet, the key was her superstitious nature. Almost everyone in sixteenth-century England believed in ghosts, spells, witches, and the like. Jennet's world view contrasts nicely with Lady Appleton's more rational outlook on life. As a bonus, it offers the opportunity for comic relief. In *Face Down Beneath the Eleanor Cross*, Lady Appleton is accused of murdering her husband. In an attempt to help her mistress, Jennet questions a suspect's mother, a woman who is reputed to be a witch. When the woman realizes who Jennet is, she curses her. Jennet, fearful of what will happen as a result of that curse, is desperate enough to try a method she's assured will divert the ill-wishing—she buys a cow on its last legs so that the curse will settle on her cattle instead of on herself. The cow becomes something of a running gag for the rest of the novel, since it immediately begins to thrive. Is this crucial to the mystery? No, but it does keep the novel from unrelenting despair. And it affects the relationships of several continuing characters.

### Using a "Watson"

The use of a sidekick as a first-person narrator is a device found with some frequency in historical mysteries. In *The Name of the Rose*, very obviously following the Holmes/Watson model, Umberto Eco gives his sleuth, William of Baskerville, a secretary named Adso. He was there. He tells the story as he saw it unfold. We see the sleuth only through his eyes.

When Peter Heck chose to make Mark Twain his detective he "knew better than to try to imitate him directly." Instead he created a "Watson" in Wentworth Cabot, lawyer's son, recent graduate of Yale, and fledgling writer. As Twain's "traveling secretary," Cabot gives first-hand accounts of the mysteries "Mr. Clemens" solves. It isn't necessary for the "Watson" to look stupid in comparison to the sleuth, but this character, as narrator, does need to stay in a supporting role. Writing of Cabot on his website, Heck says: "Even in those days it was hard to get through Yale without something between the ears — but in many ways he is a true innocent."

Daniel Stashower's series features magician Harry Houdini. At first, he "had trouble finding the right voice. On the face of it, it would be hard to imagine a more natural detective hero. He was an athletic marvel. He was a born showman. He had a gift for creating and solving puzzles. He had wealth, fame, and an apparently limitless supply of useful tricks up his sleeve. This combination of attributes, however pleasant, didn't leave much room for character development." Even worse, "Houdini was famous for his arrogance, and I worried that the reader would lose patience or find him unsympathetic."

Stashower's solution was to establish "a Holmes-Watson relationship, with Houdini's younger brother, Dash Hardeen, serving as an affable narrator, human in scale, to provide a buffer between the reader and Houdini. I wanted Dash to be worldly and funny in a way that Houdini wasn't, and this opened the door to a sort of inversion of the traditional detective-and-sidekick arrangement. In my books, if not in life, Dash is the brains of the outfit. Houdini has plenty of important virtues — strength, courage and an undeniable creative genius — but Dash provides the cunning and practical know-how, not to mention the wisecracks. For me, the relationship between the two of them is what made it interesting."

## Other Secondary Characters

There will be a few characters who don't need to be developed much — mere place-holders like the messenger who delivers a letter. Unless you want them to seem more important than they are, you don't even need to give these people names. Most characters, however, have to be fleshed out a little. In writing historical mysteries, you need to place them in the hierarchy of their time and place and gauge their relationship to other characters in terms of existing social and economic barriers. A Victorian city gentleman's attitude toward servants was not the same as an Elizabethan country gentlewoman's.

Some characters in a historical mystery will be stereotypes. The word has a bad reputation, but all stereotyping really does in this case is provide a means of quick identification for the reader. A stereotype is a character who is a typical member of a group. If readers already know what the group is like, they understand a character who is a member of that group without a lot of explanation. A group name — maidservant, for example —

is sometimes all that is needed to call to mind a recognizable image. The most common stereotypes are occupations—servant, lawyer, merchant, prostitute—and those based on relationships—the confidant, the rival, the meddling relative.

For a third-string character who exists solely to perform a function in the plot—the queen who sends the sleuth to investigate a threat to the Crown—there is no need to go beyond standard expectations. For others, you can still start with the stereotype, then take the next step and develop the unique aspects of the individual. Make the character act *against* stereotype. Give him multiple functions or additional ties to other characters—a past relationship, a family connection, or a debt of honor to be repaid. To these add character traits—habitual behavior, oddities of speech, and the like—and physical description.

Describing a character's clothing, although a distraction when it is overdone, is an extremely useful device in historicals. In past times the relative richness of a person's garments often indicated a great deal about family, wealth, and position in society. In fact, some place-holders—the liveried servant, the judge in his robes and wig—can be described only by their clothes.

Here's a bit of character description, from Edward Marston's *The Devil's Apprentice*, that I wish I had written. The character's name is Egidius Pye. "Tall, scrawny, and stooping, he had an air of sustained neglect about him." He is losing his hair, his beard is graying, and his "ponderous movements" make him seem twenty years older than he is. Marston gives him a food-stained, dirt-flecked white ruff, but the telling details are these: "So close were the eyes, nose, and mouth that it looked as if all four had retreated to the center of his face out of sudden fright on the principle that there was safety in numbers."

If you want to create memorable characters you need memorable descriptions. It's not the purpose of this book to teach fiction writing in general, so I'll offer only this advice: look to books on writing, but also to those written for actors. Learn something about body language. And to understand what makes a person tick, study personality types.

### Motivating Real People

Hundreds of years later, the behavior of real historical figures sometimes seems incomprehensible. And yet, as a writer of historical fiction, you don't want to change known facts. I encountered this dilemma in writing *Face Down Before Rebel Hooves*. In 1569, two women played key roles in a rebellion against Queen Elizabeth. I could not avoid using them as characters, but they appeared to behave irrationally, and statements attributed to them did not always make sense. Worse, they seemed to be much alike. I needed to find a way to make them distinct individuals and to understand why they acted the way they did.

Jane Howard, countess of Westmorland (1537–1593), was the wife of Charles Neville, sixth earl of Westmorland (1543–1601) and the sister of the fourth duke of Norfolk. She was ambitious and well educated—she knew Greek and Latin and was a poet. She had four daughters, although their ages in 1569 are unknown. She was the oldest of three sisters and she did not flee England with her husband when the rebellion failed, but rather petitioned the queen for a pardon. She was the more outspoken of the two countesses. The comments that have come down to us are full of contradictions. Records call her "a woman of spirit."

Anne Somerset, countess of Northumberland (d. 1591) was said to be devoted to her husband, Thomas Percy, seventh earl of Northumberland (1528–1572) and had four daughters by him. She bore another one nine months after the rebellion began. "Beautiful and spirited" say the accounts. Romantic stories came out of her flight over the border into Scotland when the rebellion failed, but these have to be taken with a grain of salt.

To create distinctive and believable characters out of these two real and similar women, I relied upon Linda N. Edelstein's *The Writer's Guide to Character Traits*, classifying Lady Westmorland as a "bossy" character type and Lady Northumberland as an "adventurer." They still had much in common, but Lady Westmorland now came to be defined by her tendency toward recklessness, combativeness, and rudeness. According to Edelstein, a "bossy" is someone good at coercion and able to use others' weaknesses, someone who avoids intimacy and sees others as puppets. Although my Lady Westmorland is thick-skinned, she is still sensitive to criticism. She's also competitive, stubborn, closed-minded, mistrustful, easily frustrated, and concerned about status.

As an "adventurer," the key to Lady Northumberland's character became her bold, energetic nature and her craving for excitement. Like a "bossy," she wants her own way. Unconcerned with rules or social conventions, she is forceful, ruthless, and impulsive. Her overconfidence causes her to exhibit poor judgment. Most significant, however, is the fact that, unlike the "bossy" character type, the "adventurer" has a wide circle of friends.

Based on these character traits and on historical records, I let my Lady Northumberland run roughshod over her household, often ignoring the feelings of others. But she has attractive, admirable qualities as well—she is concerned when one of her women has an eye infection and goes out of her way to seek remedies for the condition. This also provided me with a way to introduce my sleuth, skilled as an herbalist, into the household.

### Suspects

In a mystery almost every character is a potential suspect. You may know who your villain is, but you don't want your readers to guess, not until late in the book, ideally at just about the same moment your sleuth figures it out.

Give every character you can a secret. This does not necessarily mean everyone has committed a crime. Secrets can be trivial—such as an embarrassing personal detail the suspect doesn't want to share with the sleuth—just so long as they complicate the solution to the mystery. They do, however, have to be suitable to the station and sensibility of the character. As a rule of thumb, provide your sleuth with at least three viable suspects who have motives, real or imagined, that are strong enough to result in murder.

### Victims

Anyone can become a victim. Two classic plot devices (or possibly clichés) of mystery fiction are to kill off the sleuth's nearest and dearest to provide a reason for him or her to get involved in solving the crime, and to have the sleuth's primary suspect become the murderer's next victim. There's a good reason so many fictional policemen lose partners—or spouses—in the line of duty. Murdering someone close to the sleuth has more dramatic impact and raises the stakes for the detective.

Murdering someone everyone likes also increases the stakes for the sleuth, as well as enhancing the emotional involvement of readers. On the other hand, it can be gratifying, to both writer and reader, to kill off a character no one likes. Deciding whom to murder helps determine your plot, while the character of the victim has an effect on how people, both in your novel and reading it, react to the crime.

Sometimes the identity of a victim is the result of the author's research. When M.E. Cooper was investigating real-life Confederate General W.W. Loring, she came across the fact that experts estimate that more than 4,000 women served as soldiers in the American Civil War. She knew at once that the murder victim in *Uncivil Death* would be one of these women.

### The Villain

The villain of the piece is almost as important to the story as the sleuth and needs to be carefully crafted. The motivation for the crime has to fit the historical period and reflect the criminal's probable knowledge of how things work, from the criminal justice system to the weapon of choice. A gently bred lady of the late nineteenth century might pull out a pocket pistol and shoot someone but a twelfth-century gentlewoman cannot.

As in most mystery fiction, the villain's identity and motives, unless you're writing a howdunit rather than a whodunit, must be concealed as long as possible and yet, when revealed, seem perfectly logical. The reader should feel he or she came close to solving the case. Leaving a reader feeling cheated, or frustrated, or, worse, disappointed, because the solution was obvious all along, is something to avoid at all costs.

Usually a villain will appear in only one book while the sleuth may go on to solve other cases. In one way, then, the villain is just another secondary character. On the other hand, you need to put a lot of thought into this person's background and develop a fully rounded character in order for him or her to be a worthy opponent for your sleuth.

It is a good idea for the writer to know the villain's identity and motive early on. However, there is something to be said for keeping an open mind. If a better solution to the crime—or a better character to have committed it—comes to you as you're writing, be flexible.

In plotting *Fatal as a Fallen Woman*, I thought I knew who the murderer was from the beginning. When I reached the penultimate scene, however, where this character was supposed to reveal the motive for the crime, I realized that the person I'd cast as my villain was guilty of other less serious crimes but had not committed the murder. The real culprit had been there, in the background, all along. With the insertion of a few scenes earlier in the book, I made it possible for my sleuth, Diana Spaulding, to discover the real killer's identity *after* the confrontation with my original candidate. The result was a stronger book with a better mystery.

If you don't mind spoilers, here are the specifics. Diana Spaulding is investigating the murder of her estranged father, William Torrence, a wealthy silver baron, in Denver, Colorado in 1888. Her mother is the prime suspect because when Diana's father divorced her, Elmira Torrence took up a career as the madam of a whorehouse to support herself. "Fallen women" abound in this novel, but the villain I originally chose was the sister of someone Torrence had ordered murdered years before. She has taken a job, under a false name, as a bookkeeper at the brothel. The reader meets her early on. Eventually Diana learns that this woman was in

Torrence's hotel room shortly before he was murdered. Afraid of being found out, the bookkeeper maneuvers Diana, her sleuthing partner Ben Northcote, and Elmira into a trap and seems about to kill all three of them.

And that was the point at which, as Diana was demanding explanations, I realized the bookkeeper had not killed anybody. She would never have shot William Torrence. She had a more painful revenge planned—financial ruin.

Left without a killer, I went back to the beginning of the manuscript and started looking for other possibilities. It didn't take long to find one. There was a "mysterious woman" in the background, someone with whom William Torrence was supposed to be having an affair. I'd intended her to be a red herring, and in fact had already written a scene in which Ben visits another of the brothels in Denver's red light district and discovers her identity, that of a prostitute who has left town. Now I had a better idea. What if there was no such girl? What if it was the madam herself who was involved with Torrence? And what if, having decided to run for political office, Torrence had informed the madam that he was through with her? With very little tinkering to the manuscript, the madam fit perfectly into the role of murderer. She had motive, means, and opportunity, and no compunction about lying to cover up her crime. Best of all, she'd been there all along, so I was still playing fair with the reader.

## Keeping Track of Characters

Sometimes creating a realistic background can make difficulties for the writer simply because it calls for too many people to be present at all times. If you set your story at a royal court, for example, you'll have to be careful not to trip over extras, so to speak. In many earlier eras, people simply did not take off on their own. They traveled in groups, lived in communities, even slept several to a bed.

In a series, the number of continuing characters tends to expand with each book. If your sleuth marries and has children, they also add to the cast. At some point you may have to consider killing off characters readers like, not only because it is cumbersome to have all those people around when your sleuth is trying to detect, but also because people did die younger in the past and of causes that today would mean nothing more than a quick visit to a doctor. Alternatively, some could be "out of town."

Keeping track of "a cast of thousands" can be a challenge. I use a loose-leaf notebook divided into sections labeled CURRENT BOOK, LAST BOOK, BOOK BEFORE THAT, CONTINUING CHARACTERS, and CHARACTERS NOW

DEAD. For each character I make a character sheet. The form I've devised contains the following headings: Age, Hair, Eyes, Other Facial Features, Height, Build, Other Physical Features, Distinguishing Habits, Voice Quality and Speech Patterns, Occupation or Social Position, Secrets, Significant Biographical Background (this includes special relationships to other characters), and finally, Miscellaneous Details. This is a handy reference to keep me from changing the color of someone's eyes in mid book. Continuing characters get additional pages to remind me what they've done in each book. For quick reference, I also keep a chronology that includes birth dates for the important characters. This allows me to keep track of their relative ages. In addition, when I think they may be useful, I make family trees.

Those things help *me* keep track of characters, but what about readers? Do they need a little help, especially if a historical mystery has a particularly large number of characters? You can always, as I and many authors do, include a "Cast of Characters" in the front matter. Such lists also provide an opportunity for an author to set the tone for the novel, particularly if the mystery contains humor. Selecting one of Lindsey Davis's novels about Falco at random (*Shadows in Bronze*), I found the following among the entries in the DRAMATIS PERSONAE: "Vespasian, Lord of the World (& short of cash)" and "His sons: Titus (A treasure)" and "Domitian (A trial)." There are also "Geminus, An auctioneer; who may be Falco's father but hopes he isn't," "Name unknown, A Sacred Goat," and "Nero (aka Spot), An ox enjoying his holiday."

## Characters with Children

Many sleuths are married, which brings up the problem of children. Although there were methods of birth control in the past, not everyone knew about them. In some cases religious beliefs prevented their use. And of course people were supposed to *want* a big family. If your characters are sexually active, on or off the page, children are almost inevitable. How do you prevent them in a believable way? And, if you don't, what do you do with them once they arrive?

I chose to make Lady Appleton "barren." In the sixteenth century, this was something to be ashamed of, and it adds particular poignancy to her discovery that her philandering husband has fathered a child by one of his mistresses. I now have the best of all possible worlds—a child for my sleuth to foster when she is useful for plot purposes, but one who can be sent back to her birth mother when she is in the way.

Elizabeth Peters, who gave Amelia Peabody Emerson one child, the precocious Ramses, and an adopted daughter, Nefret, comments in an interview in *Deadly Women* that she didn't write *Crocodile on the Sandbank* as the first book in a series. "If I had intended to, I might have finessed the dates and the ages of the characters, and—above all else!—not given Amelia and Emerson a child who was bound to get older with each passing year." The challenge she has had to deal with is making Ramses "a believable—well, more or less—adult and yet retain his distinctive characteristics." Current entries in the series feature the twins born to Ramses and Nefret as minor characters.

Alan Gordon's character Feste has started down the parenthood path and Gordon says he is "having great fun in writing about a married couple trying occasionally to get it on while taking care of a baby, traveling, and solving a mystery," and adds that "any couple with more than one will have a helluva time trying to solve anything outside the family squabbles."

Carola Dunn's character Daisy Dalrymple, however, who has already acquired a stepdaughter in the course of this series, gives birth to twins in *The Bloody Tower*. "Daisy herself," Dunn says, "as a child of the aristocracy, saw little of her parents as she grew up on the family estate.

> They would have spent the spring in London, the summer at house-parties, and the autumn at shooting parties. Marrying Alec, a Scotland Yard Detective Chief Inspector whose father was a bank manager, she entered the middle of the middle class. In the 1920s, such a family would expect to have a nanny to look after young children. Babies were for the most part bottle-fed, and older children, especially boys, often sent to boarding schools. This allows me to present Daisy with twins without a qualm. If she has to go off to Derbyshire to research an article, she knows the babies are being cared for by the person who is their usual caretaker. I chose to give her twins, a girl and a boy, because Alec already has a daughter and I wanted him to have a son, and I foresee the relationship between Belinda and her little half sister as providing some interesting developments, should the series continue long enough—and I didn't want to write any more books in which Daisy is pregnant.

Dunn also points out that "at the time contraception was just beginning to become respectable and reliable. Marie Stopes opened her first family planning clinic in London in 1921, which met with considerably less extreme antagonism than was roused by Margaret Sanger in New York. So Daisy had the choice of whether to have more children or stop after the twins."

Children can also be extremely useful in creating character motivation. The Gaslight Mysteries of Victoria Thompson feature Sarah Brandt, a childless midwife, as the detective—although she does adopt a child as the series progresses. When it came to creating a male counterpart for Sarah, Thompson thought, "Who better to help her solve mysteries than a police detective?" Her proposal for the series included a summary of how the relationship would work and it was only after the contracts were signed and she started doing in-depth research that she realized she had created a problem for herself. The real police in turn-of-the-century New York City were almost universally corrupt.

Committed to writing about a policeman in that era, Thompson had to find a way of explaining why he'd take bribes and refuse to investigate a crime unless he could expect to receive a reward for solving it. A firm believer that "you can make your characters do anything, as long as it is motivated properly," she knew she already had a good reason for him to have taken this particular job in the first place—there were very few other jobs available for Irish Catholic males. But to be worthy of being the hero of a series, she also needed a compelling reason for him to stay on the job once he realized what it entailed. Her solution was to give him a son who is deaf. As long as he must provide for the boy, he cannot risk losing his job. This complication not only puts him back in the "hero" mold, but allows Thompson to layer in a new level of conflict and tension.

## Animal Characters

One of the "rules" of mystery writing is "never kill a cat." Few things upset readers more. While most mystery fans will accept the brutal fictional murder of a person, they balk at reading about cruelty to animals. The quickest way to establish a character as a villain is to have him kick a dog or cat out of his way.

That said, animals also have another place in historical mystery fiction—as continuing characters. An animal can add a humanizing element, as the little dog Biondello does in Elizabeth Eyre's Renaissance mysteries featuring a tough mercenary soldier. Elizabeth Peters's "Bastet de cat" and her progeny play a role in almost every book in the Amelia Peabody series, in some cases taking on almost human qualities. They have also been known to attack the occasional villain. Susan Wittig Albert's series about Beatrix Potter takes anthropomorphism a step further. Her animals talk, albeit only to each other.

## Supporting Characters Who Want a Bigger Role

On occasion a sidekick or some other secondary character tries to take over a book as it is being written. This should, of course, be nipped in the bud, but it can also be mined for ideas for future projects. The early Amelia Peabody novels are written entirely in Amelia's point of view with first-person narration. Starting with *Seeing a Large Cat*, Ramses and/or Nefret are used as point-of-view characters though the device of letters and manuscripts supposedly discovered by the fictitious editor of Amelia's journals. These characters thus function as sleuths within the framework of the original series.

Miriam Grace Monfredo's Seneca Falls Mysteries feature librarian Glynis Tryon as the detective in the early books in the series but gradually introduce Glynis's niece, Bronwyn Llyr, an undercover agent for the government, as a sleuthing partner. Bronwyn takes over as protagonist in *Sisters of Cain* and continues in that role for the remainder of the series.

Sharan Newman does something a little different in one of the books in her Catherine LeVendeur series. In *The Outcast Dove*, Catherine's cousin Solomon is the sleuth. Although the plot involves a threat to their family, Catherine does not appear and is barely mentioned. Catherine's husband and usual sleuthing partner, Edgar, is in only one chapter. When Solomon demanded his own book, he got it.

Other minor characters from historical mysteries have solved their own cases in short stories, always a good outlet for "leftovers" from a longer mystery. Develop every secondary character fully and you never know where it will lead.

Put two characters on a page and let them talk to each other, and something is bound to develop. Their interaction is the beginning of a plot.

# 7 Plots, Subplots, and Building Suspense

"THE *mystery* novel is plot-driven. The *romance* novel is character-driven." Don't you believe it! Today's mystery novels, especially historical mysteries, contain well-rounded characters. That's why two chapters on creating believable characters came before this one. The plot, more often than not, derives from the actions of its characters. In fiction, if not in real life, the motivation behind the crime is of paramount importance in solving the mystery.

## To Outline or To Wing It, That Is the Question

How much plotting should you do before you begin to write? Some mystery writers plan every detail, filling page after page with extensive notes. According to an interview in Mystery Readers International's "At Home" series, Peter Lovesey spends a couple of months on his outline, planning "all the major events, twists, surprises." He makes all the decisions ahead of time and then writes just one draft.

Another pioneer of the historical mystery, Ellis Peters (Edith Pargeter), explained how she organized her books in an interview in *Publishers Weekly* in 1991. She "begins by studying twelfth-century chronicles, selecting historical events in which Cadfael may participate, and doing a great deal of thinking and outlining—'sometimes three or more outlines'—before she actually proceeds with setting down the text of her novel."

Other writers plan in less detail. Some prefer to wing it.

I do some serious thinking before I set fingers to keyboard, but I do not map out the entire plot. For one thing, my mind doesn't work that way. I am unable to think too far ahead. For another, there is something to be said for the writer being surprised along the way. When an idea comes along that is better than the one I started out with, I embrace it.

The best advice I can give is this: Find your own way of writing. Proceed in whatever manner works for you—months of planning, or plunging right in (after doing at least some of the research), or something in between. Find the process with which you are most comfortable. As for the physical act of writing, that's a matter of personal choice as well. We all know the stories of rough drafts of successful novels being written in longhand on yellow lined paper while commuting by train, or in an Edinburgh coffee shop while unemployed. At the other extreme are the books written in a quiet home office on state-of-the-art computer equipment. How you write is your choice. Some of what you write, however, is not.

## Crime in Historical Context

Since you're writing a mystery, deciding what crime has been committed has to be one of the earliest decisions. As has already been mentioned, that crime is usually murder simply because the stakes are higher when death is involved. Tension is automatically greater.

The method of murder must depend upon the historical period you've chosen. So must the tools at hand for solving it. Find out all you can about how crime was handled in the era you're writing about—both the law and the order. Were there police of any sort? How did they investigate? What happened to a person they took into custody? What were trials like? In many cases, not much time elapsed between arrest, trial, and execution. Your sleuth may literally have a deadline to find the real killer.

Aside from determining what weapons were in use, you also need to think in terms of which crimes were considered most vile. Murder wasn't always the worst crime a person could commit. In many societies, treason was the ultimate sin. In England in many eras a murderer would be hanged but a traitor would be hanged, drawn, and quartered. A woman who murdered her husband or a servant who killed his or her master was burnt to death. Why the harsher punishments? Because they were guilty of what was called petty treason. To rebel against an authority figure was seen as a crime against the proper order of things. Striking out against one's master, the reasoning went, was akin to attacking the sovereign.

Even veteran mystery writers like Anne Perry admit that coming up with innovative crimes is "one of the hardest things of all," especially since "there are very few believable reasons why anyone would kill." In an "At Home" interview, she explains that "simple insanity" isn't credible and she finds "simple greed very boring" as a motive. "Complicated greed for subtle reason," however, is another matter.

### Serial Killers

Jack the Ripper is often said to be the world's first serial killer, with H.H. Holmes, tried in Philadelphia in 1895, as America's first. But is that really true? It turns out there was a serial killer in Austin, Texas in 1884, "the servant girl annihilator," now somewhat better known because of Steven Saylor's historical mystery novel, A *Twist at the End.*

Were there serial killers before that, say in medieval or Roman times? There were certainly mass murderers well before the nineteenth century. There is some question as to whether Gilles de Rais was guilty or not, but he was accused of kidnapping, torturing, and killing as many as two hundred children between the ages of six and eighteen over a ten-year period in fifteenth-century France. After a graphic confession, made under threat of being tortured himself, he was convicted of and executed for those crimes in 1440.

The earliest accounts of Elizabeth Bathory, "the Blood Countess," (1560–c.1614) who supposedly killed as many as forty young women and bathed in their blood, derive from publications in 1744 and 1796. Even those dates, however, indicate a familiarity with the concept of a female serial killer that predates the nineteenth century. And she didn't even use poison as a weapon! Famous women poisoners exist in even earlier periods, though the number of their crimes may well be exaggerated. Roberta Gellis presents Lucrezia Borgia as sleuth rather than murderer in *Lucrezia Borgia and the Mother of Poisons.*

If you want to use a serial killer in a historical mystery, there's no reason not to. The thing you have to be careful about is giving your sleuth a knowledge of today's methods of profiling. Someone can spot a pattern (a murder committed in the same way on victims of similar appearance, for example), but if your medieval sleuth goes looking for a suspect who set fires or tortured animals as a child, somehow *knowing* that those are likely habits for many who later go on to commit murder, you would be venturing into an area where a detective from that era simply would not—could not—go.

One reason writers of historical mysteries often give for not writing contemporaries is that they don't want to deal with modern forensic science. Unfortunately, you can't completely ignore it. Since your readers know—or think they know—something about profiling serial killers, you need to understand the typical behavior of such people. In the same way that you can't ignore what we now know about the effects of a particular poisonous herb on the human body, you must also become familiar with whatever aspects of modern forensic science relate to your plot. Your characters may not know what makes the villain behave as he or she does, but *you* should.

### Solving Historical Crimes

Real-life notorious or unsolved murders are always tempting to write about because they engage popular interest. They also tend to provoke strong opinions. However, readers, including reviewers, are also more likely to be critical if your solution to a real case doesn't agree with what they believe happened. In addition, it would be difficult to come up with a solution to any well-known mystery that hasn't already been suggested. In short, if you use a real case, with all the real people involved as characters, you may be making the job of writing a historical mystery novel more difficult for yourself.

That said, many writers do use true crime stories in their novels. Paul Doherty has based many of his historical mysteries (written under a variety of pseudonyms) on real cases, including the murders of Lord Darnley and of King Edward II and the mystery surrounding the disappearance of Richard III's nephews from the Tower of London. Doherty's medieval detective, Hugh Corbett, had his origin in a real robbery that took place in 1303. A clerk, John de Droxford, was sent by Edward I to investigate the matter. Droxford inspired Doherty to create Hugh, and much later, to write a nonfiction account of the incident, *The Great Crown Jewels Robbery of 1303.*

Bill and Susan Wittig Albert, writing as Robin Paige, are among the historical mystery writers who have made use of the case of Jack the Ripper. Bill Albert comments that "historical crimes are an excellent hook to catch the reader's attention, but they come with some built-in challenges.

> Most readers instantly recognize the word "Ripper" and are willing to invest hours of reading time in a book about the killings, even if that is not the main focus of the plot. They enjoy matching the details in the novel against the story they already know. The Ripper killings, however, come with an extraordinary amount of baggage. For one thing, there is the challenge of getting the details right—and there are plenty of ways to get them wrong. For another, readers may have already accepted a solution to the crime, or have some personal animosity toward a particular solution. There is always something in a book that triggers some readers' prior assumptions. The writer who uses a well-known historical crime in a realistic setting runs the risk of pulling that trigger in a big way.

The mystery in *Death at Whitechapel* is "a crime-within-a-crime: an 1898 blackmail plot targeting Jennie Churchill and her son Winston because of Randolph Churchill's alleged participation in the Ripper killings of 1888.

Our only obligation was to resolve the blackmail plot and to suggest a plausible solution to the Ripper killings. Among several possible approaches to the Ripper, we adopted (and adapted) the one that proposes Randolph Churchill as one of a group of Masonic Rippers in a series of killings aimed at covering up the marriage between Prince Eddy (the Duke of Clarence, second in line to Victoria's throne) and a Catholic shop-girl. It gave us a stage upon which we could confront our central characters—Jennie and Winston Churchill—with a frightening threat to the Churchill family reputation, which they have to resolve (and cover up) in order to save the family reputation and Winston's future political life.

"Some people wrote lengthy letters to us," Albert adds, "telling us why Randolph Churchill would never commit a murder, while others suggested that we were merely engaging in 'Royal bashing.' Masons wrote to tell us how angry they were at the ridiculous idea that a Mason might kill someone." One reader even accused them of being anti-Semitic "because one of our characters mentioned a particular Masonic belief about the Jews and Jesus Christ."

No matter how much or how little is known about a real crime, writing about one restricts the writer's freedom to make things up. Using an authentic case as your inspiration and changing the details, or simply inventing a crime out of whole cloth will probably be easier. Still, if you're passionate about a particular historical incident and feel you have a new take on it, by all means give it a try. In the end success or failure comes down to only one thing—good storytelling.

## Beginnings

Once you have determined the elements of your historical mystery—the "when," "where," "who," and "what crime"—you are still left with a major decision—how do you open your story?

### The Latter-Day Editor

Some historical mysteries use prologues in which a present-day "editor" explains how the story to follow came into his or her hands. *The Name of the Rose* begins this way. The fictitious author, writing in 1983, tells of acquiring a nineteenth-century book that is, in turn, a reproduction of a fourteenth-century manuscript. The novel is a "translation" of this find.

The "editor" of Amelia Peabody Emerson's memoirs, who does not put in an appearance until *The Mummy Case*, the third book in Elizabeth Peters's series, explains in the Foreword that Emerson is not the author's real name and goes on to disclaim responsibility for "the opinions expressed herein" and for "certain minor errors of fact, which are due in part to Mrs. 'Emerson's' faulty memory and in even larger part to her personal eccentricities and prejudices." Such disclaimers become even more heated in subsequent books.

Laurie R. King, as the supposed editor of Mary Russell's manuscripts, is even more outspoken on the subject. Her Editor's Preface to *The Beekeeper's Apprentice* begins with these words: "The first thing I want the reader to know is that I had nothing to do with this book you have in your hand."

In a variation of this technique, Carole Nelson Douglas starts *Good Night, Mr. Holmes* in 1894 with a scene between Sherlock Holmes and Dr. Watson in Watson's point of view, and then shifts back to 1881 and Irene Adler's "Watson," Nell Huxleigh. Then Douglas adds a Scholarly Afterword in which, in the guise of "Fiona Witherspoon, Ph.D, F.I.A." (Friends of Irene Adler) she reveals where the diaries of Penelope Huxleigh were found, insists that both Sherlock Holmes and Irene Adler were real people and that Sir Arthur Conan Doyle "acted as literary agent for the actual, retiring—if not completely anonymous—Dr. Watson," and explains away discrepancies between "the foregoing collation" and the Holmes Canon.

The literary device of starting a novel at a date later than the events in the body of the story, then taking the reader back in time is frequently used in historical mysteries. *The Name of the Rose* adds another layer to the storytelling by having the narrator, Adso, write the account of his youthful adventure from the perspective of an old man looking back on events many years earlier. Daniel Stashower uses a similar technique in a series setting: each year on the anniversary of Harry Houdini's death, an interviewer coaxes another story out of Houdini's brother, by then an old man in a nursing home. In Caleb Carr's *The Alienist*, a team of detectives reunites at the funeral of Theodore Roosevelt in 1919, where they realize that the story of their pursuit of a serial killer, which could not be told when it happened in the 1890s, can now be recounted. The variations on this way of starting a story are endless. The only risk is falling into the "had-I-but-known" trap while telling the tale.

### Plunging into the Past

You can also, of course, plunge right into your story at the date when it really begins. This is probably the most common way of starting a historical mystery novel. If it is written in first person, unless the format is a series of journal entries, the story is obviously being told after the successful conclusion of the events in the novel, but not necessarily very long afterward. Jane Finnis writes her Roman Empire mystery *Get Out or Die* in the form of "an official report to the Governor of the province of Britannia." The narrator, a female innkeeper, records her experiences during a murder investigation in first person and in her own distinctive voice.

### Start with the Day That Is Different

Whatever the setup for telling the story, you will have to pick a starting point for the actual narrative. Begin with the day that is in some way *different*. That may or may not mean the day a murder took place.

Many mystery novels do start with the murder, or at least with a body. This has certain advantages. It leaves no doubt in the reader's mind that this is a mystery. On the other hand, in a historical mystery, it is equally important to establish a sense of time and place. Can you do both? Certainly. Some writers use a dateline with the time and place of the action at the start of Chapter One. Whether or not there are also significant tipoffs in the opening paragraphs, this makes it clear to the reader when and where your mystery is set. Reactions to the discovery of the body and the actions taken by those in authority will also tell your reader a great deal about the milieu.

Reviewer and lecturer Molly Weston offers this advice on the subject of beginnings: "Remember, a mystery involves a crime! Get the crime in early and let the rest of the book unfold as a result of the crime. In the phrase 'historical mystery,' historical is an adjective. 'Mystery' is the noun, and to be a mystery, there must be a crime!

"Maybe this would be of help to you. It was attributed to me, but I don't think I said it—it's too good. Invoke the rule of 100 in your reading. Subtract your age from 100. The result is how many pages you read before making a decision as to whether you should keep reading a book."

Opening with a murder does get things off to a fast start and keeps the reader turning pages. It also tends to motivate most of the characters. Some want to solve the crime. Others try to hide things from those investigating. At least one person will instantly become downright dangerous to anyone who gets too close to the truth.

There is also something to be said, however, for introducing characters and their relationships first. The death of a character readers have gotten to know, especially one they like, gives them a vested interest in the detective's hunt for the killer. The outcome matters more on a personal level and they will keep reading not only to find out the villain's identity but also for the satisfaction of seeing justice done.

There is no hard and fast rule about when the crime should occur in a mystery novel. It may even take place before the story opens. Your characters may never see a dead body. What you do need to do from page one, however, is to draw both your sleuth and your readers into the events that will eventually lead to the solution of the crime.

### Involving Your Sleuth

At whatever point in the plot you have the crime occur, think carefully once again about your reasons for involving the sleuth. There would be no plot if your detective did not want to solve the crime.

One compelling reason for a person to turn amateur detective is for him or her to be suspected of the crime. Although this is a motive that has been overused in the mystery genre, it does have the advantage of putting your sleuth at risk and giving him or her a great deal to lose. The threat of imprisonment or execution is a great motivator.

Making a suspect someone who is important to your sleuth is another possibility. Whether a family member, a close friend, or a love interest, this gives the detective a little extra motivation to solve the crime. If you are writing a series, however, it is unrealistic to think that every suspect in every crime the sleuth encounters will be someone with whom they have a personal connection. The historical equivalent of "Cabot Cove Syndrome" in *Murder, She Wrote*, where everyone Jessica Fletcher has ever met seems to end up either dead or accused of murder, is something you want to avoid. Simply making your sleuth a busybody is probably not such a great idea, either.

The challenge of writing about an amateur detective is that you have to keep coming up with good reasons for your sleuth to become involved with murder. Why is your protagonist on the scene? What is at stake? Why does s/he choose to look for the killer? Your readers must believe your detective is motivated to solve the crime or your story will fall apart at the start.

## Subplots

In historical mystery short stories, there is no room for subplots, but novel-length fiction usually has at least one. It frequently concerns the personal life of the sleuth. It may also grow out of one of those secrets you gave to secondary characters.

The goal of any subplot is to enhance the main plot and complicate the crime's solution. If possible, plot and subplots should be wrapped up as close to simultaneously as possible.

### Romance

One of the most common and most useful subplots introduces a note of romance into the mystery. You can have your sleuth fall in love, with all the complications and conflicts that entails, or give secondary characters a love story. Almost all of Ellis Peters's Cadfael novels feature a pair of star-crossed lovers in a subplot. In her Amelia Peabody novels, Elizabeth Peters both honors and spoofs this tradition, to the point where Peabody's husband complains of the frequency with which they encounter young lovers.

I use a romance subplot in most of my Face Down mysteries, usually between two minor characters. Their relationship complicates Susanna Appleton's life and often serves to obscure clues. In the Diana Spaulding Mysteries, the first book involves Diana herself in a dangerous romance. The succeeding volumes lead up to her marriage at the end of the fourth and last book. In that one, while the main plot centers on murder, a subplot involves Diana's imminent wedding. Dissension among relatives provides comic relief.

### Political Intrigue and Espionage

The second subplot in most of my Face Down books has to do with spies, treason, and politics. This works particularly well in historical mysteries. By making Sir Robert Appleton an "intelligence gatherer" for the Crown, I linked him to historical events and gave him, and later his widow, a connection to people with the clout to help out in an murder investigation.

Political intrigue was a fact of life in most historical periods. From Lynda S. Robinson's Ancient Egypt to Anne Perry's Victorian London, both real and fictional schemes to undermine the government abound.

## Keeping Track of Plot Points

With a main plot and two subplots to keep straight, I generally make a chart of WHO KNOWS WHAT WHEN as I write. Both false clues—red herrings—and real clues need to be carefully planted.

Since you are writing a historical mystery, the plotting process must also take into account what was going in the real world at the time. Even if you've created a fictional location within a real country and all fictional characters, you still need to know if anything out of the ordinary took place in the neighborhood. If there was a major earthquake, for example, or a battle, or the queen passed by on her annual progress, your characters can't be ignorant of such events. If characters are to visit another place, check to see what would have been going on every year at that time as well as in that specific year. If there was an annual fair, for example, you may be able to use that fact. By and large, what you find will not present an obstacle to the story you want to tell. Such discoveries, worked into the plot, generally enhance it.

During my research, I keep an eye out for anything that has a date and make a note of it. I also keep a list of significant dates, year by year. A note I made back in the 1970s about Oxford University being closed by the plague during the summer of 1571 came in handy later when I was writing a mystery set in that year. It isn't crucial to the plot but it provides a useful detail to flesh out the story and helps explain why a certain group of people were available to gather together where I wanted them.

## Motivation as Plot Device

A crime has to be motivated by something believable. Motivation is part of character development, because every suspect has a motive, but it is also a key ingredient in plot. When you get right down to it, there aren't all that many motives for murder. Monetary gain/greed is one — to acquire property or an inheritance or do away with competition in business. There is self-protection — to cover up some lesser illegal activity. There is passion/thwarted love, which includes double murder, single murder, and murder-suicide scenarios based on the "if I can't have her, no one can" theme. Passion is also behind the murder of an unwanted spouse or lover or the murder to protect a loved one. But one of the most popular motives in historical mysteries is revenge.

The trigger for an act of revenge can be real or imagined; the one taking revenge a cold, calculating, horribly sane person or someone suffering from a recognizable — by the modern reader — mental illness. In historical mysteries, incidentally, characters don't have to worry about being politically correct. Even the sleuth may be motivated by a desire for revenge. This may take the more acceptable form of "seeking justice," but the urge to punish the villain, whether through the law or outside of it, can at times be as much a quest for vengeance as the criminal behavior that provoked it.

## Building Suspense

Suspense goes back to character in the sense that the reader should worry about what's going to happen to the sleuth. There's always a threat that getting too close to the killer will lead your detective into danger. Accentuate this where you can.

There may also be other threats — is the church or the state likely to interfere for reasons other than the crime itself? Does something in the sleuth's personal life give cause for alarm? In addition, uncovering a secret completely unrelated to the murder can also put your sleuth in danger.

Many techniques for creating suspense are purely technical and are often a simple matter of pacing. End chapters with cliffhangers. Have something suspicious happen to break up any long stretch of the sleuth's frustration at finding no new clues. Show the reader, but not the sleuth, a shadowy figure lurking in the background, a source of imminent danger if the detective opens the wrong door or enters the deserted churchyard.

In Rhys Bowen's Agatha-nominated *Death of Riley*, fledgling detective Molly Murphy is trying to discover who murdered her employer, Paddy Riley. The building suspense nicely parallels Molly's journey of self-discovery as she goes through Paddy's open cases in search of suspects. She starts with the relatively harmless — a divorce case — and works her way up to the truly terrifying prospect of an anarchist plot. Each possibility suggests a stronger motive for murder and presents a greater risk for Molly herself. Suspense builds naturally but steadily with each new discovery.

A classic way to increase suspense (in multiple point-of-view books) is through the use of "secret villain" scenes. Written in the villain's point of view, they reveal nothing about the identity of that character, not even gender, but they let the reader know that the villain is aware of the sleuth's activities and that the sleuth will become the villain's target if he or she gets too close to the truth. The trick, of course, is to put the sleuth in jeopardy without stumbling over the line into either melodrama or farce... unless you intend to, that is.

If you have a plot with plenty of twists and turns, suspense tends to come naturally. As your sleuth gets closer to catching the villain, setbacks occur, each one more serious — and perhaps more potentially dangerous to your detective — than the one before.

The time frame of your mystery, especially if there is a deadline for finding answers, can also increase suspense. The events in *The Name of the Rose*, long as that novel is, take place in only a little over a week's time

When you revise, you can increase suspense by rearranging scenes, eliminating places where you telegraph too much of what's ahead, and cutting excess description that slows things down. Just making sentences shorter can have an effect. In revision you can also reassess clues and red herrings. Too many? Too few? Either problem can be fixed, and should be. Mysteries with sagging middles lose readers who put them down and don't feel inspired to pick them up again.

## Endings

Suspense is the art of making your reader think: "Don't go in there!" or "Look behind you!" as your sleuth wavers on the brink of falling into a trap or being ambushed. If the villain gets hold of your detective or some other important character, the stakes rise even higher. This is the sort of thing, however, that belongs toward the end of the story (unless you are writing a thriller). Such a scene leads directly to the climax of the tale — a rescue, a fight, possibly even the death of the villain or some other character.

It is up to you how much detail to show when you put someone in mortal danger. If you have written a traditional, domestic-oriented mystery up until this point, it is probably best not to suddenly veer off into the horrific. In any case, hinting at what terrible things may be happening is often more frightening than describing them in graphic terms. Ideally, readers should be biting their nails as they turn the page to see what happens next. You do *not* want them to toss the book aside in disgust. If you must describe the use of a medieval torture device in loving detail, then the tone of earlier scenes should prepare your readers for graphic violence to come. If your aim is to shock and horrify your readers, then make sure you succeed in that goal. If you simply gross them out, you will have achieved nothing but the loss of potential fans. Historical mystery readers do not like to be misled about the kind of book they're getting.

In the best of all possible worlds, plot, subplots, and any loose ends are wrapped up in the last couple of pages of the book and the reader closes the novel feeling satisfied. Once everything is explained, it becomes apparent that the clues were there all along. The solution makes sense. The reader figured it out at about the same time the sleuth did or, failing that, now realizes that the answers were only just out of reach. The author played fair.

How do you manage the explanations? Very carefully. Some novels use "the obligatory spilling of the beans," a phrase coined by syndicated columnist Joel Achenbach to mean the scene "where the villain explains his diabolical plot to rule the world, a moment of braggadocio that will lead to his downfall once the hero escapes." In mystery novels, this is the point at which the villain confesses to all his crimes and willingly answers any remaining questions, usually because he plans, momentarily, to kill the sleuth. Alternatively, the sleuth works out what must have happened and explains to someone who still doesn't understand. Either way, *if* readers have already figured out whodunit and why, your sleuth will seem slow or even stupid.

On the other hand, it isn't realistic to think that one person can be so brilliant that they can solve crime after crime with nary a misstep. Your sleuth can be misled, even come up with a completely wrong explanation for the crime at first, in the middle of the story. As soon as all the information is available, however, he or she should be able to put the pieces of the puzzle together correctly.

Holding some information back may be the hardest thing a writer of mysteries has to do. Once you have worked out what really happened it is only natural to want to share that information. To do so too early, even to hint too strongly at the villain's identity, will spoil the story for readers. Careful planning and/or a lot of revision are the only ways to get this just right.

Is the "spilling of the beans" overused? Certainly the old gather-every-one-in-the-library ending to mystery novels feels contrived these days. But the same plot devices are used over and over again for two reasons. First, they work. And second, there just aren't that many ways to bring a mystery novel to a satisfying conclusion. The way you write the revelation scene can still be fresh. A greater sin than falling back on the villain spilling the beans or the sleuth explaining what happened to the gathered suspects or a friend would be to leave loose ends.

What if the sleuth identifies the killer fifty pages before the end of the book? Is that necessarily a bad thing? No—you've just left room for a few more twists and turns. The sleuth might have the right villain but the wrong motive, necessitating more sleuthing at greater risk, since the villain may realize s/he's under suspicion. Or the villain may become desperate enough to do something totally unexpected. Twists and double twists at the end of a mystery novel are a good thing. In *Face Down Among the Winchester Geese*, the discovery of my killer's motive leads to a last-minute revelation of another person's involvement in all that has gone before. The clues are there, but if I did my job correctly, that second person's identity should come as a complete shock to the reader.

There is one more thing to consider at the end of the book. If this is part of a mystery series, you need to find a subtle way to set the stage for the next book in the series. This isn't easy. You don't want to be too obvious about it. Chances are, however, that as you've been writing this historical mystery, you've been making mental notes about possibilities for others. If you can, drop a hint about what is to come.

## Rethinking Plots

It is a rare writer who can plan the entire novel in advance and stick to that plan from start to finish. If you are one of those lucky few, more power to you. Most of us are stuck with rewriting and revising.

Whatever doesn't work in the rough draft of a novel can be fixed in revision. The order of scenes can be changed. So can the point of view they are written in. Subplots can be added or deleted and suspense heightened. You can even change your mind about the identity of the villain. My rough drafts are always ragged, full of notes to myself like "add humor here" and "Susanna says something to make the murderer think she knows who he is."

If you can give yourself some breathing room between drafts, do so. I try to set my rough draft aside for at least a month. When I go back to it, I have some perspective. I can be objective about what needs fixing. I've had time to find answers to those pesky research questions I didn't anticipate. And often my subconscious has come up with the perfect solution to some troublesome plot point.

There is no pat answer to how to plot a historical mystery, only a few common-sense ground rules. A mystery must be mysterious. It must contain suspense. And it must leave the reader feeling satisfied with the solution.

# 8 It's in the Details: Creating a Sense of Time and Place

IN HISTORICAL mysteries, especially those with no dateline and no "editor" writing a foreword, it is the function of a few carefully chosen descriptive details to transport readers to the time and place of the story. The excerpts that follow illustrate a variety of ways this can be done. They are not all the first lines of the novel in question, but they do come from the first page of each book.

## Variations on an Opening Theme

> When the girl came rushing up the steps, I decided she was wearing far too many clothes. It was late summer. Rome frizzled like a pancake on a griddleplate. People unlaced their shoes but had to keep them on; not even an elephant could cross the streets unshod.
> —Lindsey Davis, *The Silver Pigs*, Rome, A.D. 70

> Brother Cadfael had been up long before Prime, pricking out cabbage seedlings before the day was aired, and his thoughts were all on birth, growth and fertility, not at all on graves and reliquaries and violent deaths, whether of saints, sinners or ordinary decent, fallible men like himself.
> —Ellis Peters, *A Morbid Taste for Bones*, England, 1136

> Brother Wulfstan checked the color of his patient's eyes, tasted his sweat. The physick had only weakened the man. The Infirmarian feared he might lose this pilgrim. Trembling with disappointment, Wulfstan sat himself down at his worktable to think through the problem.
> —Candace Robb, *The Apothecary Rose*, England, 1363

> Before the first crow of the cock the scullery maid at the Triple Crown awoke to the rustle of mice in the thatch and the moon

flowing through the cracks in the timbers like strands of golden wire. She lay motionless, savoring the warmth of the straw.

—Leonard Tourney, *The Player's Boy is Dead*, England, 1591

Take this down… "At the stroke of 8 o'clock this morning, while the night-watch Charlies still slept in their boxes, the Honorable Marmaduke Smallwood tied a knot with tongue which he can never untie with his teeth. To whit, he married a common Covent Garden trollop."

—Fidelis Morgan, *Unnatural Fire*, England, 1699

Sergeant Cribb sat with his pint of Bass East India, moodily watching the froth disperse. A glass at the Ratcatcher, supped in solitude after work, was his usual antidote for a hard day. Murder, or arson, rape or robbery, he would seldom allow duty to break the routine.

—Peter Lovesey, *The Detective Wore Silk Drawers*, Victorian England

I know what people say about me: that I am willful and opinionated, shockingly eccentric in my manner of dress (this because I will not wear a corset), altogether a trial to my father. These things are true except the last.

—Dianne Day, *The Strange Files of Fremont Jones*, California, 1905

In this quiet part of Warwickshire death came as frequently as it did anywhere else in England.… Sons and fathers had died in the Great War; the terrible influenza epidemic had scythed the country…and murder was not unheard of even here in Upper Streetham.

—Charles Todd, *A Test of Wills*, England, 1919

## Getting the Details Right

What sort of details do you need to accumulate in order to create a sense of time and place? Rhys Bowen hands out a list of questions for authors to fill in for themselves when she gives talks on writing. After asking where and when the story takes place, what major events took place and what famous people lived at the same time, she concentrates on details of the main character's life. Does he or she have an unusual occupation for the time? Is s/he well respected? An outcast? A ruler? A peasant? Where does s/he live? What kind of house? Village or town?

Narrowing in on place, she asks what that village or town is like. Are the streets cobbled? Muddy? Paved? Is traffic on horseback? On foot? Are there trams? Where is the drain? Do they tip slops into it? What is the landscape like? What are the farming methods? Are there woods? How many rooms in the house? What furniture? How is the house heated? Is the house lit by candles, gas brackets, electric light, kerosene lamps, or oil lamps? What were the bathroom arrangements?

Bowen's list addresses how often people washed and how they arranged their hair. She asks, "What is the fashion of the time?" and advises her audience to check the year, since fashion changes quickly. What about undergarments? Shoes and boots? Is the sleuth "part of the fashionable set?" Does he or she have servants? What do the servants do? Is the social hierarchy rigid? How do people of different classes interact?

She has questions, too, about cooking arrangements. What, when, where, and how did they eat? Have forks been invented? Is there any protocol observed, such as men sitting first and women serving? Do dogs lie under the tables and get the bones? And speaking of animals, which ones will be around? How are they treated?

A writer needs to know details of marriage and courtship at the time. How are marriages arranged? How are they celebrated? How are children treated? What relationship is typical between husband and wife? How do they address each other? To the question "What are the forms of address used in society?" Bowen adds the warning "Watch out for bloopers." (I'll be discussing forms of address in Chapter Nine.)

Since you're writing a mystery, you need to know about punishments, laws, jails, and police. What are the social taboos? What happens if you break them? What about doctors, sickness, and medicines? Last on Bowen's list are entertainment (How much free time do people have? What do they do with their leisure? Are there public holidays?) and religion (How important is religion in this society?).

All these questions, and many more, should have answers before you proceed very far with writing your historical mystery. You'll only use a fraction of the details you accumulate, but you need to have them all at your fingertips in order to select the ones that will make the milieu of your story come alive.

## Making Details "Historical"

In some ways, details are details—they evoke all five senses and bring the reader into the scene. Obviously, in a historical novel, the writer chooses details that also evoke a specific time and place. The sound of horses' hooves and carriage wheels on cobblestones—clattering? Clopping? An occasional whuffle from the horse in question? And what smells go with that? (The streets were *not* clean.)

But would your character notice the smell of horse dung? Probably only if it were fresh and s/he almost stepped in it. Whether you have only one point-of-view character or many, you are telling the story through their eyes. Someone who lives in a town with a paper mill is not aware of the smell. Only someone coming in from outside will notice it. The same is true of sounds. Medieval people were accustomed to bells ringing at all hours. Unless they had a reason to respond to one particular signal—a death knell, for example—they'd go about their business without taking particular notice of the sound. Just as someone who lives by a major high-way does not, for the most part, see or hear the cars passing by or smell the exhaust, a nineteenth-century New Yorker who lives near the elevated rail-way would have grown accustomed to the noise and the shaking and the cinders. Only if the vibration of a passing train causes something to fall and break or if a spark starts a fire will the El be worthy of comment from that character's point of view.

## Picking and Choosing Which Ones to Use

Early in my career, an article written for *School Library Journal* by Joan W. Blos (editor, critic, lecturer, teacher, and Newbery-Medal winner) titled "The Overstuffed Sentence" made a deep impression on me. Blos states: "Nothing should be commented on or described by a character un-less it would be appropriate for that person to do so." She offers this test: "Ask whether the equivalent detail would be reported by an equivalent character in a contemporary novel."

Just as you wouldn't include all the steps in loading the dishwasher or grilling a steak, don't have a character in a historical mystery go over the process involved in something similarly ordinary to him or her, such as making bread. These details should be included only if the person is learning a new task or if the point-of-view character is watching another person at work and is admiring, or criticizing, the process.

In *Face Down Under the Wych Elm*, I describe women doing laundry in quite a bit of detail. I did so because the villain was about to tip the scalding contents of a laundry tub over onto my sleuth. In *Face Down Across the Western Sea*, two characters visit a brewhouse in an effort to dis-cover why the last batch of beer was bitter. Neither the answer nor details of the process of brewing beer have anything to do with the mystery, but letting Jennet, Lady Appleton's housekeeper, grill the brewer about her technique provides a bit of comic relief. It also gives Jennet's companion, a suspect, a false sense of security. She relaxes, joins in the discussion, and gives me the opportunity to plant a clue having to do with something entirely different in the suspect's past.

Critic Molly Weston focuses on "the story and the characters" when she writes reviews of mystery novels and gives this advice to historical mystery writers:

> It's imperative that the story move, and the faster, the better. Pedantic teaching and long descriptions don't cut it for me. I like the author to be clever about giving clues to the history that's important to the story, dropping references to real events and people rather than reporting them. For instance, instead of describing how muddy a road is during a long rainy trip, the author could let the character look out at the dreary countryside and the mud splashing on the horse's legs and think about the warmth of the fire in the inn where she will spend the night. Rather than describe the grandeur of a castle, the character might mentally contrast it with the hovel of the blacksmith who just shod his horse. Imparting action, even if mental, involves both the character and the reader, and it still gives the description. Whenever description is necessary, make it alive.

Details do seem to be the key to winning over reviewers. Jon L. Breen, a novelist as well as a critic, feels that "a good historical mystery brings its time and place alive with telling details without letting the history overwhelm the story." Reviewer Sally Fellows admires "a writer who can create a vivid picture of the period of time, so vivid that she makes it her own. The details are sufficient to make that time come alive. The second most important thing is the creation of characters who 'fit' or 'belong' in that time. When I read them I don't feel they have strayed from today. The time and the characters together allow me to lose myself in the book and 'suspend my disbelief.'" Among the writers Fellows thinks do it "just right" are Elizabeth Peters, Laurie R. King, Rennie Airth, Bruce Alexander, Victoria Thompson, Barbara Cleverly, Barbara Hambly, Rebecca Pawel, and Jacqueline Winspear.

Reviewer Barbara Franchi (www.ReviewingTheEvidence.com) agrees that historical mysteries should have a "sense of place and time." She cites Lindsey Davis, who "puts Falco in Ancient Rome with problems similar to those of today but the city is very vivid. Reed and Mayer do the same with Constantinople and John the Eunuch. David Roberts writes of a more recent time but it is fun to try and match his fictional characters with the real ones on which they are based." She also likes "books that take a time and place about which I know a little and bring it to life" and gives Lauren Belfer's *City of Light* and Andrew Taylor's series set on the Welsh border during the 1950s as good examples. Taylor "subtly sets the scene. Just the small things—ladies putting on hats and gloves before going out, rationing still on or just finished in England, people not having one car per person, etc.—make this series an excellent portrait of the period."

Steven Steinbock, review editor for *The Strand Magazine*, also believes details are crucial, explaining,

> As a mystery reviewer, the three aspects of a book I'm most concerned with are the story, the characters, and the writing style. These factors matter, whether the book is set in Tudor England, Nero's Rome, or the mean streets of Baltimore. Once those three elements are out of the way, I can take time to judge the setting and the honest (or dishonest) adherence to historical detail. But if the dialogue is too arcane, or the details dumped on my lap like leaves from an encyclopedia without advancing the plotline, I have a tough time getting past them.
>
> The matter of detail is a delicate matter of taste. In all likelihood, you will have readers that want more accurate details, and readers that want less. If all your readers are perfectly happy, it's a sure sign that you don't have enough readers. I approach every historical mystery I read with innocent eyes. If a given page contains a word I don't know, or a reference I'm not familiar with, those details can still add to my enjoyment of the book by creating an exotic milieu for me. But three or four—or nine or ten— obscure bits of vocabulary or historical detail on the same page are likely to stymie me to an extent that I may not be capable of going on to the next page.

### Elusive Details

Thorough research is the only way to locate all the details you'll need for verisimilitude. But what if you can't find some particular bit of information? Do you make an educated guess? Or do you gloss over the details and move on? Either works. The real trick is to avoid describing something in intricate detail and finding out after the book is published that your guess was completely wrong!

Jane Finnis writes: "My books are set in first-century Roman Britain, partly because it interests me, but also because quite a lot of its history isn't known, so there's room for imagination to let rip. Looking at life in Roman times is like standing in the dark outside a large house (a villa perhaps?) and trying to peer in through the windows to examine the many rooms inside…. Parts of the house are plainly visible in great detail, but not all, and the lighted rooms are scattered, not adjacent. Similarly, we know only certain aspects of the history of Britannia in real depth. Our knowledge is growing all the time, but can never be complete. That's both a pain and a challenge."

At one time I was in a critique group. One of the other writers had written a scene in which village women were plucking chickens. Having no firsthand experience with this herself, my friend went into some detail about how the women applied just the right amount of torque to twist off the feathers prior to cooking. My grandparents owned a poultry farm in the 1950s. I have a vivid memory—complete with the smell—of my grandmother dunking a decapitated chicken in boiling water to loosen the feathers before attempting to remove them. I'm sure I'm not the only one of my friend's potential readers who'd know that detail and have serious doubts about the technique she invented.

When Caroline Roe began to write *Remedy for Treason*, set in fourteenth-century Spain, she "became obsessed with detail." She had recently fallen into conversation with a horse-breeder who'd told her that when he came across a detail to do with horses in a mystery novel that was dead wrong, he put the book down, unable to finish it, and would never buy another book by that author again. He'd assume the author got everything else wrong, too. Roe was determined to get everything right.

"For reasons essential to the plot," she recalls, "I needed a character to ride at speed from Barcelona to Girona and back with only a brief rest between—a distance of around 125 miles. Also essential was that the young man came from the poor branch of a rich and important family. The death or laming of his horse would be a disaster. I needed to know how much rest the horse would need between runs; how fast he could move at a steady gallop and for how long; and for that I needed to know what type of horse he was likely to be riding."

In search of the details, Roe consulted "a cousin who raises horses for a living and goes in for three-day eventing, a sport that challenges strength and endurance—not my cousin's but her horse's. But that was not the same sort of thing." She found information in the university library on the network of couriers who "carried messages from one end of Europe to the other in astonishingly rapid times, but by changing horses." That wasn't quite right either, but she was able to use that information to work out what sort of horse her character would be riding—"classy, quite fast, not big, with endurance and bred in Spain. A Porsche—or, in his case, a somewhat lower-priced imitation—of the horse world."

The municipal library system also provided a great deal of information on horses, "from books for horse-mad ten-year-old girls to serious journals on various aspects of equine management. Among them I found material published by a British association dedicated to endurance trials, in which the horses race for two and three days, and sometimes longer, with overnight rests. There were years and years of results of these trials by horses of varied backgrounds, showing how the length of the rests altered the results."

It took Roe a full week to get the details right for "one brief event," but when the specifics are important, it is worth the time.

In some cases, getting a detail wrong can ruin a story for readers. Dean James, former manager of Murder by the Book in Houston and a longtime reviewer for various publications, is also the award-winning author of numerous works of mystery nonfiction and the author of ten mystery novels. He loses faith in an author's credibility when that writer "demonstrates that he or she hasn't done enough (and appropriate) research." An example? "In a medieval mystery I read a few years ago, set in the late twelfth century, the author had the abbess of an English nunnery invite a knight to dine with her and all her nuns in the nunnery. It was patently ridiculous, and that demonstrated to me that the author really had done slipshod research."

Sometimes missing details aren't crucial but simply nag at the writer until they are found. When Sharan Newman was writing *Death Comes as Epiphany*, the first in her Catherine LeVendeur series, she wondered what people in twelfth-century France used instead of toilet paper, which was yet to be invented. It wasn't that Newman was planning an elaborately detailed scene in the privy, but characters do occasionally "answer the call of nature," just as they eat, drink, and have sex lives. Unaware at the time quite how much this detail would delight readers, she consulted another medieval scholar and used the answer exactly the way descriptive details are best employed—subtly, casually, and in keeping with the scene:

"'Good morning,' Catherine said. 'Where...?'

"'Out back,' Emma sniffed. 'The moss bucket is in here by the door.'"

Catherine then scoops up a handful of moss as she goes out, thinking, "Dame Emma was thoughtful to keep it inside. There was nothing worse than having to wipe oneself with an icy clump of moss."

## Figures of Speech

Similes and metaphors frequently make use of descriptive details that evoke time and place. Rather than simply saying Lord Meren's presence made a group of suspects nervous, in *Murder in the Place of Anubis* Lynda S. Robinson writes: "The name caused a stirring among them like papyrus reeds shifting in the north wind." Elsewhere a character is told not to "wheeze as though you had swallowed a whole pomegranate." Meren himself is said to be able to "scent fear as a hound scents a wounded gazelle."

In *The Right Hand of Amon*, Lauren Haney has a character scowling at Lieutenant Bak "over pyramided fingers," a nice variation on the steepled fingers found so often in detective stories, and entirely suitable in a setting that has pyramids but lacks churches.

"Fall colors were just beginning to tinge the landscape," Dale Furutani writes in *Kill the Shogun*, "like the delicate strokes of a kimono painter, touching brush to silk and watching the rich hues spread across the tightly woven, shimmering cloth." Not only is this a lovely image, but it brings readers into the place (Japan) and the time (when there were kimono painters, in this case, 1603).

There is only one caveat about using colorful language. If you come up with a turn of phrase that you find *particularly* clever, think twice about using it. If it doesn't fit in with the rest of what you've written, or if it doesn't suit the characters and the situation, it will stick out like the proverbial sore thumb. If it does, *get rid of it!* The last thing you want to do is pull the reader out of the story.

## Information Dumps and How To Avoid Them

Reviewer Steven Steinbock offers this piece of advice that applies to both colorful language and information dumps: "If you love history, and enjoy sharing it with others, it's likely that if unbridled, you would give more detail than is in the best interest of your story. Any piece of writing that you're especially proud of needs to be looked at honestly, and if it fails to advance the story, put it under the guillotine."

Historical mystery readers enjoy vivid settings and are prepared to read a great number of historical details, but they don't want them all at once. Furthermore, there must be a good reason to include these details. Do you really need to describe everything your character sees while walking from one place to another in eighteenth-century New York? Unless one of those things will turn out to be important later, or you are using the trip to give the character a chance to mull something over, then simply take him to his destination. "After a brisk walk, he arrived at the townhouse" is sufficient.

Paranormal–historical mystery writer P.N. Elrod has strong feelings on the subject of what she calls a "data dump" and a more colorful way of expressing them than I do: "The trick is not to use everything you find. (I've suffered for my art, now it's the reader's turn.) Unless it has to do with the plot, character, or is a 'light' touch to set a scene, leave it out. I don't care what people are eating and wearing, but dote on what they're doing and saying. How a rare and juicy pomegranate made its way to milady's dining table is boring. Her throwing it at someone à la one of the Three Stooges isn't."

This is the same thing that bothers Dean James most about some historical mysteries—when "the author simply can't resist the 'Gee whiz, look what I found out' factor and proceeds in mind-numbing detail about something that isn't really germane to the story." Fascinating as *you* may find the details of how something worked in the past, it can be fatal to assume your readers will be equally entranced. If you slow down the narrative just to show off what you've learned, you pull readers out of the story. They may not return. If you must share something your scholarship has revealed and it doesn't fit in with the plot, put it on your website, in a newsletter, or in a blog.

The tricky part about avoiding information dumps, however, is that the person who wrote them often has a great deal of difficulty spotting them. To you, they'll seem perfectly logical, even essential to the story. This is why it helps to set the finished manuscript aside for a time. When you go back to your book after a break, you will have some perspective, and you should be able to pick out the places that lag. Another solution is to have someone else read your manuscript and be honest about anything that results in a loss of interest in the story.

## Layering in Descriptive Details and Planting Clues

Casual mention of descriptive details is the most effective way to work them in. "Seamless" is the word some reviewers employ. Unless your point-of-view character has never seen such splendor or such squalor before, there is no reason to have him or her list every item in a room…except when there is a clue hidden among the items on it.

The following excerpt from *Face Down Below the Banqueting House* comes after a paragraph in which the point-of-view character, Winifred Baldwin, runs an assessing gaze over several pieces of expensive furniture and a tapestry:

> Atop an oval table, Holme had combined a chessboard with the pieces from a game of tables in order to play draughts. Wondering how else he passed his time, Winifred surveyed the room again, this time without regard for the monetary value of the

things she saw. A box of lutestrings. Five songbooks. But no lute. Winifred supposed it was elsewhere in the house. She frowned at a red ball but dismissed the incongruity of its presence the moment she caught sight of an open box of ginger candy.

Since Winifred has a well-established sweet tooth, the candies grab her attention. Then Holme himself enters the room to provide more distraction. Looking at this out of context, it isn't hard to spot the red ball as an item that doesn't fit. Mystery readers who really get into solving the crime may take note of it as an anomaly as they read. More casual readers won't remember it was there at all until it becomes important later in the story.

What does the red ball signify? That another member of that household, who has a little problem with kleptomania, has been at Leigh Abbey—that's the only way she could have come into possession of the red ball, since it belongs to a boy who lives there. That puts her in place to have information Lady Appleton needs to know. This doesn't solve the major mystery of the piece—the kleptomaniac is not the killer and doesn't know who is—but it moves the story along and contributes to the subplot.

In *Ragtime in Simla*, Barbara Cleverly inserts an obvious clue—a newspaper clipping—that leads both the reader and the detective to think one particular fact contained in it is important. It is…but so are two other details. Cleverly brings us back to the clipping not once, but twice, each time pointing out important information that was there all along but was overlooked.

Mary Reed and Eric Mayer successfully hide clues in plain sight in *Six For Gold*, in which John the Eunuch is charged with discovering why a sheep apparently committed suicide by cutting its own throat on a sharp blade. Melios, owner of the dead sheep, mentions in the course of showing John around his Egyptian estate that he is treating his rheumatic knees with the herb squill and that this remedy has made patches of his skin raw. This information comes during a casual exchange about gardeners. When next the dead sheep is mentioned, another character, Dedi, claims he caused the animal to kill itself through "magickal powers." Dedi later sets up a second demonstration of these powers—another sheep suicide. The sheep dies in spite of the "protective garland" it wears. This garland, however, is supplied by Melios's gardener, who also works for Dedi. As John does, the astute reader will have picked up on the fact that the gardener was previously seen pinching white flowers off what appears to be a large onion and that John's servant, Peter, got blisters on his hands after chopping another "onion." The plant is actually squill and the garland, when examined, is laced with the stuff, which irritated the sheep's skin. When the animal tried to ease the itching by rubbing against a sword, it ended up slitting its own throat—not suicide, or magic, but murder.

Sometimes it is the *lack* of something that provides a clue. Does someone leave a detail out of his account of what happened on the day of the murder? And why *didn't* the dog bark if a stranger came near?

Another use of clues, although it is one I don't much care for, is to have the sleuth discover something and emphasize its importance but not tell the reader what it is or why it is significant until much later in the book. This may work, however, if you provide a distraction at the appropriate moment, preventing the sleuth from sharing his or her thoughts with the reader.

The identity of the villain also needs to be obvious once it is revealed, but hidden until then. He or she should appear on the scene early on, but it is not necessary to have the sleuth suspect him or her until much later in the story. The best mystery writers make readers certain someone else is guilty, and give them no overt reason to suspect the real villain. Hints that the real villain is not all he or she seems are slipped into the story.

Let's say the villain is the steward in a noble household. He may do something that seems out of character or make a comment that shows he has knowledge he should not have, or he may have some secret in his past that casts doubt on his behavior in the present. As long as readers are diverted by their suspicion of someone else, these clues will go virtually unnoticed. A variant is to have the sleuth suspect the real murderer early on, then dismiss the suspicions as unfounded until new information emerges.

However you choose to plant your clues, it is a good idea to keep track of them. List what they are and where they are and what significance they have. And make sure you tie up any loose ends. If you create questions in the readers' minds, even by the use of a red herring, you have an obligation to answer them.

## Keeping Track

You never know when you are going to need a particular detail. If you've done your research, you have reams of notes and shelves full of books. If you are in the habit of putting notes on your computer, you can probably find what you want with a search function, but for some the old-fashioned way still works best.

I'm not sure it's possible to keep track of everything, but the best method I've found so far is to use a series of loose-leaf notebooks. After writing ten novels and numerous short stories in the Face Down series, I have to be very careful not to contradict myself. This means I need to keep track of what I've already said in previous books. My current loose-leaf binders are labeled HERBS, CURES, SETTING, CHARACTERS, DATES, and, with a certain irony, QUICK REFERENCE. The latter is for the work in progress and pulls pages from the others and from my three-drawer lateral file cabinet full of folders on various subjects that run from ALEHOUSES to ZENO FAMILY.

Granted, some of this material, especially details on continuing characters and the settings I reuse (Lady Appleton's various houses, Nick Baldwin's warehouse in London, and so on) makes it into computer files, but if I kept all of those updated I'd never have time to write books.

If I had to find a source for something specific in one of the earlier books, I could probably do it, but not without a long search. Fortunately, the most likely person to question accuracy of information is the copy editor, and at that point the research is still recent enough to find quickly. Reviewers, of course, often jump on things they think are wrong. Sometimes it is the reviewer who is mistaken, but there isn't any dignified way for a writer to respond to an unfair review, so it is rarely worth the bother of producing proof to refute charges of inaccuracy. The purpose of keeping files in some sort of order is so that you can find the information you need when you are actually writing the story.

## How Graphic Is Too Graphic?

One last topic related to your choice of descriptive details is the question of how "realistic" you want your historical mystery to be. Yes, you want to take your readers into the past and make it believable, but do you need to describe every open sore, every fetid smell, every vile taste?

By modern standards, hygiene in past eras was seriously lacking, violence and disease often went unchecked, and women, with fewer legal rights, had to put up with far more of what we now label as abuse. The subject of using detailed descriptions of sexual encounters in historical mysteries has already been touched upon in Chapter Five, but there are other areas in which details may be defined as "graphic" or even "gratuitous"—scenes of violence and descriptions that may sicken or disgust the reader.

Consider what is necessary to your plot. Then consider what you are comfortable writing. And finally think of your readers—what are the sensibilities of your target audience? Do they really want to know how it feels and smells to have a plague boil lanced? Do they want a blow-by-blow description of a swordfight or a brawl? And even if they'll accept the need for the latter—blood spurting from a broken nose or a slit throat may have a bearing on both character and plot—do they want to read a detailed torture or rape scene?

If your historical mystery would otherwise be described as a cozy, then don't go into all the gory details. Find other ways to establish the fact that something horrific has happened. If you want to show the gritty reality of a time and place, then your story should be written that way from the beginning. When it comes right down to it, the writer chooses which details to use and is the only one who can decide which ones are gratuitous and which are not.

Getting right the sort of details discussed in this chapter is only part of your job as a writer. The language appropriate to a historical mystery requires an entire chapter of its own.

# 9 *Language—*
## *A Sign of the Times*

ELLIS Peters once told an interviewer from *Publishers Weekly* that she always tried to "strike a balance between modern, colloquial speech and the archaic" and that the key to making Cadfael "the person next door" was avoiding "stilted language."

The author's use of language, especially in dialogue, is an essential tool in creating the right feel for a historical mystery. Complete accuracy does not work well—it sounds too stiff and formal to modern readers. Writer/reviewer Betty Webb summarizes the ideal balance quite nicely in her *Mystery Scene* review of George Rees's *An Eye of Death*, set in Elizabethan London. The novel contains what Webb calls "the era's elegant language peeled back to allow for a comfortable read."

## Historical Mysteries as Translations

Some mystery authors will say straight out that their books are "translations" of recently discovered manuscripts. This is a convenient way of excusing any inaccuracies in language that readers may find in the text, such as the author's use of words not yet coined during the period in which the story is set. In a very real sense, however, all historical mysteries are translations. Sharan Newman is not writing in medieval French. Caroline Roe is not writing in medieval Spanish. Steven Saylor is not writing in Latin. And I do not write in Elizabethan English. The sixteenth century was a period in which the language wasn't all that different from what we speak today, but if I kept to all the linguistic conventions it would sound like bad—very bad—Shakespeare, and no one wants to read that.

## The Flavor of the Language

What appears to work for most historical mysteries is the selective use of archaic language to give a sense of the time period. Use a few period words that are not in modern dictionaries. That means readers must be able to reason out what they mean from the context.

Some writers use a non-English or archaic word, followed immediately by the modern English equivalent, to make the meaning clear. Others simply drop a word or phrase in another language into the text and let the reader deduce its meaning from the context. Both techniques work, but beware of overusing either. Also make sure that if you use an archaic word, you use it correctly.

With so-called "modern" English (which dates from the sixteenth century!) you can find suitable period words and also hear the rhythm of the language by listening to the dialogue in plays written in your chosen period. You can get a feel for the spoken word from Shakespeare (sixteenth and early seventeenth centuries), Shaw (late nineteenth century and early twentieth), Noel Coward (early- to mid-twentieth century), and others. If your mysteries are set in the United States, find plays written by Americans in the years surrounding your story. If you are unable to attend a production or obtain a recorded reading of a play, then read it aloud yourself.

Letters and diaries are another source of words, but in letters the language is apt to be more formal and complex—dare I say convoluted? Also look at newspapers and magazines. The articles in many of these were actually first-person essays.

Another way to give an authentic feel to the dialogue in your historical mystery is to study linguistics. Any basic textbook on the subject will tell you that in the sixteenth century, -ly endings on words were rare and the contractions *it's* and *don't* were not yet in use. An Elizabethan would say something was *passing strange* (surpassingly strange) and use *'tis* or *it is* instead of *it's*.

Curiously, although *it's* is one of those words that tends to be invisible to the reader, *'tis* stands out. Frequent repetition tends to become annoying. For that reason, after writing several books in the Face Down series, I cut way back on the use of *'tis*. For some reason, however, I started using words like *certes* (certainly) and *gramercy* (thank you). They are correct for the sixteenth century and earlier, but like *forsooth* and *gadzooks*, are probably better avoided. To use Josephine Tey's phrase from *The Daughter of Time*, "speaking forsoothly" will only get you into trouble!

The words you choose to give the flavor of the language to your historical mystery have to be your own choices. It's a judgment call. Some readers are going to be put off by any use of archaic words or spelling. There's no winning them over, no matter how hard you try. All readers, however, pick up a historical mystery to be entertained. No one wants to struggle with unfamiliar words. Since total accuracy is impossible to obtain—even contemporary novels don't reproduce natural speech exactly—seek to imbue your language, particularly your dialogue, with a hint of the period you write about *without* going to extremes.

### Dialects, Accents, and Speech Patterns

In *Face Down Upon an Herbal*, which I will discuss in more detail in Chapter Eleven, I use dialect extensively with the character of Nan, a maidservant. There is even an important clue included in her ramblings. Is her speech historically accurate? Not completely, but I don't think it is too far off, either.

People writing in the sixteenth century didn't make much effort to record differences in regional dialects. Sometimes there are clues in the spelling, but not always. However, since regional distinctions were still obvious until the advent of television, I felt confident basing Nan's speech on information in a book written in 1898 and another published right after World War II. I also use the trick of interpreting at least some of her words through another character whose English is easier to understand.

Susan Wittig Albert does this rather cleverly in *The Tale of Hill Top Farm*, the first in her Beatrix Potter series. When a character says, "Two pounds is a girt lot of money," the next line (the "translation") is the response of one of the animal characters: "A great deal of money indeed!"

If you're writing about the more recent past, you can listen to audio records of dialects and accents. Linguistic studies discuss differences in speech from region to region, particularly in the U.S. and U.K. Peter Trudgill's *The Dialects of England*, Clive Upton and J.D.A. Widdowson's *An Atlas of English Dialects*, and Harold Orton, Stewart Sanderson, and John Widdowson's *The Linguistic Atlas of England* can be borrowed on inter-library loan. I also recommend the *Linguistic Atlas of New England* and Marvin Rubinstein's *American English Compendium*. The latter lists proverbs, American slang, and the differences between British and American terms. A drawback of Rubinstein's book is the lack of dates, but you can cross-check anything you think you might use with the *OED*.

Americans writing about England are going to make linguistic "mistakes" in British English. Don't drive yourself crazy over this. For one thing, your so-called mistake may not *be* one, given the historical period you've chosen. The great divide between British and American English came in the seventeenth century. At that time, for example, both *fall* and *autumn* were in use in England. Some "authorities" seem to think Americans exclusively and throughout history have said only *fall* while Englishmen never refer to the season as anything but *autumn*. Nonsense.

One place that studies English dialects in the U.S. is Plimoth Plantation, where the re-enactors try to duplicate the speech of the county of origin of the real persons they portray. Some of that can also be found on the video of "Muse of Fire," one episode in the PBS series *The Story of English*. The "companion book" is edited by Robert McCrum, William Cran, and Robert MacNeil. Stephen Eddy Snow's *Performing the Pilgrims: A Study of Ethnohistorical Role-Playing at Plimoth Plantation* discusses this in greater detail. And, of course, you can visit it in Plymouth, Massachusetts for yourself.

I have a little booklet titled "A Dictionary of the Queen's English," acquired back in 1972 from the Travel and Tourism Division of the North Carolina Department of Commerce. It contains three lists: Elizabethan words still used in North Carolina, North Carolina dialect, and North Carolina Expressions. What stands out for me about some of the entries, especially in the section on "North Carolina dialect," is that the same words and pronunciations have also been in use in Maine, where I live, since Colonial times—*de-ah* for dear; *furriner* for someone from outside the community. These may indeed be used in North Carolina, but they are not exclusive to that geographic region.

"A Dictionary of the Queen's English" *seems* to be a serious attempt to "translate" dialect. Why would I hesitate to rely on it? Because a fair number of spoofs have been published about language and dialects, John Gould's *Maine Lingo* and Gerald E. Lewis's *How to Talk Yankee* among them. Each contains some sound information, but the authors are humorists. They exaggerate to get a laugh. That basic rule of research applies here: never rely on only one source.

Speech patterns vary from character to character in any novel, just as they do among real people. These differences were even more pronounced (pardon the pun) in the past, when isolation and the absence of television or radio kept regional dialects intact. Class distinctions are also reflected in language and speech patterns. In an essay in *The Detective as Historian*, Linda J. Holland-Toll touches on this subject in discussing Anne Perry's Thomas and Charlotte Pitt novels: "One of the ways Perry employs dialect is as a class marker; both Gracie, Charlotte's maid, and the typical police constable drop their *h's*, render *isn't it* as *in't*, and substitute *f/v* for *th*, as in *bruvver*, reflect an intrusive *r* as in *gorn* for *gone* and *barf* for *bath*, all of which are dialectically correct."

Edward D. Hoch writes stories about Dr. Sam Hawthorne, a country doctor in 1922 Connecticut. Upon reading the first one, his editor made a suggestion Hoch found unsettling. "He wanted old Dr. Sam, in narrating the story, to speak more in a country dialect, dropping his final letters and such. Although I'd had some of the other characters doing this, especially Sheriff Lens, I'd avoided it with Dr. Sam." Hoch agreed to the change, but "over the next several stories the use of this country dialect decreased and finally Fred (Dannay, editor of *Ellery Queen's Mystery Magazine*) told me he thought the stories worked just as well without it."

If you are considering having one or more of your characters speak in dialect, keep in mind that many of today's editors, my own included, no longer consider dialect desirable in fiction. They tend to edit out more than the occasional word in favor of making the text readable.

### Slang

Using slang is even trickier than using dialect or giving a character an accent. Lists of "underground" slang included in glossaries in some secondary sources can't be trusted. One such list, in a book on crime in Elizabethan London, consists primarily of terms from a pamphlet which, although written at the time, was penned for quick money by a notorious drunk. The same list also includes the verb *halek*, meaning to have sexual relations. It implies this word was in common use. In fact, it was a term coined by Simon Forman and found only in his private diary. It was not in use by the general public.

Similarly, *Shakespeare's Bawdy* by Eric Partridge, although lauded by scholars, is severely flawed. According to Partridge, almost every word Shakespeare wrote had a double meaning. My best advice is to go back to the original sources and decide for yourself what terms will work for your characters.

### Proverbs, Sayings, Expressions...and Clichés

As with the figures of speech discussed in Chapter Eight, proverbs, sayings, and expressions used by your characters need to fit the time and place in which your historical mystery is set. In *Get Out or Die*, set in Roman Britain, Jane Finnis's innkeeper sleuth, Aurelia, quotes her grandmother as saying, "You can't judge a scroll by looking at its case." Aurelia's sister Albia begs to differ because their grandmother "never read anything in her life except wine-shippers' lists. If she'd felt the need for a corny proverb, she'd have said, you can't judge the vintage by looking at the amphora."

In past eras, picturesque language was the result of references of a Biblical, feudal, agricultural, nautical, or military nature. Trade also provided words and expressions—a tinker's dam as a thing of little worth, for example. To check exactly when a particular expression or proverb came into use, consult the OED or William Brohaugh's *English Through the Ages*, and possibly Bartlett's *Familiar Quotations*.

Some figures of speech have long histories, to the point where they have become clichés. However, in the period you're writing about, these same sayings could represent a brand new way of expressing a sentiment. In some eras, it was also considered very clever to drop quotes from the classics into conversation.

If you are trying to give a character realistic dialogue within a certain setting, the use of an occasional hackneyed phrase—and where, exactly, did "hackneyed phrase" come from?—might work very well. People do just this in normal conversation. In fact, you might even consider creating a character who *always* speaks in clichés and using that for comic effect. To do so, however, requires that you know what expressions would have been considered clichés *in your time period*.

### The Use of Expletives

To swear or not to swear? And if your characters do let out an occasional oath, what do they say? Expletives tend to be deleted in much of what has come down to us through history. They were used in conversation, not letters or official documents, although I'm sure there are exceptions. Once again, you might try looking to plays as a source of language.

Cursing and other "bad" language, like everything else in a historical mystery, has to fit into the milieu and work for the character in question. In Kerry Greenwood's *The Castlemaine Murders*, set in 1928, the fact that sleuth Phryne Fisher's sister drops her haughty airs to say, "Bugger that" marks a turning point in the relationship between the two women.

Consider which god or gods characters worship when you are looking for oaths. In *Get Out or Die*, Aurelia swears by "Holy Diana" while her handyman, Taurus, upon catching his first glimpse of a body, exclaims, "Oh, Saturn's balls! Is he dead?"

In the Face Down series I wanted to give my sleuth, Susanna, something to say when she was extremely frustrated, the Elizabethan equivalent of "Oh, shit" or "damn." In one of Shakespeare's plays I found the word "bodykins" with an editor's note saying it was "a mild curse." Perfect. Only some readers didn't think so. For them it was a peculiar word that stuck out like the proverbial sore thumb and, momentarily, stopped the story. In later books Susanna doesn't swear at all.

When it comes to swear words for other characters, I have to admit that I have not been spectacularly successful in selecting them. There is a fine line between the obscene and the absurd. Most of the Face Down characters use traditional period expressions such as "God's blood!" but there are two exceptions—Nick Baldwin and his mother. Since Nick was planned as an important continuing character, I wanted him to say something unique when he gets upset. I settled on "dragon water!" Dragon Water was a popular medicine of the age. Nick's mother, Winifred, swears "by St. Frideswide's girdle." This is my own invention, but follows the pattern of many real curses. Unfortunately, both expressions were just a little too different and attracted negative attention from reviewers. I'd have been better off sticking with "God's blood!"

In working on *Face Down O'er the Border*, which is set in Scotland, I gave a secondary character the curse "Christ aid!" It is one I turned up in my research as being in use in the sixteenth century in England. Since the character was a Scot, however, I wondered if I might not be able to find something better, perhaps in Gaelic. This seemed an ideal time to use the Internet. I typed in a few key words and promptly came up with a webpage that claimed to list Gaelic curses. I was looking for "taking the name of the Lord in vain," but this website presented me with an appalling variety of Gaelic terms for body parts and sexual acts. There was absolutely nothing equivalent to "Christ aid" or "God's bones." We won't get into the illustrated links to other websites—they definitely weren't offering what I was looking for! In the end, my character stuck with "Christ aid!"

In my Diana Spaulding Mysteries, set in 1888, I found it easier to come up with expletives. The occasional "Confound it" and "Balderdash!" don't sound quite so odd to modern ears, even though we no longer use those expressions. No one has commented on my use of either. Of course that could simply be because there are so many other Victorian-era mysteries.

Historical mystery readers are accustomed to Elizabeth Peters's character Radcliffe Emerson, "the Father of Curses," who uses both "confounded" and "balderdash" in *Crocodile on the Sandbank*, the first book in the series, along with the adjective "cursed" and the occasional "Good God" and "Bah!" His future wife, being more genteel, substitutes "Good Gad" for "Good God!" In *Tomb of the Golden Bird*, now long married and a grandfather, Emerson hasn't changed. His wife, Amelia Peabody Emerson, records the following as an example of her husband's usual discourse: "How are you, Ibraham, you old son of an incontinent camel?" Later she quotes Emerson's "Hell and damnation!" but employs parentheses when "none of his (expletive) business" comes from her own thoughts.

In another Amelia Peabody novel, *The Falcon at the Portal*, there is a scene that provides an excellent example of how to have characters swear without actually using objectionable language. Burglars have broken into the Emerson house in the middle of the night and Ramses, Amelia's son, has caught them in the act. When a gunshot wakes the rest of the household, they all go rushing downstairs. Amelia can hear Emerson's "breathless curses close behind" her. There is "a loud Damn!" from Nefret. When Emerson and Amelia run into each other in the confusion, Emerson bellows, "Where the devil…?" Then, figuring out where the sounds of a fight are coming from, Emerson says "a very bad word." They rush into the library only to find that Nefret is there ahead of them: "She jumped aside, swearing, as the burglar flung Ramses over onto his back—and onto the broken glass. His hand did not lose its grip, but the expletive that burst from his lips proved him a worthy son of his father." A few moments later, Ramses says, "Damnation!" but that is the extent of the actual swearing.

Of course, if you are writing about gangsters during Prohibition, such restraint may not be necessary. Use what is appropriate to the time and place to the extent that you are comfortable with putting those words on the page. There are only two sources of swear words I'd advise you to avoid, unless you are trying for a humorous effect. Do not use any of those Shakespearean curse-generating websites. And disregard anything you've heard in an old movie. "Zounds" may be a perfectly legitimate variant of "God's wounds" but it will always sound like a cliché.

## Characters with Distinctive Speech

Ideally, every character speaks with a distinct cadence, accent, and vocabulary. But dialect, speech impediments, and the like can easily become annoying, especially if there does not seem to be a good reason to use them. In a historical setting, almost everyone would have had a distinct regional accent. It is extremely difficult, however, to sustain such a thing with any accuracy.

One historical mystery that does succeed in this is Steve Hockensmith's *Holmes on the Range*, in which the narrator is a cowboy, Otto Amlingmeyer (Big Red) in 1893 Montana. He is Watson to his brother Gustav (Old Red)'s Sherlock Holmes. Both men use colorful language that carries the distinctive flavor of the Old West. "A fox with a mouthful of chicken feathers could hardly have looked more guilty," Big Red says. And upon examining a body and ruling out suicide, Old Red remarks: "Blastin' yourself in the skull ain't sharpshootin'. You'd have to get your hand right up against your noggin. And if you did that, not only would you end up wearin' your brains for a glove, you'd give yourself a heck of a powder burn."

Other ways to distinguish characters by their speech are to indicate different voice qualities, vary the speed and sound level at which they speak, and experiment with speech patterns. Short, choppy sentences, for example, in which the character uses only verbs, not subjects, give readers an impression of someone who is impatient and opinionated. Verbal habits like humming or snorting to express derision also reveal character.

One small consolation I take from being the age I am is that I can remember how my grandparents spoke. When I wrote the third book in the Diana Spaulding series, *No Mortal Reason*, set in the area of rural New York State where I grew up, I could hear the intonation, remember the expressions, even recollect that I once corrected my grandmother for saying "ain't" because, at eight years old, I'd been told by a teacher that it wasn't proper grammar.

For any character's speech, accuracy is important. So is consistency. If a character starts off talking like a street urchin, he shouldn't be speaking "the King's English" by the end of the book. Unless, of course, he's been in disguise all along.

## What Were Things Called *Then*?

Another language problem that may edge over into the area of anachronisms, the subject of the next chapter, is the question of which words people employed to refer to places and things at various points in history.

Place names vary from century to century. Using the modern name is certainly acceptable, for clarity, but the old ones can be found on maps contemporary to your story. The English Channel was called the Narrow Seas in medieval and Elizabethan times, although it also appears on maps as "the British Sea." The French called it *"la Manche"* ("the Sleeve"). In the same period, the Atlantic Ocean was "the Western Sea" and the North Sea was, usually, "the German Ocean." Maps are also useful for finding variant spellings, which can lend historical flavor while still being recognizable as their modern-day equivalents.

*Things* are usually harder than places for the reader to identify. The writer, familiar with a word, may not recognize it as a puzzler, but that same word can stop a reader dead. The first page of *Face Down Upon an Herbal* contains the words "aumbrys" and "armariola." In an attempt to create a sense of the historical period, I ended up sacrificing clarity. Cabinet and desk (or writing table) would have worked just as well and would have kept readers reading. I'll never know if I lost any sales, but I can imagine someone picking the book up in the store, reading that first page, and deciding that following the story would take too much effort to make the book worth buying. I *do* know that people stopped reading long enough to grab a dictionary…and then suffered the frustration of not being able to find either of these archaic words listed.

The word "herbal" was also unfamiliar to some readers, but in a title that can be an advantage. It may have made a few people stop in the bookstore and look closer, at least close enough to discover that an herbal is a book about herbs.

## What Were People Called *Then*?

Naming characters requires particular attention in historical mysteries in the same way that any other word choice does. Various times and places may have certain conventions, although as Lindsey Davis points out on her website: "The main thing you need to know about Roman names is this: There are rules, but—the Romans were not a hidebound people and they did not follow the rules!"

Middle names were rare in Elizabethan England. The exceptions, like Thomas Posthumous Hoby, stand out. Given the time and place of your setting, and the social status of your characters, would they have been likely to be christened with a whole string of names or just one? In an earlier period, would they even have surnames or were people known only as Jack the Tiler and Joan the Weaver? You need to know before you blithely start assigning names to your characters.

Simon Levack, who sets his Aztec mysteries in the reign of Emperor Montezuma, had a choice to make when it came to naming characters. "When I began writing *Demon of the Air*," he recalls,

> I searched assiduously for authentic Aztec names for my characters, and rendered them all in their own language, Nahuatl. However, my agent and my editor told me that readers would be put off by tongue-twisters such as "Tlilpotonqui" and "Miahaux-ihuitl." Even translating them into English was problematic, as I was told this would make my book read like a work of fantasy. It does not help that most Aztecs were called after their name-day, and only those days considered lucky were ever used, so in practice many ordinary people might have the same name. I could see readers getting fed up trying to work out which "One Flower" was the killer and which was the victim. So I settled for giving them the sort of nicknames that they might have given themselves.

His sleuth, Yaotl, is the slave of Montezuma's chief minister, "The unscrupulous Lord Feathered In Black."

When I do research, especially in biographies that contain genealogical tables, I write down any unusual given names and any unusual spellings for common names. Thus I know I can call a sixteenth-century woman Dousabella or Euphemia. I could also name one Philadelphia, after Philadelphia Carey, a maid of honor at the court of Elizabeth I, but that's the sort of name I hesitate to use because, although it is historically accurate, it *sounds* modern. Susanna, by the way, was a popular name among those who embraced the New Religion, while the names of lesser known saints, like Werburga and Frideswide, tended to indicate that a girl came from a recusant (Catholic) family.

If you are using real people as characters, even minor characters, make sure you find out if the names of their family members and servants are known to history. Why make up a name for someone's wife if you can find it in Burke's *Peerage* or in a genealogy on the Internet? Besides, family connections through marriage may add another layer to the story, especially if your plot or subplot involves political intrigue.

Is there ever a good reason to change real people's names? If it seems necessary to avoid confusion, yes. Some given names—John and Mary come to mind—crop up far too often in real life. But if you do substitute something more distinctive, or give a character a nickname, you might want to mention that in an author's note.

### Forms of Address

For some reason using the correct form of address for a character causes problems for many historical novelists. It shouldn't, at least not for those historicals set in England. There were and are clear-cut rules for addressing knights, peers, and royalty. My sleuth is Susanna, Lady Appleton. She is addressed as Lady Appleton (because her husband is Sir Robert Appleton), *not* Lady Susanna. The latter form of address would be appropriate only if her *father* were a nobleman (above the rank of baron).

Wherever your story is set, take the time to learn how various groups of people are addressed now and if there were differences during the period you are writing about. It wouldn't hurt, either, if you have given titles to some of your characters, to familiarize yourself with the real noble houses of the times. If there were an actual Duke of Norfolk, then it would not be a good idea to use that title for a completely fictional character.

Sadly, no matter how careful the author is to get it right, a fair number of reviewers and other readers will get it wrong when they write or talk about your book. Thus "Lady Susanna" even turned up in some of my cover copy in the past. The only thing you can do is grit your teeth, make corrections when you can, and learn to live with other people's lack of knowledge or caring the rest of the time.

## Keeping Track of Words

As with other research, take copious notes on language. Start a word list, particularly of unusual or interesting words. Mine for the sixteenth century currently runs to just under thirty single-spaced pages. An abridged version is posted on my website. Both lists include unusual words and their meanings. The thirty-page version also lists words not yet in use in the middle of the sixteenth century. If I decide to use one of these anyway, at least I'll know I'm fudging.

I also keep track of names I've already used, even those given to very minor characters. Old Mag, for example, is mentioned only once, in *Face Down Among the Winchester Geese*. She's a midwife who doctors the prostitutes at The Sign of the Smock, a whorehouse. I might use Mag as a name again sometime. If I do, I want to be sure I remember who had it before. At various times I've used an address label program to keep track of names, because it lets me index by first name, last name, or book in series (the address line). I've also used a genealogy program to make family trees for continuing characters.

For the recent Face Down books that were published by Perseverance Press, glossaries have been added to the front matter. This was the suggestion of my editor and I think it's a good one. The tricky part is figuring out which words will give readers trouble. The meaning of any unusual word should always be clear from the context, but even when the writer believes that to be the case, some readers will still stop reading just because they've come upon an unfamiliar term. At least having a glossary keeps them from putting the book down while they look for a dictionary.

## What Do Historical Mystery Readers Think About Language?

Although it is possible to lose readers by using too many archaic words, a majority of historical mystery readers seem to prefer that authors use an obscure but correct word rather than one that is more recognizable but incorrect for the historical period. Back in 2004, while writing one of her Sister Frevisse mysteries, Margaret Frazer discovered that the word *seamstress* was not in use until the 1600s. The term *sempster* was used in the 1400s. This left her in a quandary, since the word had to appear in her title. Frazer's own preference was for *The Sempster's Tale*. Her agent and editor preferred *The Seamstress's Tale*, feeling readers would not know what a sempster was. Frazer posed the question to members of CrimeThruTime and received twenty-two replies to the list. Every one of them stated a preference for *sempster* over *seamstress*.

Whatever dialects, accents, archaic words or usages you decide to sprinkle in, just remember to use a light hand. And trust your instincts, too. If a word doesn't feel right to you, even if you know it is correct, find something else that means the same thing. Chances are that if a word choice bothers you as a writer, it will bother readers, too.

# CHAPTER 10 *Anachronisms and How To Avoid Gadzookery*

ANACHRONISMS are the bane of the historical mystery writer's existence. It isn't too hard to avoid glaring errors like putting a Regency rake in doublet and hose or having a Roman matron cook on an electric stove, but there are all sorts of things that can sneak into a manuscript when you're not looking. Even if you choose to write paranormals or alternate history mysteries, you need to check facts. Alternate history depends upon history being the same up to a certain event. Just as in a regular historical mystery, dress, customs, food, and all the rest have to agree with what we know about a certain era.

What, exactly, is an anachronism? Quite simply, anachronisms are things used in the wrong time period. This can be either because they are no longer used or because they are not yet in use. No matter how careful your research, anachronisms in language and anachronistic details—things you never thought to check because you were so certain they were accurate—slip through the cracks.

## "Read until First Anachronism. Toss."

You may be wondering what happened to poetic license. We're writing fiction and there are bestsellers that are notoriously inaccurate when it comes to historical "facts." True, but as a writer of historical mysteries, you are targeting a specific audience, one that prefers their history accurate down to the smallest detail. Get it wrong and you pull them out of the story. Get it wrong and you'll hear from readers, telling you about what you did. Get it wrong and you justify comments like the one Marilyn Stasio, mystery critic for the *New York Times*, made in a 2006 review: "Here's my standard approach to historical mysteries: Open book. Read until first anachronism. Toss."

Most reviewers seem to agree that anachronisms are flaws that would prevent them from giving an otherwise well-written novel high marks. Jon L. Breen hates "obvious anachronisms of slang or other terminology. I'm most likely to find these in books about relatively recent history, in which they are paradoxically harder to avoid and more likely to be spotted. A too early use of 'shrink' for psychiatrist is one that comes up frequently." Dean James comments that "no one expects the author to write in Middle English or Norman French…but the author can still work to avoid obvious anachronisms with words that are too modern. A truly gifted writer can convey the concept without having to resort to the modern term for it."

Reviewer Steven Steinbock suggests that the authors of historical mysteries need "to find the golden mean between accuracy and accessibility. Of course, you want your book to accurately capture the essence of the period in your dialogue and description. You've done the research, and know what foods people eat, how they dress, and how social and political institutions of the period operated. If your villain carries a pump-action shotgun during the American Civil War, a few gun-buffs may catch you. But that's still a few too many. But the flipside is that too much accuracy can bog your story down. Readers want the feel of the period, but they also deserve to get to the story without having to wade through footnotes, glossaries, and endless minutiae."

## Anachronistic Words

Kim Malo, moderator of CrimeThruTime (CTT), writes: "Taken to its logical absurdity, any historical mystery set more than a hundred years or so back and written in modern English is an anachronism." As discussed in Chapter Nine, using the exact language of the time usually isn't a good idea. Better, as Kim puts it, to use "comprehensible modern English" and avoid "clear anachronisms, such as having a pair of cavaliers synchronize their watches."

Short of checking every single word in your manuscript to be certain it was actually used during the time of your historical mystery, there is no way to avoid ever using an anachronistic word. An alert copy editor may catch some, but more often than not, they are words you've already checked for yourself and found to be accurate. Check again. No point in letting a foolish error slip through. But there will be other words that will escape notice. They *sound* right for the period and it will never occur to you to make sure they are.

Steven Steinbock calls word choice a "tricky matter.

> All too often, while reading a historical mystery, I come across a term that seems so jarringly anachronistic that I dash off to the *Oxford English Dictionary* to check. I'm often surprised to find

that the author was indeed technically correct. But by that time I've lost the momentum of the story. I've been distracted away from what the author intended. Shakespeare can and did use the word "punk." But for the Elizabethan reader, it didn't mean a rude teenage boy on a skateboard. It didn't mean a boy at all. An obnoxious person might have been called a "jerk" in the 1920s, but encountering it on the printed page might jerk me in the wrong direction. For the author of historical mysteries, it isn't enough to use words that *are* appropriate to the period. The writer must choose words that *sound* accurate for the period.

The words writers need to be especially aware of, since they are sure to be caught by readers if they are used by mistake, are those derived from people's names and names of commodities. Mesmerism, for example, comes from Dr. F.A. Mesmer, born in 1734. Tea leaves and the word *tea* did not appear in England before the mid-seventeenth century. Could a character in the fifteenth century know about a drink called tea (though it would be spelled differently)? Yes...but only if he had access to information about China.

In some cases the source word for an English word of a later era was in common usage in another language, such as French or Dutch. If your character has contact with people who speak a language other than English, or has traveled abroad, then he or she may have access to additional vocabulary.

Words we associate with murder investigations also need to be checked. How early could one have an alibi? Or a motive, for that matter? And were those words used in the same sense we mean today?

When I was working on *Face Down Among the Winchester Geese*, I was unable to turn up any information concerning the disposition of unclaimed, murdered bodies in 1560s England. Was there such a thing as a morgue? The *OED* told me that the word was not yet in use and indicated that there was unlikely to have been a specific place where murder victims were customarily taken. It only seems logical that some procedure was followed, but lacking specifics, I decided to have my sleuth claim the body at the murder scene by saying it was that of a relative. I still don't have an answer to my question, but what happens in the novel is believable.

Consulting the *OED* to catch anachronisms is a must for the writer of historicals, but remember that the *OED* cites only the first occurrence of that word *in print* and *in English*. Earlier occurrences may have been lost over time. In addition, when books were rare, many words would have been in use far earlier than their first appearance in print.

In addition to the *OED*, you may find it useful to consult William Bro-haugh's *English Through the Ages* (1998). Sections are broken down by date. Some of the words that were not used in 1950 but were in use by 1960, for example, are: dust mop, exotic dancer, eye contact, gunpoint, mother hen, ploughman's lunch, press secretary, second banana, send-up (parody), spear-carrier, and stretch marks. Also listed is *gadzookery*, a British word that means using archaic words!

## The Tale of the Clocks

A topic that has been addressed more than once on the CTT listserv concerns how people told time in past ages. The most recent discussion started with a question about the accuracy of referring to the quarter hour in a monastery in the 1530s. This struck a good many people as anachronistic, myself included. How would this person know the time to that degree? Clocks were rare, weren't they? And expensive. Weren't most people still telling time by the sun or by cock crow? Or perhaps, by the ringing of church bells? But how often did those ring, and how accurate were they?

It didn't take long for the inquisitive readers on the list to chime in with their research. It turns out that sixteenth-century people were familiar with the concept of minutes and that most monasteries in the 1530s probably had water clocks. Simple, inexpensive versions of these had been available since ancient times. Is there a great deal of evidence of this in period writings? There is some, but I couldn't recall coming across any reference to water clocks in over thirty years of research into everyday life in the era. Why not? The answer, when I thought about it, was simple. People don't mention the commonplace. You wouldn't necessarily mention how your character knew it was ten past six if you were writing a mystery set in 2008. Your reader would assume your character glanced at a watch or a clock.

Omitting similar information in a historical mystery, however, can result in a true fact being questioned by readers. It must have bothered some of them quite a bit or they wouldn't have posted on CTT. So, if you have a situation akin to this one in your novel, what do you do? Do you make some reference to the water clock—or a sundial, or whatever means of telling time is appropriate—to prevent readers from wondering how the character knew? Or do you follow Joan Blos's test, cited in Chapter Eight, and leave it out because "the equivalent detail" would not be mentioned in a contemporary novel? The only answer I can offer is that you must decide on a case-by-case basis.

## Deliberate Use of Anachronistic Language

Is there ever a time when you can get away with the deliberate use of an anachronistic word? In the use of words from an earlier period, certainly. I call a lady's private chamber a solar in my sixteenth-century series, even though most sources, including the OED, say that the word was no longer in use by that time. My argument is to cite a parallel case—we no longer put parlors in today's houses, but some people still use the term, especially in rural locations.

Using words or expressions not yet invented is a trickier proposition and goes back to the "translation" discussion in Chapter Nine. It can work if you do it well and are consistent. Lindsey Davis's character Falco speaks in colloquial English. At times Falco, the Roman "private informer," sounds very much like a twentieth-century hard-boiled detective. Some readers consider that anachronistic. Others delight in the humor that results from deliberate use of anachronisms. At her website, Lindsey Davis answers some of the most persistent critics with the same wit and humor that grace her novels by remarking that "nobody has ever written to tell me I have made an error in human relationships, which ought to matter far more."

Anachronisms are also used for comic effect in Marcia Talley's short story, the humorous howdunit "Too Many Cooks." Set in Scotland in the time of Macbeth, it won the Agatha, the Anthony, and the Macavity awards for best mystery short story in 2002. Talley's deliberate use of anachronistic language, as when one of the three witches yells, "It's show time!" before they go off to confront Macbeth, works well in that context.

## Dealing with Inconvenient Historical Facts

Not surprisingly, historical mystery writers have strong opinions on this subject. Jane Finnis, whose books are set in Roman Britain, believes that "the most important rule for writing historical mysteries is: don't tamper with known historical facts to make them fit your story. Some writers think this doesn't matter, as long as they avoid the crasser anachronisms, like having Julius Caesar discussing politics with Plato. They're wrong. Unless you're writing what is clearly fantasy or science fiction, readers have every right to expect the history that comes with their mysteries to be as correct as it can be."

Steven Saylor, in the interview from Murder: Past Tense cited earlier, says that "the truth is always more interesting than anything invented. I fill in the gaps, I do my best to be creative in the unknown area, but I never change the facts." When he invents things, such as the "Pharaoh's down the Nile" game in *Rubicon*, he does so with a clear conscience because "the Romans did have board games. I could imagine a little board with crocodiles...."

There are usually creative ways around inconvenient historical facts. There are also ways, if you do decide to alter some historical detail, to head off reader outrage. Victoria Thompson's *Murder on St. Mark's Place* is set in New York City in 1896. An Author's Note at the end explains that the Elephant Hotel on Coney Island had actually been abandoned for several years by that date, but that it "was such a delightfully absurd part of Coney Island, I just had to use it in the book." Thompson then asks her readers to "forgive my lapse in accuracy for the sake of whimsy."

Sometimes, however, research reveals inconvenient facts that are much bigger than whether or not a hotel was still in business. Say you've envisioned your plot going in a certain direction and there's a battle or a natural disaster or a train wreck right in the way of the story. Ignore it? Change history? If you do, be sure to add an author's note explaining what you've done and why. But before you do, consider that this setback may present a challenge instead. See if you can figure out a way to work around the problem, or work it into your story, *without* changing history.

## The Opportunity To Be Creative

Eric Mayer, whose mysteries written with wife Mary Reed are set in sixth-century Byzantium, believes that "the fiction writer's burden of proof is the opposite of the historian's. Historians must prove what they say is true while historical writers are allowed to say just about anything that can't be proved false." He agrees, in his online essay "Writing the Historical Mystery," that historical mysteries should be accurate, but points out that "the question of accuracy is rarely simple. The historical record, not to mention common sense, would indicate that Queen Victoria didn't hunt Jack [the Ripper] down in her spare time, let alone by posing as a member of a traveling circus, but then again maybe the historians missed that. The trick to writing imaginative historical mysteries is keeping just under the radar of historians."

Mayer's contention is that sources aren't always trustworthy, and he cites the example of Procopius, who wrote panegyrics to the Emperor Justinian while in Justinian's service, but also wrote a "Secret History" painting him as "a rapacious demon without a face. When faced with such inconsistency, I prefer to choose whatever suits my purpose! This might sound like cheating but, I suspect, historians do much the same thing in a somewhat more sophisticated way. I'm not arguing that historical mystery writers have a license to be inaccurate, but rather that they should take advantage of the many available opportunities to be creative."

## "Novels Are Fiction, Not Textbooks"

Few if any historical mystery writers will deliberately distort history. On the other hand, there is no point in getting obsessive about it. Margaret L. Foxwell, in an essay on Peter Lovesey in *The Detective as Historian*, points out that "a historical mystery goes where history cannot—into the minds and hearts of living characters, breaking down the separation between times and places far from the present and in the process touching minds, hearts, and imaginations."

Although the late Michael Kilian remarked on a panel at Malice Domestic in 2004 that writers should alter history "not one whit," he also confessed to once using a "*very* fast steam packet" to get his character from one place to another. Sometimes, in the interests of good storytelling, a little fudging can be okay.

Lindsey Davis puts it even more succinctly in a "rant" titled "Historical Errors?" on her website: "It is a matter of professional pride with me to avoid historical mistakes if I can, and yet as I often point out (particularly to American teachers), novels are fiction, not textbooks.... If I stopped to check every tiny detail, the passion would be lost—and frankly I would have no incentive to write. You can have a novel a year, written with flair but a few rough edges—or a pedantically correct perfect thing, honed for a decade and checked with numerous experts."

## Anachronistic Attitudes

Far more troubling in a historical mystery novel than an anachronistic word or detail is a character's anachronistic attitude. Sad to say, some historical fiction is simply costume drama. The characters are put in a period setting, but they could act out their story in another era just as easily. Interpretation of history by an author means more than giving characters in fancy dress lines of dialogue and a plot.

Novelist and critic Jon L. Breen puts it this way: "When a historical figure appears as a character, invention is obviously inevitable but nothing should directly contradict the historical record, especially as to the person's character and attitudes." Writers of historical mysteries must always strive to keep modern opinions from creeping into the mindset of a character who is supposed to be the product of a past time. In dealing with historical issues, the fiction writer has an obligation to *try* to present the view of the characters as accurately as possible, without passing judgment.

Human nature may not change from century to century, but attitudes do. Modern opinion on such subjects as slavery, anti-Semitism, gladiatorial combat, torture, suppression of the working class, the lack of women's rights, and so on differs greatly from views held in other eras. Yes, there is some leeway, but to quote Breen again: "We have to realize that historical novels are products of the time in which they are written and may say more about that time than the time treated in the novel. But when present-day ways of thinking are imposed on characters of the past, it should not be sore-thumb obvious. This most often comes up in matters of political correctness. Historical attitudes toward women and minorities often have to be softened to appeal to a present-day audience, but it shouldn't be done in a manner so extreme as to be ridiculous."

When you put words in a character's mouth, you are expressing his or her views. They may not necessarily agree with your own. Even if there is a message hidden in your historical mystery—writing about a past war is often done, in part, as an indictment against a current conflict—don't let that underlying theme make your entire story anachronistic.

## Is the Self-Sufficient Female Sleuth an Anachronism?

Were there "liberated women" in past eras? Of course. The difference is that they could not and did not express their feelings in the same way women in the 1960s did. No corset-burnings are recorded in the nineteenth century.

Do your research. Find out what real women did and base what *could* have happened to your fictional characters on that. Women cannot be placed in roles that were, in that particular time period, exclusively reserved for men. As Lynda S. Robinson points out in her essay, "Women's Roles in the Ancient Mystery" in *Deadly Women*, she could not use a woman as her sleuth in Ancient Egypt because although pharaohs did use confidential inquiry agents, these officials were always male.

From the Middle Ages on, however, there are many female detectives in mystery fiction. Some critics say there are too many of them—intrepid, adventurous, independent-minded women who are, they claim, "unrealistic" because they would not have had the freedom, given the restrictions of the society they lived in, to investigate murders. Some call them modern women, even feminists, in costume.

Anne Perry comes in for particular attention in this area, even from critics who admire her work. In *The Detective as Historian*, Linda J. Holland-Toll labels Charlotte Ellison Pitt, her sister Emily, and their mother "too contemporary," commenting that "the Ellison women are all rule breakers: why would Perry, who well knows the boundaries of the times, create what to Victorian eyes would have been an unholy trio? The Victorian preoccupation with blood and insanity would seem likelier to dismiss the whole family as mad, rather than accept them in society."

What this critic overlooks is that most of the sleuthing done by these three women is in secret and behind the scenes. Yes, marriage to a policeman would probably banish most young gentlewomen from polite society, but when Charlotte moves in those circles, it is in borrowed finery that does not betray her current status and usually under the sponsorship of "Aunt Vespasia," an elderly society matron who has apparently earned the right to do as she likes simply by surviving as long as she has and having money. No one, not even Ms. Holland-Toll, seems to question Vespasia's believability when she decides to help out with an investigation.

There is, however, no simple way to dispute charges that a female sleuth is too modern in her actions or her outlook. Most of those who make these claims aren't about to be convinced by the facts. The best you can do is trust your own research. If you've based a female sleuth and other fictional female characters on what you have discovered about the real women of the same period, then let your readers know your sources through author's notes, blogs, speaking engagements, website extras, and any other means at your disposal. You might even make subtle mention of some of your role models in the text.

Paul C. Doherty categorizes the real-life detectives of medieval England as "monks or friars"—like his Athelstan—and "clerks, civil servants, men who attended the schools at Oxford and Cambridge"—like his Hugh Corbett. But Doherty doesn't stop at enumerating the sort of men who might make good sleuths. For years he has cited two female physicians, Mathilde of Westminster (Edward II's physician in 1322) and Cecily of Oxford (personal physician of Edward III in the 1330s) as examples of real women who might well have been called upon to investigate a murder. In *The Cup of Ghosts*, he uses Mathilde as his sleuth.

Rhys Bowen based her character Molly Murphy on her great aunt "who thought herself the equal of any man. Although women in 1900 were still restricted by the mores of society, many of them were attempting to break free of these restrictions. Women's colleges were turning out young graduates who had learned to trust their own intellect and judgment. Louise Boyd led an expedition to the North Pole in 1910 and the NYPD was already employing real-life female detectives."

Ask any author of a historical mystery series featuring a strong woman and they will tell you that real women of the same era could do and often *did* many of the same things as the fictional characters in their historical mysteries.

### Making Her Stand Out

She will need to be unique. Don't repeat what's already been done with fictional women in your historical period. Yes, your character can have some of the same traits as other detectives, but she must also have a quality (or a skill) or be in a situation that makes her different.

Aside from working in an unusual profession or craft, a female sleuth can be distinctive because of her circumstances. Give her no choice but to solve the crime and her actions automatically become believable. If she is about to be arrested, or someone she loves is accused of the crime, then she has a strong motivation to solve it herself, even if it means stepping outside the bounds of her usual existence.

Yet another way to make a female sleuth unique while keeping her true to her times is to create conflict in her personal life. Is she an abandoned wife? Does she have an eccentric grandmother to care for? Is she running away from an abusive home life? A heroine hiding a murder she committed in the past has been used in a number of historical mysteries already, so you might want to avoid that one, but there are still plenty of "personal problems" available. Today's readers—witness the success of Jacqueline Winspear's Maisie Dobbs series—are frequently as interested in the psychological makeup of the sleuth as they are in her ability to solve mysteries.

## What "Everybody Knows"

There will always be readers (and reviewers) who are certain they know better than the author. Jeffrey Marks has run into "countless readers who want to tell me what I did wrong about the Civil War. In 99% of the instances, what they think they know is incorrect. Trying to write for what readers *think* they know…can be extremely difficult."

Margaret Frazer has encountered this same phenomenon. "For the one series, the main character is a Benedictine nun in England in the 1400s. I always make the story fit the reality, not the other way around. I even try to keep my vocabulary pre-1500, which helps me stay in the characters' mindsets. And then I get something like one Amazon.com comment about *The Sempster's Tale*—that some of the characters have modern attitudes. The attitudes they have may be modern, yes, but those were attitudes held by some medieval people, too, and I found them in my research." A review of Frazer's other series, featuring a traveling player, praised "how well I detail how things were done in medieval theater—when much of that I *am* making up because there's so much we simply don't know and I have to extrapolate."

## Bloopers and What To Do about Them

Sometimes readers will find mistakes you really have made. As you continue to do research in your chosen historical period, after the publication of one or more books in your series, you may also come across sources that contradict "facts" you've already used. It's far too late to go back and change your text, although you may be able to make a correction in a reprint edition, so is there anything you can do about these errors? Yes—have fun with them.

I have a "Bloopers Page" at my website. There I freely confess to such errors as calling a certain poison *Aqua Toffana* in *Face Down In the Marrow-Bone Pie*. That book is set in 1559, but it turns out that *Aqua Toffana* is a sort of brand name for that particular poison. An individual named Toffana began to sell it in special bottles in the 1650s...almost a hundred years after my mystery takes place.

I know what you're thinking—picky, picky, picky. Who notices stuff like that? You'd be surprised. Granted, most readers are prepared to overlook almost anything if the story is good enough, but there are others who react violently to what they perceive as mistakes—the toss-the-book-across-the-room types.

A polite reply to a letter or e-mail pointing out a mistake in one of your books is never amiss. Whether the fan is in error or you really did get a detail wrong, you can follow up by circulating the real historical facts in newsletters, interviews, blogs, and, yes, blooper pages. But be prepared to encounter readers (and reviewers) who will flatly refuse to accept that your understanding of the way things were in a particular era is more thorough than theirs. There's nothing you can do about such people or their unwarranted criticism except ignore them.

On a more positive note, most readers just want the same thing you do, to make sure all the details are right, as an e-mail I received illustrates. Face Down fan Lin Jenkins writes: "I just finished *Face Down Beside St Anne's Well* and enjoyed it quite a bit.

> But I think I have found a relatively minor error. And, following Miss DeVine's example in *Gaudy Night*, I'm communicating with the author rather than announcing it to the world.
> The matter is this: at the end of Chapter 15, Will produces the note that he thought was from Rosamund, described as a

page torn from a commonplace book. Such books were around at the end of the 16th century and were full of blank pages, and I suppose a dastardly villain wouldn't mind ripping out a page! They were printed on cheap paper and you describe the page as "paper" both on that page (102) and again at the top of 107 when it is missing. But in the next paragraph on 107, you describe it as parchment, and mention in an aside how parchment was often scraped and reused. True, but paper wasn't. The cheap paper used in commonplace books, which was also very soft because of its high linen rag content, would have just shredded. Parchment, on the other hand, was made from animal hide, was much tougher, and so was often used several times over. But it wasn't bound in commonplace books—and if it had been, our villain would have had a heck of a time ripping a page out for a message!

Oops! I just plain missed the contradiction. I suspect that I added the details on parchment in one of my revisions, having forgotten I'd already been so specific about the source of the note. Although I should have, I didn't catch the discrepancy in subsequent read-throughs, and this is not the kind of thing an editor or copy editor could be expected to notice. My reaction to this e-mail, besides embarrassment, was to thank Lin profusely for pointing out the error and to ask her permission to tell the story here and on the Bloopers Page.

When it comes to anachronisms, as with any "blooper," it isn't always possible to get everything right, but it *is* possible to put forward your best effort in that direction. That, after all, is the point of all your research, and part of the challenge of writing good historical fiction.

# 11 Case Study– Face Down Upon an Herbal

NOW that you've been introduced to the basics, you may be interested to hear how they work in practice. If not, skip to the next chapter. This one is devoted to an account of the creation of one of my own historical mysteries.

## The Setup

In the Face Down series my sleuth is Susanna, Lady Appleton, a well-educated sixteenth-century gentlewoman. I based her upbringing on that given to a number of real gentlewomen and noblewomen of the period. Since single women did not have much freedom of movement, I gave her a husband, but because widows had even more independence than wives, I planned from the first to kill him off a few books into the series. Arranged marriages were common in those days and in this case created an antagonism between husband and wife that served a useful purpose in the plot, preventing them from comparing notes on clues as quickly as they might have if they got along. Although they function in some ways as a sleuthing couple, Susanna is clearly the one with the brains and she is the one who solves the crimes.

Most sixteenth-century women were trained in home remedies, but to allow Susanna to investigate murders, I gave her a special interest in poisonous herbs. Because her younger sister died as a result of eating poisonous berries, she has compiled what she calls a "cautionary herbal" intended to help housewives and cooks avoid accidentally poisoning someone. What she doesn't realize until later is that she has written a manual for murder.

## The Proposal

To sell the series I wrote the first book (*Face Down In the Marrow-Bone Pie*) and submitted the finished manuscript, together with a short synopsis of each of the next two books, proposed titles for three more, and the first chapter of the second book. This is my description of my overall plan for the series:

> The sleuth in this series of historical mysteries is a sixteenth-century gentlewoman, Susanna Appleton. Her husband, Sir Robert, is frequently away on the queen's business, leaving Susanna to her own devices. They are a childless couple, and although her father had Susanna educated in the manner of Sir Thomas More's daughters, her avid interest in scholarship is not enough to fill the time she has free after seeing to the management of their estates.
>
> Susanna's quick-wittedness and her skill as an herbalist once enabled her to do a service for Elizabeth Tudor, before that lady became queen of England. In this mystery series, the queen's knowledge of her abilities is an important factor, although Susanna herself never meets Elizabeth.
>
> The first book takes place at the beginning of Elizabeth's reign. I project a long life for Susanna, extending throughout the years 1558 to 1603. Like her queen, Susanna is in her mid-twenties in 1559.
>
> Susanna will be widowed at the end of the third book in the series and will not remarry. Widows at this time had many legal advantages over wives and a widowed gentlewoman sleuth will be able to operate with nearly complete freedom in future books in the series, a decided advantage.

Let me insert an aside here. A few things changed between the proposal and the finished product. One of them was that Robert takes credit for what Susanna did for the queen, and I leave unclear whether Elizabeth Tudor knows the real story or not. Also several character names changed.

The original proposal for the second book (*Face Down Upon an Herbal*), at that time titled *Dangerous Knowledge*, went as follows:

> This time Lady Appleton is asked to solve a mystery by Queen Elizabeth herself. She sends Susanna to Madderly Castle in the Cotswolds, where a minor Scots nobleman (Lord Glenelg) has been stabbed to death with his own bye-knife. Sir Robert is dispatched to Scotland, there to dance attendance on Mary, queen of Scots. Mary has just returned to her homeland from France and seems determined to stir up trouble for England.
>
> To hide her real purpose at Madderly Castle, Susanna pretends she is only there to assist Lady Madderly in compiling a

definitive herbal. Margaret Madderly, the baron's second wife, has been working on the project for some time and welcomes Susanna as an expert in the field.

Susanna takes Catherine Denholm with her to Madderly Castle. Catherine is actually Robert's half sister, a secret Susanna learned in the course of discovering the identity of the murderer in Book One. Catherine's romantic involvement with one of the present suspects, a mysterious young man named Gilbert Russell, complicates Susanna's investigation, especially after Susanna finds Lady Madderly bludgeoned to death with a silver candlestick in her tower workroom.

Unable to rely upon her knowledge of poisons to solve this case, Lady Appleton falls back on her scholar's skills. She begins to dig into the past, and uncovers more secrets than she anticipated. Lady Madderly was not what she seemed. Then some curious documents come to light, documents with official seals that turn out to be forgeries. Bit by bit, Susanna Appleton discovers the truth, that at Madderly Castle someone is making counterfeit seals and signet rings in a complex plot to use them on documents whose contents will undermine the English government.

Robert's presence in Scotland proves crucial to the solution of the crimes, even though Susanna can only communicate with him by letter. Her decision to trust Gilbert Russell at the penultimate moment is a risk she must take, but one that pays off. The killer is caught and Catherine and Gilbert seem likely to live happily ever after.

As a result of this proposal, St. Martin's Press made an offer for the first two books in the series and expressed an interest in continuing the series after that. A revision letter followed—nothing too onerous—and a request for a new title for the second book.

## How "Face Down" Came About

The title *Face Down In the Marrow-Bone Pie* (Book One)came out of a 1991 proposal for a historical romance, *Unquiet Hearts*. I originally intended that it feature Cordell Allington, the sleuth from my earlier historical-mystery-turned-historical-romance, *Winter Tapestry*, in a supporting role. In the end, Cordell was written out in order to keep the focus on romantic suspense rather than the mystery elements in the plot. However, the proposal originally contained this sentence: "Lady Allington points out that when her host falls over dead in the remains of his marrow-bone pie and most of his guests look relieved by that sudden turn of events, she can hardly be blamed for thinking there may have been foul play." That sentence—and that image—inspired the Face Down series.

With the request for a new title for the second book, it occurred to me that continuity in titles would increase the recognition factor, always a good thing. The obvious choice was to start each title with the same words, in this case *Face Down*. An Internet search turned up only one other title with those words in it, a Western. Another author later came out with *Facedown in the Park*, a contemporary mystery, which caused some temporary confusion among booksellers, but between the deliberate choice of "face down" rather than "facedown" and the number of titles in the series, this is no longer a problem.

The list of possible titles I considered for the second book included *Face Down in a Plum-Colored Doublet, Face Down on a Crested Dagger, Face Down on a Crested Bye-Knife, Face Down on a Crested Bodkin, Face Down on the Foolscap, Face Down on the Vellum Pages, Face Down on the Writing Table, Face Down on a Bee and Thistle, Face Down in M'Lord's Closet, Face Down on an Herbal, Face Down on an Herbal Crest,* and *Face Down in Green Velvet.*

The last was a nod to an Elizabeth Peters novel. The others had something to do with the murder weapon or the place where the body was found. Foolscap, incidentally, is an anachronism in this period, but I didn't know that then.

I ended up with *Face Down Upon an Herbal*—not exactly inspired, but the best I could do—and the one the editor liked. Once that was settled, I started thinking about *Face Down* names for future books and decided that I'd also vary the third word in the sequence. I'd used "in" and "upon." I was able to list more than twenty additional choices, but if I'd had any sense, I'd have stuck with "in." Reviewers seem to have particular difficulty getting the titles right, even though they presumably have the book in front of them. It isn't always that easy to have the body on its face, either. Still, the benefits of a catchy, recognizable title are worth the trouble. So far I've used *Face Down Among the Winchester Geese, Face Down Beneath the Eleanor Cross, Face Down Under the Wych Elm, Face Down Before Rebel Hooves, Face Down Across the Western Sea, Face Down Below the Banqueting House, Face Down Beside St. Anne's Well,* and *Face Down O'er the Border.*

## Pre-Writing

*Face Down Upon an Herbal* is in one way atypical of my historical mysteries. Before it was a Lady Appleton mystery, the story belonged to a contemporary novel, my first attempt at writing straight mystery for an adult audience (as opposed to romantic suspense and children's mysteries). This early effort did not sell, but since I had spent a great deal of time and effort developing characters and plot twists, it seemed a shame to waste them. I'm a firm believer in recycling.

Unlikely as it might seem at first glance, some things can be shifted, with remarkably few changes, from 1980s Maine to 1560s England. As I said earlier, I *don't* recommend just dressing modern characters in historical costumes, but the fact remains that motives for murder have not changed over the centuries and neither has human nature. The modern story and relationships between characters provided not the actual events but the inspiration to create a parallel situation in a historical setting.

In *Face Down Upon an Herbal*, a murder is committed to cover up another crime. In the contemporary version, this crime was the production and sale of phony college transcripts—obviously not something that would work in Tudor England. There was, however, a sixteenth-century equivalent: forgery has been around for a long time. So have con men.

In the first book in the series, I had established that some sixteenth-century Englishwomen were extremely well educated. Even though there was no historical situation exactly like the one I created for this book—a group of women working together to produce a comprehensive herbal—such a thing would not have been out of the question. Lord Madderly's library is modeled on the book collection of a real Elizabethan nobleman, Lord Lumley.

From that atypical beginning, I proceeded in my usual manner. This may or may not work for you. I offer it only as a suggestion. I start by jotting down ideas to guide me as I write and questions that I'll need to answer before the book is finished.

My first list was of characters whose point of view (POV) I would use. Susanna, Lady Appleton is featured in the majority of chapters, but I also wanted to write in the POV of Catherine Denholm. In addition, some chapters are written in the POV of Gilbert Russell, gentleman usher to Lord Madderly; Magdalen, waiting gentlewoman to Lady Madderly; and Sir Robert Appleton, Susanna's husband. The POV of Walter Pendennis, intelligence gatherer for the queen, is also used briefly, because I wanted to describe Susanna as he meets her for the first time. His admiration of her is designed to contrast with Robert's indifference.

My second list was titled PEOPLE LADY APPLETON SUSPECTS and includes her reasons for thinking they might have killed Lord Glenelg. First up was Margaret, Lady Madderly. I wrote, "If Glenelg was blackmailing her, she wanted to stop him. When she becomes the second victim,

Susanna thinks she was killed by Gilbert to avenge Glenelg's death. Susanna has to visit the city where Margaret was born in order to uncover her past? Also finds personal notes with notes for the herbal?"

Suspect number two was Gilbert—"He has been in the household since August but is suspiciously lacking in the servile attitude that should go with his position; later Susanna learns he profited by Glenelg's death and she also thinks he may be Arabella's lover."

Third was Lord Madderly—"Motivated by his desire to end the blackmail of his wife. This rests on the assumption that he knew she was being blackmailed and thought Lord Glenelg was the one who knew about her past. Note: Madderly collects letters as well as books and maps and therefore has signatures that can be used to create forgeries. Can I have both forged letters and counterfeit seals or will that be too confusing?"

Fourth was Arabella—"Her secretiveness is suspicious until she's also murdered."

Fifth came Magdalen—"Was she warding off a sexual advance by Glenelg? She does have a secret but it has nothing to do with Glenelg. She's a poet and is trying to get her poems published, even if it must be anonymously." Other less obvious suspects were Otto Harleigh, Magdalen's husband, "motivated by his desire to avenge a slight to his wife?" and the real villain, "Master Wheelwright, tutor to Lord Madderly's sons." He has "no apparent motive but no one likes him except his pet ferret."

Just to be thorough, Susanna also lists "one of the children," "one of the servants," and "someone from outside the household." In fact, eager to embrace this solution, the local authorities later arrest the local cunning woman and charge her with murder. She is the proverbial innocent bystander, but turns out to possess a vital clue.

My third list was PEOPLE GILBERT SUSPECTS. The love story of Catherine and Gilbert forms a subplot for this novel and since Robert Appleton spends most of the book in Scotland, Gilbert also fills Robert's previous role as a sleuthing and sparring partner for Susanna.

Gilbert suspects Lord Madderly, thinking that he may have killed Lord Glenelg to save himself and then killed his own wife because he found out she deceived him about her past. He suspects Madderly's sister Arabella because he knows she was jealous of Lady Madderly. And he suspects Lady Appleton. Gilbert knows she could not have killed Glenelg—she was far away in Kent when that murder took place—but she might have killed both Margaret and Arabella in order to gain control of the herbal project. Wheelwright is also on Gilbert's list, but only because he doesn't like the man, and Magdalen is there because Gilbert is aware that she is keeping *something* secret.

My notes then read: "The third murder changes everything. Arabella is no longer a suspect, but a closer look at her secrets will lead to the real killer. Who was she meeting? Susanna thinks it was Gilbert. It was really Wheelwright."

My fourth and possibly most important list is WHO KNOWS WHAT WHEN?

"No one knows Lady Appleton's purpose at Madderly Castle at first, not even Lady Appleton. The queen has sent Walter Pendennis to ask Lady Appleton to go there to assist Lady Madderly with the preparation of a comprehensive herbal and ordered Robert to visit at Christmas, using that visit as an excuse to investigate Lord Glenelg's death. Glenelg was carrying papers and a seal which are now missing and may have an impact on delicate English/Scottish relations." This last was modified somewhat, but the murder in England of Glenelg, a Scots lord, still creates a ticklish diplomatic situation. I continued,

> No one knows Gilbert is the new Lord Glenelg. Or does Parlan [Lord Glenelg's servant]? He has to have a reason to let Gilbert search Glenelg's belongings after the murder. But Wheelwright got there first and took the evidence. Madderly knows Gilbert hoped to catch Glenelg in treason and stays to see if he can discover the identity of the murderer. Madderly was cooperating with the Scots because of a Scots friend (need to identify?) and to allay suspicion he might be involved in something treasonous, though he doesn't know what that might be. His effort to appear innocent makes him look suspicious.
>
> Scots Protestants were aware of Glenelg's schemes by the time Mary Stewart arrived back in Scotland and have sent Gilbert Russell to Madderly Castle as their agent. He is posing as Madderly's gentleman usher with Madderly's consent.
>
> English authorities are unaware of any problem until Glenelg is murdered. Lady Appleton is sent to Madderly Castle to give Robert an excuse to investigate. Lord Madderly's loyalty is suspect. Lady Appleton is supposed to think she's there only to help with an herbal project in which the queen takes an interest.
>
> Lord Madderly does not know his wife's secret past, or that Wheelwright was blackmailing her, or that Glenelg and Wheelwright were working together on forgeries. He thinks Glenelg came to sell him books and Wheelwright is only what he seems—a tutor. He doesn't know Gilbert is Glenelg's heir, though he does know Gilbert came to Madderly Castle to keep an eye on Glenelg and is staying in hope of finding out who killed him.

My fifth list was of QUESTIONS TO ANSWER: "Why was Glenelg murdered? Where are Wheelwright's loyalties? Why is Margaret murdered? Why is solving Glenelg's murder important to Queen Elizabeth? Who is Glenelg? Is Wheelwright involved for political reasons? Why is Arabella murdered?" I wrote down what I *thought* the answers were. Most changed during the writing of the novel.

That's pretty much all I start with when I write. Sometimes I have less. I figure out twists and turns as I go along, throw out things that don't work, and think of new things to put in.

## Outline? What Outline?

I do not make outlines. Truthfully, I can't think that far ahead. After I've started writing, however, I do make notes concerning the proposed content of each chapter, mostly to remind myself what I intend to do in each. The following is as detailed as it usually gets for any of the books:

**Chapter One** Madderly Castle, October, 1561 (Monday, October 13)
    Magdalen's POV—Lord Madderly's library—she's reading Susanna's
        herbal
    Characters introduced:
        1. Magdalen—she sighs and scratches; set up hidden door
        2. Edward and Philip—set up their father's "special" collection
        3. Lord Glenelg—set up his bye-knife, Magdalen having a secret,
            and Glenelg's confiscation of Lady Appleton's herbal
        4. Beatrice—Magdalen is envious of her
        5. Wheelwright— his ability to blend in
            Mention: "S.A." who wrote herbal, Lord and Lady Madderly,
            Otto, and the fact that Lord Madderly's study is off limits

**Chapter Two** Later that afternoon—murderer's POV [secret villain scene]

**Chapter Three** Supper that evening through discovery of body
    Gilbert's POV
    Meet Lord and Lady Madderly, Otto, and Wheelwright's ferret

**Chapter Four** Leigh Abbey, three weeks later (Monday, November 3)
    Walter's POV for part of chapter with a switch to Susanna's POV
    Meet Catherine and Jennet

**Chapter Five** Edinburgh (Saturday, November 8)
    Robert's POV
    Meet Robert's mistress, Annabel

**Chapter Six** Madderly Castle (Monday, November 10)
    Catherine's POV—she and Susanna compare their observations and Catherine reveals a romantic interest in Gilbert.

My "notes" on the remaining thirty-six chapters are limited to whose POV is used in the scene, the location, and the date. These details change a fair amount during the writing process. The climax, however, was always scheduled to occur in Chapter Forty-one, in Susanna's POV. Events in that chapter take place on February 6. Chapter Forty-two, a very short one, takes place the following June at Catherine and Gilbert's wedding. It is in Robert's POV so that, in addition to tying up loose ends, it sets up his growing discontent, which is further developed in the third book.

## Research

I've been fascinated by sixteenth-century England for over forty years, but I still have to do specific research for each book in the series. When I decided to place Madderly Castle in the Cotswolds I read everything I could find about that area. Among several "scenes of the Cotswolds" books I found one that gave examples of the local dialect. The differences in the way people from various areas of England spoke in those days, much more distinctive than nowadays, provided the basis for a significant clue, one that leads Catherine—who was born and bred in rural Lancashire and has worked hard to lose her own country accent—to the murderer.

I did not know I would do this in advance. In fact, I rarely know what twists and turns the story will take ahead of time. This leaves me room to be pleasantly surprised. I'm open to serendipity. I also end up doing a lot of revising before I finally get things right.

## Revisions

I usually write a complete rough draft just to find out if the plot will work. Then I insert things as I revise. These insertions can be as short as a single descriptive detail or as long as an entire chapter, whatever is needed, but each draft ends up longer than the previous version. I may also switch the order of chapters around. My list of questions to myself gets longer and I make another list of things I may need to expand upon. Sometimes, on rereading, I decide the writing is fine as is. Other times, considerably more research and revision are called for.

Between drafts, I try to let the manuscript sit as long as possible, at least a few weeks and preferably a few months. My goal is to be far enough removed from the story to spot gaps, bloopers, typos, and so on. I find it beneficial to work on something completely different in the interim. This allows me to go back to the Face Down manuscript recharged and ready to tackle whatever changes need to be made.

When I *do* go back to it, I try not to make large changes right away. I just mark places where there may be problems and write questions to myself. I stick in Post-its, just the way a copy editor does. Why? Because I may have forgotten that I already dealt with that particular problem a bit later in the manuscript.

After the complete read-through, I make choices. I go back and add material. I ask myself why each character, even a minor one, does and says certain things. Sometimes the answers lead to new plot twists. There are times during the research stage that I come across some specific detail I know I want to work in—something that is simply too good not to use—but it may be the revision stage before I figure out how to do it. With plenty of time for the book to "rest" between each revision, I am able to think of things that will work better than what I originally had planned.

And sometimes I take things out. Even a huge chunk should go, if removing it will make the book better. Nothing is ever wasted—what comes out of one novel can always be recycled into a future project.

At the time I wrote *Herbal* I was a member of a five-person manuscript critique group and also had a critique-by-mail partner. When I was reasonably happy with the manuscript, I gave copies to each of them and asked for their input. I also asked each of them to make a note at the point where they figured out whodunit. If I'd been too obvious, I'd have to go back and do a better job of hiding clues.

Not all critiques will be equally helpful. The most useful will come from people who are historical mystery fans familiar with the subgenre. A reader who is more accustomed to reading romantic suspense may well find straight mystery lacking and may attempt to turn your mystery into something it was never intended to be. Genres overlap, especially these two, but there are differences in focus. Similarly, readers who prefer contemporary novels may have a difficult time with historicals. Consider the source of a suggestion before you actually make a change. Ultimately, you'll have to trust your own instincts about what works and what doesn't.

At the final revision stage, I usually drive myself crazy with details—not just playing with word choices and trying to cut down on repetitious words, but also searching for things I know I read somewhere and now can't find.

Did I do things in *Face Down Upon an Herbal* that I now wish I could change? Of course. Jennet, Lady Appleton's maid, provides comic relief in the first book. She appears in only in one chapter in this one. My failure to use her more left me struggling to keep *Herbal* from getting too dark. And I should have done more research on ferrets. They were popular pets in the sixteenth century, as evidenced by their appearance in at least one portrait of a gentlewoman. I used Wheelwright's ferret, Bede, as a device to reveal something about his character, but overlooked Bede's potential as an interesting character in his own right.

Were there any bloopers? Yes, at least one. After the novel was published I got hold of a copy of Phillis Cunnington's *Costumes of Household Servants from the Middle Ages to 1900*. According to this book, written by a renowned expert on historical clothing, head coverings were worn indoors by most people in the sixteenth century—except by liveried servants. Gilbert, while serving in Lord Madderly's household, should not have been wearing a hat indoors. I not only gave him one, I had Catherine call attention to it.

## Miscellaneous Statistics

After having written ten Face Down books and four Diana Spaulding Mysteries, my "system" for writing a historical mystery is fairly well established. I spend several weeks beforehand on research—plus *years* before that. I don't know how long that would take if I were starting from scratch.

A look at my daybooks for the period when I was working on another of the Face Downs does give some idea of how long it took me to pull that particular book together. I spent parts of five days planning, spread out over a month, then puttered with the first chapter on one day in one week and on two days during the next—all the while, of course, while working on other projects. Once I really got into the book, however, I spent an average of three to five hours a day, five to seven days a week, on that one project.

After about three weeks, I had roughed out the first ten of forty-two chapters and had notes for Eleven through Fourteen. At that point I went back to the beginning and made changes. A week later I had once again reached Chapter Eleven. Two weeks after that I had eighteen chapters and started revising at Chapter One for the second time. Nine days later I was back at Chapter Eighteen and could start to rough out Chapters Nineteen through Thirty-nine. Two weeks later, it was back to Chapter One again, but this time I kept going through to the end of the rough draft. That took a little more than two weeks and I ended up with a 271-page manuscript.

Although this was too short, the book was "finished" as far as containing a fully worked-out plot and character development. All I had left to do was fine-tuning. I put the manuscript away and did not look at it again for more than three months. By the time I came back to it, I could—almost—look at it as if someone else had written it. That makes it a lot easier to spot things that need to be fixed.

The first overall revision took about two weeks and at the end of that period I had a manuscript 312 pages long. A second revision, during which I also double-checked for continuity with the other books in the series, took ten days and produced a 319-page draft. Another "rest" followed, during which this particular book was read by two people I trusted to give me honest critiques and help me catch typos. Keeping their comments in mind, I did a "last" read during which I tried to pretend I'd just bought this book in a store and was reading it for the first time. This only took a couple of days. That done, and just about a year after I'd started writing the book, I was able to send a 321-page draft to my agent to send to my editor.

You'll notice I've been talking in terms of number of pages in the manuscript rather than number of words. I find this useful because it takes into account the amount of white space I leave, something a word count does not. I generally aim for 310–330 pages, but my historical mysteries are on the short side.

Since word processing programs make it easy to do word counts, I do know how long my published Face Down novels are. The first, *Face Down In the Marrow-Bone Pie*, is 66,034 words. *Face Down Beneath the Eleanor Cross* is the longest so far, at 70,804 words, and *Face Down Under the Wych Elm* is the shortest, 63,676 words. How long *should* a historical mystery be? As long—or as short—as it needs to be to tell your story.

And speaking of short...

# 12 Historical Mystery Short Stories

THE historical mystery short story differs in both technique and style from longer fiction. A short story has its own demands, both in length and content. In other words, the ability to write novel-length historical mystery fiction does not automatically mean you can successfully write historical mystery short stories.

Why, if your focus is on writing novels, would you bother with writing stories? Several reasons. It can be an additional source of income. It allows the author of a mystery series set in one era to write something completely different. Two historical mystery short stories that have won awards, Marcia Talley's "Too Many Cooks" and Rhys Bowen's "Doppleganger," are quite different from what those authors usually write. Conversely, it can provide the opportunity to use secondary characters as the sleuths, or to fill in the gap between two books in a series. In the case of P.N. Elrod's "Death in Dover," it let her eighteenth-century vampire, Jonathan Barrett, solve a mystery while he was still human. They may also attract new readers for your novels. And since short story rights return to the author, in general, a year after publication, you can post a previously published story on your website in its entirety, as a writing sample or as a teaser for books that feature some of the same characters.

Some historical mystery authors specialize in short stories, preferring this form to the novel. If, after reading this chapter, you want to try your hand at short stories, I suggest you read some of the stories mentioned here and also that you learn more about short story writing in general, since it is not the purpose of this volume to teach the basics. This chapter concerns what distinguishes historical mystery short stories from contemporary ones, and from novel-length historical mysteries.

## Inspiration

Even more than with novels, inspiration for a short story can come from just about anything. Edward D. Hoch's first story about Dr. Sam Hawthorne was inspired by a January 1974 calendar illustration of a covered bridge in winter. "Pretty soon I got to wondering what would happen if a horse and carriage went in one side of the bridge and never came out the other side. Some pondering over the next day or two produced a solution and a plot to go with it. All I needed was a detective."

He created Dr. Sam Hawthorne, recent graduate of medical school and proud possessor of a 1921 Pierce-Arrow Runabout. The story, set in March of 1922, sold to *Ellery Queen's Mystery Magazine*, as did a sequel that also involved an "impossible" crime. At that point editor Fred Dannay (half of author "Ellery Queen") suggested that all Dr. Sam stories should be "locked room" or impossible crime mysteries. All the Dr. Sam Hawthorne stories since then have been. There have been a few changes, though. The character has aged, so that the most recent tales are set in the 1940s, and where the earliest stories were set within a framework—an opening with an elderly Dr. Sam welcoming a friend to hear a story and an ending that contains a hint about the next case—now, "in an attempt to speed up the stories a bit," Hoch shortens the opening and omits the closing preview entirely.

Mary Reed and Eric Mayer's novels about John the Eunuch had their origin in a short story. Anthologist Mike Ashley asked them to contribute to a collection he was editing. Reed recalls that they "were delighted by the request, but there was a catch. The deadline was only a few weeks away. As it happened Eric was interested in the Byzantine Era and owned several books about it, so we had the basic information to hand. Then, too, being a married couple, a writing collaboration was an extension of every day life. John made his debut in 'A Byzantine Mystery' in *The Mammoth Book of Historical Whodunnits*. 'Byzantine Mystery' is an extremely short work, only a couple of thousand words. Our objective was to construct a classic puzzle story with a bit of a twist at the end. We didn't give a great deal of thought to our protagonist, aside from our needing someone qualified to carry out the plot we had in mind." They didn't plan to write more John the Eunuch stories or branch out into novels, but "John decided otherwise."

## Research

There seem to be two different takes on research as it relates to writing historical mystery short stories. One is that it *is* important but since it is for a short story it cannot be as extensive as what one would do for a novel. Selected sources are deemed sufficient. This makes sense for writers who use a variety of settings in their short stories. Roberta Rogow, whose novels take place in late Victorian England, set her short story "Death in the Gardens" in Ancient Babylon. Her research consisted of Biblical texts, Josephus's *History of the Jews* in a nineteenth-century translation, and visits to an exhibit at the Metropolitan Museum in New York City.

In an interview at www.mysteryfile.com Edward D. Hoch confessed to preferring to write short stories rather than novels because he'd get "bored with the books before I finished them, anxious to get back to short stories." For Hoch, "widely varying backgrounds help keep the stories fresh. I've never visited most of the places I write about, but I rely heavily on the Internet and guide books, especially ones with good maps and street photographs." With hundreds of stories to his credit, however, Hoch has ended up using some settings more than once. He has created several series characters, two of whom, Dr. Sam Hawthorne and Alexander Swift, do their crime solving in the past. The latter solves crimes at the behest of President George Washington. Hoch loves doing the research, which he considers the number-one requirement for writing historical mysteries. For the Swift series, he consults, in particular, biographies of historical figures who appear in the stories.

The second take on research comes from writers who set all or most of their historical mysteries in one historical period. Marianne Wilski Strong's short stories take place in the fifth century and feature Kleides of Athens. Since she concentrates on one detective and one historical period, she has been able to devote as much time to her research as any novelist. Her goal has been to make Kleides "a living, breathing character in the brief space a short story allows." To do this, she needed "to understand how Kleides saw his world…. The rest—what clothes the characters wear, what food eat, what curses hurl, what taverns frequent—the writer must absolutely know all that, but it is the skin, not the flesh and blood of the characters."

Kleides is "a sophist in democratic Periclean Athens. But, as in all historical periods, Kleides encounters people who have other world views, often hostile to his own: people who believe in the gods and the old myths; who despise the sophists' clever use of language." Understanding Kleides' world, what Strong calls "the tone of the times," allows her to "choose the conflicts that a modern reader could quickly relate to: the survival of democracy, the clash between the new scientific outlook and the old mythic religion, the resentment of other city-states of powerful Athens. Then, with a few bold strokes, I could create characters with conflicts: a fellow philosopher whose despair over sophist skepticism about the gods led him to murder; an aristocratic politician who despises the new democracy.

Only after understanding how Kleides and others in his world think could I create the courtesan with whom he falls in love; the friends, such as Socrates, with whom he converses; the half brother who firmly believes in Zeus. I knew how they would react to Kleides and he to them."

## Simplify

Clayton Emery, who writes two historical mystery short story series—as well as many other things—has this tip for writers: "Take pity on readers. With a ton of facts and characters flung in their face, they can flounder and sink. Following a foreign stranger through an ancient setting is confusing enough. Trying to follow clues to solve a mystery at the same time can seem impossible."

Emery, whose Joseph Fisher mysteries are set in Colonial America, advises short story writers to "explain on the run"—don't save all the sleuth's conclusions until the end. He also writes short stories featuring Robin Hood and his wife, Marian, as sleuths. These are complex tales, and yet Emery follows his own advice to "simplify." How? "Only name the principal characters.

> Just label everyone else. "Lot's Wife. The Fishing Master. The Mother Superior. The King-at-Arms. The librarian." If they're not central to the plot, who cares about their names? One name only, please. Dostoevsky gave every character three names, then one or two nicknames, then used them in different combinations. But Fyodor didn't write mysteries. And vary the names. Never use the same first letter twice. "Sir Tristan, Sir Kay, Sir Balthazar." Not "Sirs Archibald, Arthnot, and Arn." Buy baby-name books and consult often. Reinforce the characters with ID tags. Clark Kent wears a blue suit and red tie. Adam and Eve are always naked. Good cowboys wear white hats. Why? Easy reader identification: "Sir Varnor, burly in blue; the Mohawk spokesman Apram; Lady Margaret the Elder; Anthony, Elmira's cousin." Help the reader remember your characters.

On simplifying plot details, Emery offers this advice: "Lose some research.

> Irrelevant details detract. A carriage can be a brougham, a cabriolet, or a dray, but unless the hero needs to hang from one or two axles, keep it a carriage. Put details where you need them. If the knife stuck in the gent's back is a teak-hafted parong from Mandalay, that's a clue. If it's a bread knife from the kitchen, it's

not. If the hostess wears a fire opal brooch, the murderer better have just returned from Australia, or the reader will know you're showing off. Mix universal motives with period-specific facts. The motives for murder are always love, money, or revenge. The father might have smothered his daughter as an Islamic honor killing—or her brother might just want the whole inheritance. The retainer slew the king because he violated a sacred grove and offended the ancient gods—but the retainer can grab the throne, too.

### Limiting a "Cast of Thousands"

Lillian Stewart Carl, who writes contemporary and historical short stories and contemporary mystery novels, feels that "one of the basic skills of short-story writing is focusing tightly on one situation, one setting, and one group of characters, keeping the story immediate rather than sounding like the synopsis of a novel. It goes without saying that a mystery short story, historical or otherwise, will not have nearly as many red herrings or as intricate an investigative process as a novel will have."

Carl uses "one strong point of view to tell the story, and through this person's thoughts and observations drop in just enough description to set the scene. I have to clue the reader in to the time and the place very quickly with, say, 'The Luftwaffe was hammering the dockyards at Bristol again.' I can't tell the entire history of the period in a short story."

Keeping characters to a reasonable number in a short story is essential. For writers accustomed to crafting longer historical mystery fiction, it is also a challenge. Since historical mysteries tend to have large casts, how do you reduce the number of characters?

Carl introduces "secondary characters with just one quick identifier, not a full backstory" and limits "the number of characters to those needed for the plot, ignoring all the others who would have been there at the time." In "A Mimicry of Mockingbirds," she was dealing with "several historical characters as well as my imaginary ones. The protagonist is Thomas Jefferson as a young man living in Williamsburg, Virginia. By having Jefferson interact with only one person at a time—until the 'who done it' revelation, at least—I was able to keep the story in focus."

In "The Rag and Bone Man," however, Carl "ended up with a mob of characters. A pilgrim is murdered during a visit to the shrine at medieval Walsingham Priory. Here I had to not only set up the members of the pilgrim group, but also the prior and his staff. One pilgrim is identified as Isabella, 'the king's mother.' Tempting as it was to give her entire backstory—and quite a story it is, if badly mangled in the film *Braveheart*—what was important to the story was that she was still wealthy and influential in retirement, and that she was a member of the French royal family."

One technique Carl finds helpful is to imagine herself "as a movie cameraman, focusing on a character or a clue and letting everything else fuzz out behind the main actors. Even if those blurry shapes are intriguing historical details or characters, if they're outside the scope of the story, then they're out!"

## Short Story Editors Speak out on Historical Accuracy

I asked Tekno Books fiction editor and author John Helfers, *Ellery Queen's Mystery Magazine* editor Janet Hutchings, and *Alfred Hitchcock's Mystery Magazine* editor Linda Landrigan how important they feel historical accuracy is in a short story and how they feel about anachronisms, including their deliberate use for comic effect.

Helfers qualifies his answer by saying that "since we deal primarily with theme anthologies, the real qualification is that the story be a mystery story, with the historical setting a secondary concern." However, he's quick to add that he's "not fond of authors changing [historical] details, or not researching the period, for no good reason. Considering myself a fairly educated editor, if someone misses something in their historical story (or novel, for that matter), that I catch as being incorrect, my first question is: what else have they gotten wrong? Of course, no one is going to get every last detail right, but the overall effect should be to create a picture of the time that appears plausible, so that there is no reason for the reader to suspect that anything is amiss."

Hutchings reports that at *EQMM*, "We carefully check everything we can (and that's been made easier by the Internet) but I don't want our proofreaders to have to do the author's work. So my advice to authors would be to make sure they've got it right, unless they have a specific artistic reason for the inaccuracy."

Landrigan agrees, saying, "As an editor, I don't check every detail in a historical mystery that I'm going to publish, although I do as much as I can. But I have to trust the author for a lot of that, and it is my inclination to do so. After all, it was the author who did the research. However, if the author has skimped on that research, it will be obvious not only to me but also to the average reader. Under-researched stories will fail to convey that sense of authenticity."

She adds that "on a practical note, it is enormously helpful to an editor if the author provides a style sheet, a list of usages or expressions that may be historically accurate but which I, or my proofreaders, might not recognize.

I do try to honor my authors' preferences in such cases, though as an editor, I might not agree as to what is appropriate for a contemporary audience."

The question of anachronisms, not unexpectedly, triggers strong opinions. Helfers feels that the use of anachronisms for humorous effect is "a bit like dressing a bull in a tutu and shoving it on stage; in other words, what's the point? If an author cannot draw humor from the lives of the historical people and events (and it existed in some form, no matter what time frame is being written about) and has to resort to inserting another device to gain the desired effect, then why even write about that time period in the first place? (This is assuming that the entire book isn't a farce to begin with, where nothing is to be taken seriously.) Humor in fiction should come organically from the characters, settings, and events that are already in play, not from a *deus ex machina* inserted that, to me, therefore exists solely to draw laughs or another reaction that wouldn't be considered appropriate for the time period."

Landrigan finds the situation "akin to the rules of grammar: the writer must know the facts before he or she can begin to bend them. A departure from the historical record that is nevertheless grounded in well-researched historical detail can still convey an overall sense of authority."

Hutchings has a slightly different take on the subject. Although she knows "that some of our readers are purists when it comes to historical accuracy," she is not. "Sometimes historicals that are intentionally anachronistic are a lot of fun to read. If the anachronisms are intentional and the author successfully uses those anachronisms (including speech) to create a comic effect, I say more power to him (or her). If, on the other hand, the inaccuracy comes from laziness, and there is no purpose served by the errors, then I may well reject an otherwise good story for that reason."

## Markets for Historical Mystery Short Stories
### Anthologies

Collections of short stories by various authors are published with some regularity. Most editors, however, obtain the stories by inviting selected writers to contribute a story. In other words, they are by invitation only, and not an option for an unpublished writer. These generally have a theme—a connection to a famous writer (*Much Ado About Murder: All-New Shakespeare Inspired Mystery Stories*) or a time period (*Murder Most Medieval*), or a common thread (*Mr. President, Private Eye* or *Cat Crimes Through Time*).

In the U.S., Martin H. Greenberg and John Helfers at Tekno Books package a variety of mystery anthologies containing original short stories, sometimes with "celebrity" editors. In Great Britain, both Mike Ashley and Maxim Jakubowski regularly edit similar collections.

In addition, groups such as Mystery Writers of America and local chapters of Sisters in Crime occasionally publish anthologies of short stories. Some of these are also by invitation only, but others are open to submissions. There are also single-author collections, such as those published by Crippen & Landru. I was invited to collect my Face Down short stories into an anthology with them when I had enough to fill a book. They have also published, among others, two collections of Edward D. Hoch's Dr. Sam Hawthorne stories, a collection of Edward Marston's short stories set in both the past and the present, and *Renowned Be Thy Grave: The Murderous Miss Mooney*, P.M. Carlson's tales of Bridget Mooney, a fictional nineteenth-century actress who encounters a variety of real historical figures from U.S. Grant to Lillie Langtry.

### Periodicals

As I was working on an early draft of this chapter, the May 2006 issue of *Ellery Queen's Mystery Magazine* hit news stands. It featured four historical mysteries with settings ranging from seventh-century Ireland to the Roaring Twenties. The December 2004 issue of *Alfred Hitchcock's Mystery Magazine* was similarly oriented. Three of the seven new stories it contained were historicals, taking readers from ancient Japan to Elizabethan England to the Great Depression.

The editors of both magazines like historical mysteries, but I was curious as to whether a historical mystery story would be harder to sell to them than a contemporary. For Janet Hutchings, "The question of whether a story is historical or contemporary doesn't enter into my decision to buy or reject it. A good story is a good story and it doesn't matter to us at *EQMM* what the time period is. The author is going to have to be a good storyteller to make the sale, either way. Occasionally I'll pass on a historical because the author knows his history but not how to make the history come alive. Sometimes writers of historical fiction get so caught up in relaying facts they've learned that they forget that their main task is to tell a story, and the work becomes dry." She adds that another reason to reject a historical mystery is "because the writer doesn't convey a sense of authority about the history."

Linda Landrigan finds historical mystery fiction to be "a special pleasure." She enjoys "seeing the history played out on the stage of the story and integrated into the daily lives of the characters.

The interplay between the plot and the frame of actual events—barely noticeable when it's done well—deepens the story or novel with another level of pleasure.

I've noticed that the historical mystery short stories submitted to *Alfred Hitchcock's Mystery Magazine* often employ a greater level of detail than contemporaries, making these stories "feel" more authentic. Even the characters are often more fully developed, with secondary characters that are as individual as the main characters. I suspect historical mystery stories are more fully imagined because the time that the authors have spent researching their respective eras has also allowed for more "idle" daydreaming and reimagining of events with their fictional characters involved.

Nevertheless, historicals pose particular challenges for writers and editors. For one thing, the historical mystery has twice the expository burden of a contemporary mystery. The author has to provide both a narrative and a historical background, and do so in a lively way without making it sound like a lecture. The author must decide how much historical context is necessary, and to do so, he or she must consider: 1) How much does the reader need to know in order to understand the story, and 2) What can be safely assumed most readers will already know about this time and place. For example, an author might assume that a U.S. audience might know a great deal about the American Revolution, but somewhat less about the Age of Enlightenment that gave rise to it.

In a short story, which necessarily needs to be taut and pared to essentials, the deft use of particularizing detail is always crucial, and this is no less true in the use of historical detail. It seems to me that skilled selection of appropriate details will capture the historical context almost imagistically. I think to be able to do that well, the author's research must be very, very thorough. From my conversations with writers, I know they immerse themselves in a variety of resources. One of my authors reads letters and dramas of the era, for example, to get a sense of how people actually spoke. In fact, balancing contemporary and historical rhetoric and diction is another challenge for the historical mystery author. This issue comes up in writing narrative as well as dialogue. In either case, it is easy to fall into contemporary locutions, which can be jarring to the reader. On the other hand, if the dialogue, especially, is too much of the period, it might not appeal to modern readers. My own rule of thumb is that a little goes a long way—give readers a taste of the period language and allow them to read the rest in that frame of mind.

*EQMM* and *AHMM* publish the majority of short mystery fiction found in magazines. Other periodicals, such as *The Strand Magazine,* include fewer stories and are published less frequently. Additional markets pay only in copies and an increasing number now publish only in electronic format. The best advice I can give is this: Before submitting anywhere, get hold of a copy of the most recent edition of *Novel and Short Story Writer's Market,* a book that will also be of use in selling your historical mystery novel.

# CHAPTER 13 *Selling Your Historical Mystery Novel*

YOU will hear that historicals of all kinds are dead. You will also hear that "historical mysteries remain as popular as ever, but new settings and time periods are attracting authors."

Which is true? Darned if I know, but I do know that the popularity of any genre runs in cycles, and the advantage of a historical is that it doesn't "date" the way a contemporary novel can. If you want to write historical mysteries, do it. Worry about trying to sell your manuscript after it's finished.

## An Overview of the Market

The quote above is by Jo Ann Vicarel in the February 1, 2006 issue of *Library Journal*. Vicarel singled out historical mysteries set in Paris in 1790 (Susanne Alleyn's *Game of Patience*), 1950s Mississippi (Carolyn Haines's *Penumbra*), and Franco's Spain (Rebecca Pawel's *The Summer Snow*) as evidence for her assertion, and went on to say that "if you think that medieval England is losing ground in the publishing stakes, look at Roberta Gellis's *Chains of Folly* to see how an accomplished writer can bring a fresh approach to a much-written-about time period."

Further proof that historical mysteries are popular comes from the success of Jacqueline Winspear's *Maisie Dobbs* and its sequels. Set just after World War I, the first in the series was nominated for numerous awards and won the Agatha Award for Best First Novel. It was also on the *Publishers Weekly* list of Top Ten Mysteries of 2003.

By the time *How to Write Killer Historical Mysteries* is published in 2008, the success of *Maisie Dobbs* will be five years in the past, but there will be other success stories. Historical mystery readers aren't going anywhere, and every once in a while, general readers hop on the historical bandwagon. Trends in publishing are cyclical. Even if the historical mystery market seems to be in a slump when you read this, take heart in the fact that, eventually, publishers will start buying historical mysteries again.

One of the most knowledgeable people in the mystery field is Barbara Peters of The Poisoned Pen, an independent mystery bookstore, and Poisoned Pen Press, an independent mystery press. The latter publishes a good many historical mysteries for a niche market. Peters feels that "history will always sell and be read, it just shape-shifts. Right now it's doing better as fiction than as mystery; fifteen years ago it was the opposite." Writing in August of 2006, Peters observed that "Dan Brown [*The Da Vinci Code*] popularized the form of viewing the past through a window from the present and I'm seeing a lot of that. The historical novel is making a big comeback, proving the genre cycle is still turning. I see a lot of big books reminiscent of [mid-twentieth-century authors] Anya Seton or Samuel Shellabarger. All the way from prehistory to World War II and the Cold War with expanded takes. This is in part because faction, the blend of fiction and fact, hooks reviewers and readers." However, "In mystery, the historical has cooled down."

Has there actually been a decrease in the number of history mystery titles being published? A count of all the new (as opposed to paperback reprints) historical mysteries published in the U.S. by traditional (print) publishers for 2003–2006, as recorded in CrimeThruTime's "Recent HM Releases" webpages, shows that the numbers are almost identical—right around 100 titles each year. The vast majority of them are books in a mystery series, which means there are nowhere near 100 slots open to new writers. On the other hand, series do come to an end, and there is always room for a truly exceptional novel. Will the number of historical mysteries decline in 2007? In 2008? Possibly. It may also increase.

If you are considering writing historical mysteries at all, it is probably because that is what you want to write more than anything else. For whatever reason, you are drawn to the past, not the present. As Gillian Linscott put it in an essay for *Mystery Readers Journal* back in 1993, "I write historical rather than modern day whodunits for much the same reasons that I prefer riding a horse to driving an automobile—the pace suits me and the views are better."

So, you've written an exciting, appealing, historically accurate historical mystery. Now what? How do you go about getting it published? Frankly, selling what you've written is likely to be far more frustrating than writing the book, mostly because there are so many aspects of the process over which you have no control. This chapter is designed to increase your chance of success, but comes with no guarantees.

## The Product—General Advice for Submitting any Manuscript

Before you attempt to sell your book, write the whole thing. Unless you are already a multi-published author in the mystery genre, there is no point in approaching an agent or an editor with just an idea or even a few chapters. In almost every case, they will want to see the finished product—and see exactly how you resolved the central mystery of your plot—*before* they will consider making an offer for it.

So, write it, polish it, and have it ready to submit. That means your manuscript is in hard copy on white paper—double-spaced on only one side of the page with at least one-inch margins all around and in an easy-to-read font (black, with serifs) and font size (at least ten-point). This is standard practice and it is to your advantage. If a first reader gets eyestrain trying to read a manuscript printed in a tiny or unconventional font, that manuscript is unlikely to make it out of the slush pile.

Gimmicks will never help you sell your book. Do not print on colored or scented paper—aside from that being unprofessional, some editors have allergies. The day when a handwritten manuscript could sell is so far in the past that it could be a plot point in a historical mystery novel. Fancy fonts that resemble handwriting are an equally bad idea. Publishing is a business. Treat it as one. Be professional.

Although this next piece of advice should be a matter of common sense, I'll say it anyway—make sure you keep an identical printed copy for yourself, together with back-up copies in electronic format. Most writers are obsessive about this and should be. Better safe than sorry.

If there is anyone out there protesting that word "electronic," get over it. Most publishers these days expect to receive an electronic copy of the manuscript once the book is accepted for publication. For one thing, this saves them the expense of hiring a typesetter. This requirement may even be in your contract. In addition, most editors and agents nowadays communicate by e-mail as often as they do by telephone or letter. On a brighter note, it probably won't matter what word processing program you use. You can convert most into the one your publisher prefers. And you can write your early drafts in crayon if you want to. Just make sure the final version is typed into a computer by you or someone you hire.

### Getting an Editor's Attention

The publishing industry is constantly changing. What is "hot" one year may not be the next. If you spot a trend and try to capitalize on that by writing a book that fits into it, you are courting failure. Manuscripts are commonly purchased more than a year before they are published. By the time you write yours, sell it, and it comes out, any trend you spotted beforehand is likely to be over.

Sad to say, there is also a strong "dumb luck" factor involved in the fate of your manuscript. Everyone who reads it may think it is brilliant, but if someone else just came out with a similar book a month earlier, you're probably not going to be able to sell yours...unless the first book was a blockbuster, of course, and the publisher decides this is the start of a new trend.

Patience and persistence are the keys to success in both writing and selling a manuscript. And as I've already mentioned, there is one big advantage to writing a historical mystery—the story won't become dated the way a contemporary story can. I wrote the first draft of what eventually became *Deadlier Than the Pen* in 1987. At first I was told, "East Coast Gilded Age settings don't sell." After a trip to Denver, I tried reworking the plot in a western setting. At about that time, westerns went out of fashion. I tried both romance and mystery markets, since the story had a "gothic" feel. My timing was terrible. Just using the terms "gothic," "woman in jeopardy," or "romantic suspense" could kill a potential sale. By the time romantic suspense made a comeback, I was doing other things, and this book was still a little too different to fit into the newest incarnation of the romantic suspense subgenre. Finally, in 2004, *Deadlier Than the Pen* was published as a historical mystery by a small press—as the first book in a four-book series. For this particular project, a big New York publisher just wasn't in the cards.

### Query Letters

The most common way to sell a historical mystery, whether it be single title or series, to any size publisher, is to send a query to a specific editor at the publishing house. Finding out who this person is may take a bit of research. Who is publishing historical mystery? Which editors at that house are editing it? Does one person seem to have a particular fondness for the type of historical mystery you've written? You can sometimes discover this by reading acknowledgment pages in similar historical mysteries. Magazines like *The Writer* and *Writer's Digest* are a good source of information on publishers and also provide numerous how-to articles on the basics of selling fiction. Publisher websites may also include names and mailing addresses. Whether you know the editor's particular tastes or not, it is always best to direct correspondence to a specific person. And in this case, correspondence means a letter, not an e-mail, fax, or phone call.

What if you find the warning NO UNSOLICITED MANUSCRIPTS or AGENT-ED MANUSCRIPTS ONLY in a publisher's guidelines? The query letter is your way around the ban on "unsolicited" manuscripts. If that editor is interested and asks to see the entire manuscript or a partial (usually three chapters and a synopsis, but this can vary), then you have officially been "solicited."

Entire books have been written on how to draft a query letter, so I won't spend time on that subject here, except to say that since you've written a historical mystery, you should include something in the query to convince the editor that you are qualified to write about your particular historical period. If you have formal training as a historian, say so. If not, give some indication of what it is you find so fascinating about the setting and how you went about delving into it. Keep it short, but don't be afraid to let your enthusiasm for the subject show. You're selling yourself as well as your manuscript.

It is considered unprofessional to submit the same manuscript to more than one editor at the same time. If two (or more) of them are interested, you run the risk of alienating both when you have to admit that you sent out multiple submissions. Yes, sometimes it is possible to use this situation to advantage and auction a book off to the highest bidder, but that is extremely unlikely to happen to an unagented first-time novelist in the historical mystery fiction genre. Even if you think this is a stupid rule, adhere to it. You can and should, however, feel free to send out multiple *queries*.

### Do You Need an Agent?

Eventually you probably do, but finding the right agent can be as difficult as finding a publisher. In fact, you go about it the same way, by sending out query letters.

The important thing to remember is that your agent works for you. Handle the selection process the same way you would handle hiring any employee who is going to be directly involved in your finances. Stay away from any agent who asks for a reading fee. Look for enthusiasm. An agent who has only lukewarm feelings about something you've written is unlikely to make much effort on its behalf and this can do serious damage to your career. You've written a historical mystery, so make sure your agent not only likes reading historical mysteries but also has some experience in selling them. Since most agents today require a multi-year contract, you want to be very careful during the selection process.

### Contests, Conferences, and Conventions

Aside from having an agent to handle everything or writing query letters to editors yourself, there are two other ways to bring yourself and your manuscript to the attention of an editor. The first is to enter contests that are judged by editors. The best known in the mystery genre are the two run by St. Martin's Press. One, for the traditional mystery novel, is in conjunction with the Malice Domestic convention and the other, for private eye novels, is associated with the Bouchercon convention. Only the winner is guaranteed publication, but judges see other submissions as well. If your historical mystery also fits the criteria for a traditional mystery or a private eye novel, give it a shot.

Attending writers' conferences and mystery conventions is another way to meet editors. They often appear on panels, and some conferences offer registrants the opportunity to schedule appointments with attending editors (and agents). In addition, conventions may provide opportunities like the one that gave Maureen Jennings's series about William Murdoch a jump start. Jennings attended Left Coast Crime 1995 in Scottsdale, Arizona as a fan, but since she had completed the first book in what was to become a historical mystery series set in Toronto in 1895, she also signed up for a pre-conference workshop for unpublished authors run by Miriam Grace Monfredo. When she read the prologue from *Except the Dying* aloud, she not only impressed Monfredo (who later blurbed the book) and the unpublished writers participating in the workshop, but also several publishers' representatives. Although it took another year for the book to sell, in part because of the Canadian setting, attending that convention and taking part in that workshop provided the key that opened an editor's door.

### Other Entrées to the Editor's Desk

Grants programs for writers are available from various sources. One especially worth checking into is sponsored by Malice Domestic. The Malice Grants program awards financial assistance to writers working on a "traditional" mystery novel. Winners are announced at the convention. They are also featured in the Malice Domestic newsletter, bringing them to the attention of editors and agents who receive it. Although no historical mystery entries have won as of 2006, there is no reason why one couldn't. Check the website at www.malicedomestic.org for details.

Like Mary Reed and Eric Mayer's series, Peter Tremayne's Sister Fidelma novels came about because of the short stories he had written about this character. As he relates the story in an interview in the Historical

Novel Society's *Solander* magazine, he wrote the first one for an anthology edited by Peter Haining and "word of my character spread" even before it was published. As a result, in October of 1993, four different anthologies appeared, each containing a Fidelma story. "A short time later my agent phoned saying Headline wanted to know if I could write a novel featuring the character and were prepared to offer me a three-book contract." The first book in the series appeared just under a year later.

Can a new writer do that? Probably not. Tremayne was already a published novelist, under his own name and the Tremayne pseudonym. But if you've had short stories published about your sleuth, and now have the completed manuscript of a historical mystery novel, use the success of those short stories as a selling point for the longer work.

Victoria Thompson, author of the Gaslight Mysteries, had an earlier career writing historical romances with mystery subplots. Because of this, she entered the historical mystery field in a somewhat unusual manner. It was the *publisher* who came up with the idea for the series, not Thompson herself. She was recruited, though her agent, to write a proposal incorporating certain elements and creating others. What had already been decided? That the setting should be turn-of-the-century New York City and the sleuth a midwife named Sarah Brandt.

"It just so happened," Thompson recalls, "that I was working for the March of Dimes and knew some midwives personally and my daughter was going to NYU and so we'd spent a lot of time in Greenwich Village and my husband and I had gone to the Barnes and Noble there and bought some books on the history of Greenwich Village, so I thought, 'Ah—kismet!' But I must confess that had my agent said that the series is set in medieval Mesopotamia and the heroine is a potter, I would still have said, 'Ah—kismet!' That's how much I really wanted to write again."

Although the publisher may have the initial idea, it is still the writer who makes or breaks a series. Originally, Sarah was going to be a poor relation raised by wealthy relatives. Thompson pointed out that, in order to solve mysteries, the character would have to be able to move in all classes of society. In her hands, Sarah Brandt became the rebellious daughter of wealthy parents who married a doctor and shared his idealism about dealing with the less fortunate. She's widowed when the series opens. Although she's still a rebel, she has contacts. Thanks to her privileged upbringing, she is personally acquainted with Teddy Roosevelt, who was instrumental in cleaning up New York's police department in the early days of the twentieth century. In Thompson's fictional world, Sarah and Teddy shared dancing classes when they were young.

## What Editors Look for

To gain more insight into the odds of selling a historical mystery, I solicited the opinions of six experienced mystery editors. I asked first, what qualities a historical mystery would need to convince them to buy it over a contemporary in today's market.

Carolyn Marino, senior vice president and executive editor at Harper Collins Publishers, doesn't "set a historical mystery against a contemporary one. What matters is how strong the manuscript is, whatever the genre or subgenre."

Meredith Phillips of Perseverance Press replies: "I have to actively like and enjoy the book, rather than just think it'll sell well, since I'll be working on it for a year and reading it half a dozen times. As for qualities: convincing period feel without too much research crammed in, dialogue giving flavor without being slavishly authentic, recognizable characters, colorful setting."

Hope Dellon, executive editor at St. Martin's Press, says, "One of the things I like most about publishing is that every book is different. When I am considering a new mystery, I don't pay particular attention to whether it's historical or contemporary, but rather to whether it seems distinctive and engaging enough to command attention in an extremely crowded field. For example, my colleagues and I were all very enthusiastic about a new mystery series recently that happened to be set in the sixteenth century—but what we loved were the same things we'd love in any novel: the characters and prose and plotting. I truly believe the most interesting mysteries defy any generalizations."

For John Scognamiglio at Kensington Mystery, it's the "hook." He looks for something to "appeal to readers to draw them in. For instance, the Stephanie Barron mysteries feature Jane Austen as a sleuth. Very clever!"

Ellen Edwards, Executive Editor of New American Library, a division of Penguin Group (USA) Inc., admits to being "personally drawn to historical mysteries," but finds them "a challenge to publish. In my recent experience, it's almost impossible to publish them as mass market originals. They must come out in hardcover followed by paperback or, possibly, as trade paperback originals. The writing must be exceptional and/or they must offer a story/setting/characters that would appeal to a wide audience. It helps if in story/setting/characters they can be legitimately compared to a bestselling series, or if they seem to fill a niche of the historical mystery market that isn't already covered and has proven to have some consumer appeal."

She goes on to give two examples, the Jade del Cameron Mystery series by Suzanne Arruda, starting with *Mark of the Lion*, and the Sebastian St. Cyr Mystery series by C.S. Harris, starting with *What Angels Fear*. In the case of the former, "the success of the movie *Out of Africa*, and literary fiction by Isak Dinesen and Beryl Markham among others, plus the perennial appeal of British colonialists in foreign settings, suggested that there would be a strong market for the book." The Sebastian St. Cyr series is set during the English Regency period (early 1800s) and Edwards describes it as "a big, juicy historical mystery." She adds that they "don't expect huge hardcover sales but do hope the paperback editions will expand the audience."

John Helfers, in acquiring for Five Star Mysteries, looks first for "quality of writing, no matter what the genre. With that caveat aside, a compelling time period or voice can often raise a historical mystery over a contemporary one. After all, to a certain extent, contemporary mysteries have a certain sameness about them—private eye, police officer, amateur sleuth, etc. in New York, L.A., Chicago, Florida, etc. However, when a writer takes the time to research, say, nineteenth-century hansom cab drivers in London and create a mystery with that character as the sleuth, if done properly (as that one was, since it was accepted for the mystery line), then that can often give an author a leg up."

I then asked if a historical mystery was likely to break out of midlist. Dellon feels, "It is difficult for any novel—in any genre, whether contemporary or historical—to break out of the midlist these days, because to do so requires large commitments from the bookstore chains." Scognamiglio believes it is possible, but that "it depends on the author's previous sales history and track record. You need to have sales numbers to build upon and the packaging needs to communicate 'bigger' book to the audience that might not have read the author in the past." Marino is even more positive about the possibility: "Yes, I do think historical mysteries can break out to a wider audience," but "that may depend on various factors, including the subject, word of mouth, how the book is marketed, the author's profile, and whether previous books by the author have built critical mass."

Edwards also thinks it is possible, but "only rarely and with lots of hard work and good luck. That said, we probably wouldn't be publishing historical mysteries at all if we didn't believe that it's possible to hit the jackpot and grow a series to the point where it 'breaks out' or otherwise establishes very healthy sales levels. Our job is to package the books well, get them into the right hands, and support the series in whatever way we can. After that, the consumer determines which ones really catch on."

"Given the state of genre reading today," Helfers is "not nearly as sanguine about the possibilities of an author being able to transcend the midlist, especially in mystery, with a historical mystery.

> I believe the last people to do that were Anne Perry and Elizabeth Peters, both of whom broke out about fifteen years ago.... While there are several authors making pretty good money doing historicals (Peter Tremayne comes to mind), and occasionally the brilliant one- or two-off comes along (Caleb Carr's *The Alienist* being a prime example) as far as I know, no one's doing it consistently (as a living) today except for the two authors mentioned above.
>
> The historical genre has its fans, but I don't think it will ever be considered a subgenre that can "break out" authors any more, not when the current emphasis is on global thrillers and modern mystery and crime novels. When one thinks about the authors of the past decade that have become best-sellers—Ridley Pearson, Jeffery Deaver, James Patterson, Michael Connelly, Mary Higgins Clark—all great writers, mind you, but their historical fiction, if they've even done any, is not what first comes to mind. With the midlist getting squeezed more and more, forcing wonderful historical authors like Roberta Gellis (Five Star was fortunate enough to pick up *Chains of Folly*, the most recent novel in her medieval historical series) to smaller publishers, it's hard to see the genre picking up any more clout in the marketplace any time soon, which is unfortunate.

My final question to editors was this: When you do buy a historical mystery, do you automatically think in terms of a series? Edwards answers: "Yes. Unless the book has the potential to be a huge blockbuster all on its own, a series is needed to give the consumer time to discover the author and the books, then go back and read the previously published books. That's the only way I know of to grow a readership so that, in theory at least, each successive book attracts a larger audience and the bottom line becomes increasingly healthy. In some ways, a series is also easier on the writer, who must produce a book a year or risk losing momentum; the primary settings, major characters, and much of the background research are already established in the writer's mind, so coming up with new stories within a tight time frame becomes more realistic."

Scognamiglio also comes down solidly on the side of series books: "Mystery readers want continuing characters. If it's a stand-alone, it's not being published as a mystery. It's being published as a suspense novel or a historical novel. It depends on the content of the book." Marino feels "it depends on whether the material lends itself to being continued or, especially, whether the characters have more life in them." Phillips agrees: "If the story and characters lend themselves to a continuing series, all the better, but I wouldn't rule out a stand-alone." However, Dellon points out that "a series can be a mixed blessing: If it works exceptionally well, it can keep building more and more of an audience (the Brother Cadfael series is the example that comes immediately to mind), but it can also get stuck in a rather small niche."

## Publishing Options

In general, mystery editors are fairly open to any time period if the mystery itself is engaging and the sleuth is a strong character, but hardcover and small press publishers may be more likely than mass market paperback houses to take a chance on an unusual setting, primarily because of the difference in sales expectations. In hardcover or trade paper only 3000–4000 copies of the book need to sell in order for the publisher to make a respectable profit. A typical mass market paperback print run would be at least 30,000 copies and probably much higher.

The companies publishing these different formats range from worldwide conglomerates to small presses. There's no point in my listing publishers or the editors who work for them here. Too many changes take place too fast. Smaller companies are absorbed by larger ones. New publishers take the plunge and start publishing books. Editors change jobs or get out of the business entirely. Check the latest *Novel and Short Story Writer's Market* and publishers' websites for the most up-to-date information. You may also want to consult the list of PUBLISHERS ACCEPTED BY MWA FOR ACTIVE MEMBERSHIP at the Mystery Writers of America website at http://www.mysterywriters.org.

### Large Publishers

In very general terms, large publishers, especially those that are multinational, are selling a product. They are interested in the bottom line. They expect their editors to buy books that will earn out whatever advance the author receives and then some. If your books don't make money as fast as they hope, you will be dropped. In the recent past, entire mystery imprints have been discontinued for lack of adequate sales.

In some cases, a publisher has a single target market. Five Star Mysteries is part of a much larger company that sells primarily to libraries. Five Star is also unique in that editing is handled by a packager, Tekno Books.

Both advances and print runs are low, but often Five Star will take a chance on a book when a more traditional publisher won't.

Usually, the money is better with a large publisher. On the other hand, don't expect to be offered one of those million-dollar contracts the characters in books and movies always seem to get.

Publishers don't share information on advances and print runs, so I can only offer my own experience with big New York houses. My first Face Down contract, signed in 1996, was for hardcover editions of two books with an option for a third. I turned down an offer of $3000 for each and ended up receiving an advance of $7500 for both. The print run was 4000 copies for each book. *Face Down In the Marrow-Bone Pie* had a second printing of 1000 copies. Conversations with other writers lead me to believe this was not (and sadly, *still* is not) particularly low for a first historical mystery, although some writers certainly do considerably better. In 2000, after reprint rights were sold by my publisher to another company, the first mass market paperback edition of *Face Down In the Marrow-Bone Pie* came out with a print run of 15,000 copies.

### Independent, Regional, and Small Presses

One of the largest publishers of historical mysteries today is an independent, Poisoned Pen Press. They publish only mysteries. Founded in 1997 by the owners of The Poisoned Pen bookstore in Arizona, they have grown so rapidly that they can no longer be considered a "small press."

Independent simply means a press that is not part of a conglomerate. It can still have several branches and can vary greatly in size from others. A few historical mysteries are also published by regional presses. These are independents that focus on books with a connection to the part of the country where the regional press is located.

"Small press" is a catch-all term for publishers who do not bring out very many books in the course of a year. They run the gamut from folks who set up their own publishing companies in order to self-publish to companies who've been in business for decades, consistently publishing quality fiction and nonfiction. Some focus on very specific areas—all reprints of older mysteries, all short-story anthologies—but others are receptive to new writers.

Independent, regional, and small presses may be more open to unusual projects, more willing to take a chance on a character or a setting that a big conglomerate doesn't think will sell well enough to make a profit, but they are also less likely to launch a writer into a high-profile career. If you offer your manuscript to a small press, don't expect fame or fortune.

Advances will be lower and print runs are also small, usually a few thousand in hardcover or trade paperback. A mass market paperback is not an option for them since so many copies would have to be printed in order to keep the price low enough to compete with the big publishing houses.

Distribution is often a problem for smaller presses. Your local bookstore may have to special-order copies in order for you to do a signing there. Some chain stores make this more difficult than others. If the small press has a "no returns" policy, many bookstores will not order the book at all.

Don't get me wrong. I've personally had very good experiences with several small, independent presses, but there are risks. Some small presses, even with the best of intentions, have a tough time surviving in a highly competitive marketplace. If they overextend themselves and go out of business, their authors may never see any royalty checks, even if their books sold well.

### Vanity Presses

Vanity presses have their uses, but if you want to be taken seriously as a writer of historical mysteries, they are not the way to go. You'll save yourself considerable time if you learn to distinguish vanity presses from other small presses. Most websites contain the basic information, although you may have to hunt a bit to locate all the details. iUniverse and Xlibris are two examples of vanity presses.

What you want instead is a publisher who will pay you an advance against royalties, even if it is only a small one. The publisher should also provide you with an editor, commission cover art, and engage in some sort of promotion. In other words, your publisher takes on all the expenses of publication and distribution, including sending out review copies. As the author of the work, you are paid royalties and receive a statement at least once a year.

If you are asked to pay the publisher, you are dealing with a vanity press. In general, in this sort of arrangement, you not only have to shell out your hard-earned cash, but you are then stuck with trying to get your book reviewed and trying to get bookstores to carry it. Good luck! You'll also have to store however many copies you agreed to pay to have printed.

If you are that desperate to be a published author, you'd be better off with the next option.

### Self-publishing

You may remember an ad on television a few years ago—one in which a smart-alec student informs his professor that anyone can be published with modern technology. Print on demand (POD), a process that allows for the production of one book at a time and eliminates the need to store inventory, does make this possible. But is it a good idea?

As with so much else to do with technology, change comes quickly. What's true today may not be tomorrow. From the beginning, some legitimate small presses adopted the POD process to publish their books. POD in itself is not the problem. The problem is that self-publishing, which has always been an option open to writers, is now much easier and much more tempting...but no less problematic.

Here are some of the things you generally do not get if you self-publish: an ISBN number; an editor to suggest ways to improve your novel overall; a copy editor to catch those annoying little errors, grammatical and otherwise, that slip into even the best writers' work; a publicity department to make sure review copies are sent out so that bookstores and libraries hear about your novel; a production team to design the cover and the interior of the book; a sales team to get the book to distributors so that stores will have copies on their shelves. If you self-publish, you are on your own—and it usually shows. In addition, most reviewers will not review self-published books. Most bookstores will not carry them.

There are exceptions, but they are few and far between: individuals who are willing to spend a great deal of time learning what to do and how to do it right. If you decide to self-publish, make it a point to study all the ins and outs of production and promotion. And hire a free-lance editor to go over your work. One self-published writer I know auditioned three—she sent each the first chapter of her historical mystery and paid them to edit it. Then she hired the one she thought did the best job to edit the rest of the manuscript. A good editor is expensive, but well worth the investment. The most frequent criticism leveled against self-published books is that they contain errors an editor would have caught.

M.E. Cooper is the founder of Padlock Mystery Press. She is also the author of all the Padlock Mystery Press books, which range from true crime to mystery novels, both contemporary and historical. She chose this route after her "first three books were published by small presses who promptly went out of business owing me money.

> My husband heard me moaning and said, "Hon, I'll pay to publish your books." Which is when we established Padlock Mystery Press in 1997. Thirteen books later, I can share some

wisdom learned from experience. For one thing, historical mysteries are a natural for a small publisher. They don't depend on current events to make them timely. And even more important, historical mysteries are not as dependent on mass markets to make them profitable. You have a target market for your work. Readers interested in a particular time in history will seek out books that cover that time period. Other readers simply enjoy being transported to another time and place in history.

If you decide to go the self-publishing route, you would do well to read *The Complete Guide to Self Publishing* by Tom and Marilyn Ross and follow their guidelines. Be prepared for more work after you finish writing the book. Promotion and marketing will take up a great deal of your time. Also be prepared to sell your books in non-traditional places.

### Ebooks

All the publishing options I've mentioned so far have resulted in books in print format. What about ebooks? Most large publishers nowadays also buy electronic rights. Smaller publishers leave those rights with the author so that, *after print publication*, you can make your historical mystery available with any of several legitimate websites specializing in selling ebook "reprints" of published books, usually sold as downloads. This is not the same thing as selling your manuscript to an ebook publisher. You don't want to do that. Yes, there are a few very rare cases of an ebook later making it into print with a large commercial publisher. But your chances of doing so with a historical mystery are about the same as your historical mystery selling for a million-dollar advance.

Beware of unscrupulous ebook publishers for first publication. Even the ones who offer a fair deal, with editorial services, royalties, and the possibility of a POD hard copy to sell at book signings, do not favor the writer. If you are desperate to have something you've written appear online, consider submitting to an established ezine. Write an article or a short story or a review or do interviews. Or set up your own website and make any of those available there. Or blog. Whatever you do, think long and hard before you all but give away an entire historical mystery novel.

There is one other thing to consider, too: the majority of readers still prefer their books on paper.

### Shooting Yourself in the Foot

I've met a lot of people over the years who are wonderful writers but have never sold a book. In far too many cases, it was their own fault.

If an editor shows interest in your manuscript but asks if you'll change something, for goodness sake consider doing so. I'm not saying you should automatically take every suggestion a editor makes, especially if it is made before the offer of a contract, but don't dig in your heels either. Publishing a book is a collaborative effort. Granted, there are a few bad apples, but most editors want what is best for your book and have some experience in what works in fiction and what doesn't. Their suggestions are intended to make the end result better. To be truthful, there are very few books that cannot be improved by skillful editing. Oblige or don't, it's up to you, but at least consider making each change before you say no.

How else do writers shoot themselves in the foot? Far and away the most common means is procrastination. They'll say, "More research," or "One more revision," or "It's not quite ready to submit yet." If you expect your manuscript to be published, you have to send it out into the world, usually more than once. Do it, then begin work on another book. No manuscript ever sold while sitting in a desk drawer.

There is a market out there, and you now know how to reach that market. What happens next is up to you. And after you find a publisher? Your job still isn't finished. To learn what comes next, read on.

# 14   *Getting the Word out to Historical Mystery Readers*

ONCE your book has been sold to a publisher, it will be a year, maybe two, before it is in bookstores. That doesn't mean you won't be busy. First, if you haven't already, start writing another book. Second, find out what deadlines you'll have for line edits and copy edits and be prepared for the possibility you may have to argue for your word choices at both stages. (If you do, make *sure* you are right.) Third, start thinking about what's jokingly called BSP—Blatant Self-Promotion. Once your historical mystery is in print, BSP is the only thing you can control in relation to the book's success or failure.

## Don't Quit Your Day Job

Very few historical mystery writers can live on what they earn from historical mystery royalties alone. In fact, I cannot say with absolute certainty that *any* historical mystery writer makes a living just from the royalties on his or her historical mysteries.

Let's get a few discouraging facts out of the way. According to a 1995 National Writers Union survey of 1,143 freelance writers, their median income from writing totaled only $4000 a year. You can see details of the report at http://members.aol.com/nancyds/wlot1.html. In the years since, what most writers are paid has not increased very much. In fact, some writers have been asked to take a smaller advance on later books than they received on the first book in a series. Why? There are too many reasons, some of them quite complex, to go into here. Suffice it to say that publishers are in the business to make money and most writers are not in a position to make many demands.

In 2004, Nielsen Bookscan tracked sales of 1.2 million books in the U.S. Of those 1.2 million, 950,000 titles sold fewer than ninety-nine copies each. Another 200,000 sold fewer than 1,000 copies. Only 25,000 titles sold more than 5,000 copies. Fewer than 500 sold more than 100,000 copies. Only ten books sold more than a million copies each. Taking all those figures into account, the average book published in the U.S. sells only about 500 copies.

On the bright side, most historical mystery novels do better than that, but if you have been writing while working at a non-writing job, don't give it up quite yet, not unless you have a supportive (in both senses of the word) spouse. One with health insurance.

## Blurbs

Blurbs are quotes from other authors praising your new book. Having been both a blurber and a blurbee, I have mixed feelings about this practice. Most of the time the praise is genuine, but there are notorious examples of blurbs from famous writers who never even bothered to read the book before giving it high marks. And what does it matter, really, what Ms. Famous Author thinks of a book? It is just one person's opinion.

Still, once you've sold your historical mystery, your editor will undoubtedly ask you to suggest the names of other writers, preferably well known, who can be approached about a blurb. There is no escape. You may as well start thinking about this ahead of time.

If you have attended writers' conferences or mystery conventions (more on these below) and met other mystery writers, you will have a pool of professional acquaintances to choose from. It is polite to ask if they mind your giving their name to your editor, even if it is the editor who is going to do the actual asking. Sometimes it isn't; sometimes the author is expected to make the request. Either way, as soon as published copies of the book are available, the author or publisher traditionally sends each person who blurbed the book a signed copy with appropriate words of thanks.

Be prepared for refusal. There are any number of reasons another writer might have for saying no to the opportunity to blurb your book, none of these having anything to do with your writing ability. The potential blurber might have tight deadlines for the foreseeable future and no spare time to read. S/he may have given too many quotes over the last few months and been told by an editor or agent not to give any more. Or it may have something to do with the setting of your novel. If you approach a writer who has an irrational dislike for the era in which you have set your historical mystery, be glad if s/he turns you down.

I don't like to blurb books set in periods I know nothing about because if there were anachronisms, I wouldn't be able to spot them. (Neither do I blurb books set in exactly the periods I write about, for the opposite reason—I'd be entirely too picky—although other writers will.)

What if someone agrees to blurb your book, reads it, and for whatever reason, changes his or her mind about giving you a quote? Again, it is probably nothing to do with your ability as a writer. After all, a publisher bought this book and is going to publish it. It's unfortunate to lose a potential blurb, but it's better than getting one so vague that it ends up damning your work with faint praise. The most likely reason a writer changes his or her mind after agreeing to blurb is that the novel inadvertently hit one of his or her personal hot buttons. Perhaps it is simply a matter of too much violence for that blurber's taste, or that he or she doesn't care for books featuring herbalists, or nuns…or peanut farmers. I once agreed to critique a friend's novel and then was unable to get past Chapter One because it was written in present tense ("I go to the door. I see the man lurking across the street.") and I simply couldn't tolerate reading an entire novel written that way. I've made an effort to conquer this aversion since, and have even enjoyed a couple of books written in present tense, but I wouldn't want to blurb one.

## ARCs

One extremely useful publicity tool is the ARC—the Advance Reading Copy, usually printed and bound in a sort of "limited edition" paperback before the final proofreading is done. If you are published in hardcover, the publisher will almost always provide these advance reading copies to reviewers well in advance of publication. Not all editors will tell you this, but at some of the larger publishing companies, the writer can request copies of ARCs. (Bear in mind that small publishers may print limited numbers of ARCs, and they will all be carefully allocated.) Why would you want extra ARCs? To send to reviewers and bookstore owners the big publisher does not think are worth courting.

If you have a publicist assigned to you, and can actually get that person on the phone, find out where your publisher regularly sends review copies. Almost every publisher sends ARCs to *Publishers Weekly*, *Kirkus Reviews*, *Library Journal*, and *Booklist*, and to major metropolitan newspapers. If they have experience in publishing mysteries, they will also get copies to reviewers at periodicals that cover the mystery scene. On the local level, however, you may have to take charge yourself. You will probably have filled in a questionnaire that included a space to list local newspapers and local bookstores, but this information doesn't always result in review copies being sent to those places. If you know a local reviewer's name, it doesn't hurt to send that person an autographed ARC, even if they do end up getting another one from the publisher.

If there is some special audience you think your historical mystery may appeal to—those of Scottish heritage, for example—then try to get review copies to publications that cater to that group. You might even consider running an ad in *Scottish Life* or *The Highlander*. Other writers do. And if your mystery has a love story in a subplot, don't forget the review publications aimed at romance readers. Some of them even have separate mystery sections. Start thinking about these possibilities well in advance of publication. Some magazines need to have review copies as much as six months ahead of time. Also find out in which format their reviewers will read books. In some cases, in lieu of an ARC, you can send "faux galleys"—computer printouts formatted to look like the pages of a book. In others, although this will mean a review coming out well after your book is available in stores, a copy of the actual book can be sent instead of an ARC.

## Promotional Materials

How much should you spend on self-promotion? One piece of advice you're sure to hear is to dedicate your entire advance to publicity. Of course, since advances vary wildly, this isn't really a very useful rule of thumb.

What is universal is that only rarely will a publisher do much promotion for a new author. Many do none at all. Even if you are assigned a publicist, don't expect much. Ask for what you want, by all means, just don't be surprised when the answer is no.

So, what *can* you do to promote your book? Since it is likely you were a historical mystery reader before you decided to write one, you already know how you find out about new books. Should you have postcards printed with your cover on them and do a mailing? Print bookmarks to hand out? You can print your own if you are sufficiently computer-savvy. What about giveaway items with your name or your book's title on them—pencils, magnets, keychains, and the like? You can spend a small fortune on that sort of thing, but there is really no way to tell if it helps sales of your book. Besides, you want people to remember you for your novel, not your gimmick.

Fortunately for those who don't see the point in the above-mentioned promotional materials or who simply can't afford them, there are many alternatives when it comes to publicity. You can join various groups that will help spread the word about your book. You can go out and meet potential readers in person. Or you can reach out to those same readers from the comfort of your own home.

## Groups You Can Join To Spread the Word
### Historical Mystery Readers' Groups

There are many mystery readers' groups. Among the largest and longest-established is DorothyL, a listserv on the Internet originating at Kent State University. Do not join this group simply to promote your book. "Lurk" long enough to find out what it is all about, then join in the discussions if you have something to say. Check the archives for taboo subjects and those that have already been discussed to death. Then, when the three thousand mystery readers on this list have gotten to know you a little from your posts on other books, you may include a *moderate* amount of BSP in the form of a signature line and the occasional post about your book's release date and upcoming signings.

Mystery Readers International is best known for the annual Macavity Awards and for publishing *Mystery Readers Journal*. Each issue has a theme. Coincidentally, the theme for the issues just before this volume appears in print is historical mysteries. Anyone can join this group, and authors are invited to contribute essays to *MRJ* if their mysteries lend themselves to that issue's subject.

The greatest concentration of *historical* mystery readers can be found at the CrimeThruTime Yahoo group, where posting news about your historical mystery is always acceptable. A close runner-up is the Historical Novel Society. HNS is based in Great Britain but has an American branch. American conferences were held in Salt Lake City in 2005 and in Albany, New York in 2007. HNS publishes *The Historical Novels Review* and the magazine *Solander*.

### Sisters in Crime

Sisters in Crime is probably the most useful organization a mystery writer of either sex can join. Membership is not limited to published authors, but they are entitled to participate in a variety of promotional opportunities, from signings at regional booksellers' and librarians' conferences to group ads in trade journals and an entry in the annual *Sisters in Crime Books in Print*, which is sent out to libraries all over the country. Although Sisters in Crime was originally organized over a gender issue (mysteries by women were, and still are, less frequently reviewed than those written by men), men are welcome to join the organization, and do. SinC holds regular meetings in New York during Edgars Week, at Malice Domestic, and at Bouchercon.

On the local level, Sisters in Crime chapters organize programs in libraries or other meeting places, usually with the stipulation that books be available for sale after the panel. Some also sponsor conferences, such as the New England Crime Bake (a joint effort with the local chapter of Mystery Writers of America). There are sometimes local newsletters, in addition to the national quarterly, *InSinC.*

### Professional Mystery Writers' Organizations

There are two professional writers' organizations for U.S. mystery writers. There are benefits to joining both, but if you are strapped for cash and have to make a choice when it comes to membership dues, I'd advise joining Sisters in Crime before either one.

Mystery Writers of America (MWA) is the largest group of mystery writers in the U.S. and presents the Edgar Award, which is voted on by committees established for each category, in the spring in New York City. They generally sponsor a day-long symposium the day before the Edgars are awarded. There is a monthly newsletter. Local chapters vary in how much they offer. There are different levels of membership, based on published work. You do not have to be a member to be nominated for an Edgar. More on that in a minute.

Membership in the American Crime Writers' League (ACWL) is limited to published mystery writers and there are other membership requirements designed to keep the group professional. They do not give awards for mystery writing, although they do present the Ellen Nehr award for unbiased mystery reviewing. A small, fairly informal group, ACWL holds meetings, usually, at Malice Domestic and at Bouchercon.

## Getting out and Meeting Your Public
### Signings and Readings

Once your book is available, most publishers expect you to promote it by doing book-signings. Depending upon where you live and your own personality, these may be great fun or sheer torture. Even the most successful writers have had the experience of sitting all alone at a table in a bookstore and directing people to the rest-rooms. Stores don't always publicize author events, especially chains, and especially for new and unknown authors. If the signing is in your home town, you can generate some publicity yourself, but if you are on the road, this is considerably more difficult.

Don't expect your publisher to send you on tour. This is only done for authors who are already established and making a great deal of money for their publishers. Historical mysteries do not often fall into the breakout bestseller category. It may be possible to get your publisher to come up with a poster of your cover or even pay for a rental car, but don't count on it. Expect to pay your own way.

If you live in a rural area with no big population base, scheduling lots of book-signings, especially in chain bookstores, may be a waste of time and energy. Worse, if a store orders a great many more copies of your book than they sell, they will be returning most of them to the publisher the next day. Returns are not a good thing. They are an even greater disaster if you are published in mass-market paperback. Only the cover goes back. The rest of the book goes in the recycle bin. If this happens too often, it affects sales figures for your book.

So, how do you get around the obvious disadvantages of book-signings? First, if at all possible, do signings at independent bookstores, especially those that specialize in mystery. They will hand-sell a book if they know about it and like it and will try even harder if they know the author. I've met many mystery bookstore owners by attending mystery fan conventions, in particular Malice Domestic in the spring and Bouchercon in the fall. Going to conventions, getting on panels, and tooting your own horn directly to the readers is probably more cost effective in the long run than trying to do a series of book-signings, especially if you have to travel great distances to reach the bookstores.

Second, do group signings. This takes the pressure off and usually brings in bigger crowds. Signings at conventions fall into this category, but so do special occasions at bookstores—Valentine's Day, especially if there is romance in your mystery; Christmas season, Halloween, Midsummer Madness Days—and community events such as Heritage Days.

Don't forget libraries. Even small libraries frequently sponsor programs and talks. Sometimes they can offer a small honorarium but even if they are unable to, they provide the opportunity for free publicity. Newspapers are generally more willing to write up a library event than one at a bookstore. (Bookstores are expected to pay for an ad if they want publicity.) In addition, most libraries will either arrange for a local bookstore to sell your books at a signing after your talk, or if there is no bookstore in town, will agree to let you bring copies of your book to sell yourself. You can give a formal talk or a reading, hold a question-and-answer session, or do all three together, solo or as part of a panel. Choose the sort of program that suits you best.

Finally, going back to the historical mystery set in Scotland I used as an example earlier, consider the possibility of arranging a signing at a Scottish Festival. If there are no booksellers there, see if one of the clans will invite you to sell books out of their booth. Similarly, if you write about the

American Revolution or the Civil War, seek out re-enactment groups. Medieval or Renaissance setting? Check into the Society for Creative Anachronism events and the schedule of Renaissance Faires. If your sleuth knows herbs, look up gardening societies. If embroidery plays a big role in the mystery, consider craft shops and fairs. The possibilities are endless.

### Fan Conventions

If it is at all possible, start attending mystery fan conventions before your book comes out. Here you will meet potential readers. In addition, fan conventions have book rooms. This gives you a chance to meet several mystery booksellers, and after your book is available, to sign stock—any copies of your book that are left over at the end of the convention. Always ask before you do this, incidentally, although it is rare that a bookseller will say no.

Mystery fan conventions provide tables where authors can set out promotional materials. You don't need to go for the expensive stuff. Business cards or postcard-size promotional cards you print yourself will do. Or a brightly colored tri-fold brochure, which you can also do at home. Attendees will pick up anything that looks interesting. Yes, a lot of it will end up in the trash, but some will be held out long enough to place an order at Amazon.com or some other discount online bookseller's site. This isn't good for the dealers in the book room, but a sale is a sale.

One of the larger mystery conventions, Malice Domestic, is held every spring in the Washington, D.C. area. As are most mystery conventions, it is run by fans. When you register, if your mystery is going to be in print by the convention, fill out the second form for published authors. If you register early enough, this will usually earn you a place on a panel. If it is your first mystery, you will be invited to a special breakfast for those authors and be given a chance to plug your book there. In addition, you can request a book-signing and you usually have the option of scheduling a reading. Published authors write a short autobiography and send a photo for the program book. Also consider placing an ad in the program, or asking your publisher to do so. These are all good opportunities to publicize your historical mystery.

You may be asked to contribute something to the charity auction. This is not only an opportunity for good publicity for your book, it is a way to let fans get to know you. Among the most popular auction items are a signed ARC, the chance to name a character in a forthcoming book, or a theme basket. The latter come in great variety but always include a copy of the author's book together with items related to it. To publicize *How To Write Killer Historical Mysteries* a year in advance, I auctioned off the chance to be quoted here. The winner, Kim Gray, told me that her "love of historical mysteries began with the gift of one of Anne Perry's Charlotte and Thomas Pitt novels." She had always been hesitant about reading historical mysteries, thinking she wouldn't be able to relate to them, but the story and mystery were so good that she forgot she was reading a historical. That first taste made Kim "interested in finding more historical novels with females in strong roles, such as those by Dianne Day and Laurie R. King."

Malice Domestic ends with a tea party and a hat contest. If you are clever with crafts and aren't shy, decorate a hat with mystery things or those related to your historical mystery and enter the contest. By the time you leave for home, if you have taken advantage of the above opportunities for promotion, you will have made an impression on other attendees. Some of them will buy your book. If you're very, very, lucky and it qualifies, some of them may even nominate it for the following year's Agatha award (voted on by registered members) for Best First Mystery.

Bouchercon, the largest of the fan conventions, moves from region to region. As many as 2000 people may attend, including fans, writers, editors, agents, librarians, and booksellers. The award given at Bouchercon is the Anthony (both it and the convention were named for critic Anthony Boucher) but Bouchercon also provides opportunities for other organizations to present awards—the Shamus, the Barry, the Macavity, and so on. Most of the same promotional opportunities at Malice Domestic are available at Bouchercon, from panels and signings to meeting booksellers face to face.

Smaller than Bouchercon, Left Coast Crime also moves from place to place...on the West Coast. On one occasion that was the west coast of England, but it is more usual for this convention to be held in the western U.S. Self-promotion opportunities are similar to those at Malice Domestic.

There are also a number of small weekend and one-day mystery gatherings every year. Some have been around for a while: Sleuthfest, Mayhem in the Midlands, and Magna Cum Murder. Others, like the Great Manhattan [Kansas] Mystery Conclave and Murder in the Grove are more recent entries. All of them are worth attending if you can afford to travel to them. Historical mystery writers are usually in the minority at these smaller conventions, but that should guarantee you a place on a historical mystery panel. And with only one track of programming (instead of four to eight), you'll have a bigger audience.

You can find more information on conferences and conventions and the organizations that sponsor them at their websites. For a shortcut to many mystery links, go to www.cluelass.com.

## Awards

You don't have any control over being nominated for an award for your writing, but you can make sure your publisher submits your book in the proper Edgar category. If that is not done (you can check on the MWA website), you can send copies to members of the appropriate committee yourself. Edgars are given for Best Mystery, Best First Mystery, and Best Paperback Original. Several historical mysteries have been finalists in all three categories in recent years. David Liss's *A Conspiracy of Paper* won Best First Mystery in 2001. Jason Goodwin's *The Janissary Tree* won Best Mystery in 2007. Check the MWA websites (www.TheEdgars.com and www.mysterywriters.org) for more information.

Sadly, in competition with all other mystery novels, few historicals have won awards other than the Agatha, presented by Malice Domestic. The Best First Mystery Agatha went to Rosemary Stevens for *Death on a Silver Tray* in 2001, to Rhys Bowen for *Murphy's Law* in 2002, and to Jacqueline Winspear for *Maisie Dobbs* in 2004. Winspear won the Best Mystery Agatha the following year for *Birds of a Feather*. Kate Ross also won the Best Mystery Agatha, posthumously, for *The Devil in Music* in 1998, and Carolyn G. Hart took home an Agatha in 2004 for her World War II novel, *Letter from Home*.

Awards given exclusively to historical mysteries by fan conventions and other fan groups seem to appear and vanish rather rapidly. The Bruce Alexander History Mystery Award was presented at Left Coast Crime in three successive years and went to Rhys Bowen's *For the Love of Mike* in 2004, Sharan Newman's *The Witch in the Well* in 2005, and Tony Broadbent's *Spectres in the Smoke* in 2006. It was not given at Left Coast Crime 2007. The Sue Feder Macavity Award, given by MRI at Bouchercon, was presented for the first time in 2006; Jacqueline Winspear won for *Pardonable Lies*. Earlier Macavity awards, for Best First Mystery, went to Winspear for *Maisie Dobbs* in 2004 and to David Liss's *A Conspiracy of Paper* in 2001. The Herodotus Awards, presented at Bouchercon from 1999–2002 by the now-disbanded Historical Mystery Appreciation Society, is no longer awarded.

## Promotion You Can Do from Home

If you are not able to attend conventions, or are not comfortable dealing with large numbers of people (and even if you are), how else can you reach potential readers? Extensive mailing lists are available through Sisters in Crime and Mystery Writers of America, but sending out a great many pieces of mail can be expensive. If your publisher will send postcards, great. If not, think long and hard before you budget for printing and postage costs.

Postcards are the most common item sent to mailing lists, but another option is a flyer, especially if you are sending it to bookstores or libraries. If you want to mail directly to fans, however, your best bet is probably a newsletter.

### *Newsletters*

Soon after the Face Down series broke into print, I created a fan-oriented newsletter I called *Face Down Update*. Since I do attend conventions and schedule signings, I took sign-up sheets to these events and collected names and addresses of fans interested in being on my mailing list. My thinking was that I didn't want to waste postage on people who weren't going to buy my books anyway. This kept my mailing list fairly small, which may have been a mistake. The larger the number of pieces in a mailing, the cheaper both printing and postage become. Not that it is ever cheap, you understand, even if you do all the folding, stapling, and stamping yourself.

A newsletter provides a link to fans and is a promotional tool, but it also serves another function. *Face Down Update* gave me an outlet for some of the research that didn't make it into the novels, and a place to expand on historical details that did. For a number of years, I produced a newsletter of four to eight pages two or three times a year, depending on the publication dates of the hardcovers and the paperback reprints. I used the newsletter template in my word processing program, then converted into pdf format to have it printed. The finished product went out to some 300 readers, almost all of whom seemed likely to buy the new hardcover or share the newsletter with friends or their local library. When I was about to attend a convention, I had extras made to leave on the freebies table.

I no longer send out a printed newsletter. The cost became prohibitive, in particular for postage. Instead, I switched to an e-version of the newsletter and continued to send a hard copy (printed at home) only to those few fans who did not have e-mail and specifically requested it. Was this shortsighted? Is it costing me sales? I have no way of knowing, but I do know the percentage of the price of a new book that comes to me as royalties. Hard economic fact: there is no point in spending more than that to make one sale, not at this stage. Is it, for the first book of a projected series? That's something you'll have to decide for yourself.

Creating a mailing list, whether or not you intend to do many mailings, is a good idea. Keep track of fans' addresses, both snail mail and e-mail. If they've contacted you, they're interested. On the other hand, beware of becoming a spammer. Make sure everyone getting e-mail from you wants to be on your mailing list. Give them a way to opt out. As technology, especially spamkillers, continues to evolve, writers need to change with it. What works one year may not work the next. What won't change is the advantage to the writer of keeping in touch with fans.

### Your Own Domain—the Value of a Website

These days a website is the best marketing tool you can have. Acquire your own domain name if at all possible. Mine is KathyLynnEmerson.com. If .com is unavailable, you can also go with .net, .info, or .biz, or set up a site using your sleuth's name or a book title. The important thing is that people looking for information on your books can find it.

Website hosts come in all types and price ranges and many of them will also design and maintain your website. Take a look at what other historical mystery writers have done and figure out what will work best for you and your books. It may also be worthwhile to sign on with a hosting service that serves a community of writers. Many of these offer the opportunity to participate in online chats and other promotional events arranged by the webhost. Web rings are another way to link your site to other similar ones, as is the simple exchange of links with other sites. Incidentally, there is no need to pay someone to have your site appear in search engines. Any search engine worth using will find and list your site.

Should you hire a webmaster to design and maintain a website for you or do it yourself? Designing effective websites is a skill not all authors possess. It is also time-consuming to update webpages, more so if you choose to run contests. However, cost may be a factor. Good web designers don't come cheap, and you'll have hosting fees for your website whether you do it yourself or not.

The appearance of your website will probably be the deciding factor. If you want "bells and whistles" you are better off hiring someone with experience to handle the job. On the other hand, a website should be user-friendly. Many readers appreciate simple and straightforward text that doesn't take forever to download. That's easy enough to create using the software that comes with most word processing programs.

I design and maintain my own website. There is so little a writer can control once a book is in print that I refuse to relinquish this job to others. Besides, I'm frugal. I don't want to spend the money to let someone else do it, especially since that route comes with built-in lag time. I can make additions and changes simply by typing them into a file and sending it to the website—a few minutes or a few hours, depending on how extensive the updates are.

What should every writer's website have? Information on your latest book is the most important item. After that come your backlist, e-mail contact information, your schedule of appearances, biographical information, and photos. You should include reviews and perhaps an excerpt from the new book.

Contests are an option. The best way to decide if you want to run them or not is to look at those other authors hold. Usually the prize is an autographed copy of your book. Contests are a good way to attract people to your website, but you don't want them there just to enter and run. Design a contest that encourages visitors to your site to stay and take a look around—ask them to answer a question about the site, for example, in order to qualify to win in a drawing for one of your books.

A website can also provide another outlet for sharing historical information that didn't make it into your novel. Among other things, mine features "Lady Appleton's Who's Who" and excerpts from past newsletters. I also include bibliographies for both the Face Down Series and the Diana Spaulding Mysteries.

There is one negative aspect to a website. It can attract stalkers as well as fans. Be careful what personal information you include. For that matter, be careful what personal information you give out when you acquire your website in the first place. Yes, you want fans to be able to send you e-mail. Yes, you want booksellers and librarians to be able to contact you about appearances. But be sensible. Get a post office box to use for a mailing address, and don't include a map showing the location of your house or photos of your children on your bio page. Don't list your phone number.

### Other Internet Promotional Opportunities

In addition to discussion groups such as DorothyL and CrimeThru-Time, there are several other opportunities for online publicity. Do interviews with online magazines. Find lists—Renaissance mysteries, historical mysteries, mysteries with female sleuths, etc.—that your book should be on. If it isn't, introduce yourself to the webmaster by e-mail and ask to be included. Take advantage of the opportunity, when it is offered, to post comments (such as an Amazon.com "letter from the author") about your book at online bookstores. However, do *not* try to answer negative remarks in reader reviews at these sites.

The latest addition to the list of promotional opportunities is a blog. Whether or not you want to post an online diary that anyone in cyberspace can read is entirely up to you, but if you do decide to blog, keep that definition in mind. *Anyone* can read what you write. Don't give out personal information. And don't say anything about another person, especially another author, an editor, or an agent, that you wouldn't say to his or her face.

## Make Your Own Choices

When it comes to promotion, do what works best for you in getting the word out about your book. If you have panic attacks at the thought of speaking in public, let alone reading aloud from your novel, don't torture yourself by doing either. Choose other ways to reach the reading public.

## Book Two and Beyond

If you have made the decision to write more books about the same characters or if you already have a multi-book contract, then you'll want to promote your series, not just the first book, from the beginning. In some ways, a series is easier to promote than a single title, but it still takes time to build a readership. Fans have to "discover" you. Any publicity—even a bad review—is good publicity. You *can* spend your entire advance on promotional items, but to be truthful, the best means of creating a buzz about your book cannot be bought. This is word-of-mouth, when one reader recommends a book to another. How do you generate word-of-mouth? You don't. All you can do is write the best book you can, make readers aware of it, and hope they will take to it.

To write historical mysteries, especially a series of historical mysteries, you'll need to commit to the long haul, and to the fictional people and places you create. You won't be able to count on making a living at it. On the other hand, there is nothing more fulfilling than returning, time after time, to the past as you've created it…especially when you can take a host of faithful readers with you.

# Appendix–
# A Sampling of Historical Mysteries

THIS list is not intended to be comprehensive. Only historical mysteries are listed, even though some authors also write contemporary mysteries. Authors with multiple series may not have them all listed. Only the series titles are listed for extremely prolific authors. For much more complete lists of historical mystery writers and their books, visit the "library" at www.CrimeThruTime.com.

**Susan Wittig Albert** writes mysteries set in England in 1905+ and featuring Beatrix Potter and her animals. Titles: *The Tale of Hill Top Farm, The Tale of Holly How, The Tale of Cuckoo Brow Wood, The Tale of Hawthorne House*

**Stephanie Barron** writes mysteries set in Regency England, featuring the writer Jane Austen. Titles: *Jane and the Unpleasantness at Scargrove Manor, Jane and the Man of the Cloth, Jane and the Wandering Eye, Jane and the Genius of the Place, Jane and the Stillroom Maid, Jane and the Prisoner of Wool House, Jane and the Ghosts of Netley, Jane and His Lordship's Legacy, Jane and the Barque of Frailty*

**Carrie Bebris** writes mysteries set in Regency England featuring Mr. & Mrs. (Elizabeth Bennett) Darcy. Titles: *Pride and Prescience, Suspense and Sensibility, North by Northanger*

**Rhys Bowen** writes mysteries set in New York City in 1901+ featuring Molly Murphy, new Irish immigrant turned private investigator. Titles: *Murphy's Law, Death of Riley, For the Love of Mike, In Like Flynn, Oh Danny Boy, In Dublin's Fair City*

**Lillian Stewart Carl** writes short stories featuring various settings and sleuths, collected as *The Muse and Other Stories of History, Mystery and Magic*

**Barbara Cleverly** writes mysteries set in 1920s India and London featuring Joe Sandilands, Scotland Yard detective. Titles: *The Last Kashmiri*

Rose, Ragtime in Simla, The Damascened Blade, The Palace Tiger, The Bee's Kiss, Tug of War

**M.E. Cooper** writes mysteries set in 1489 Italy featuring Avisa Boylatoni, locksmith. Titles: *Key Deceptions, Key Confrontations*. She also writes mysteries set in 1862 Virginia featuring Confederate General W.W. Loring. Titles: *Uncivil Death, Uncivil Death in Norfolk*

**Jeanne M. Dams** writes mysteries set in South Bend, Indiana in 1900+ featuring Hilda Johansson, a housemaid. Titles: *Death in Lacquer Red, The Red, White, and Blue Murders, Green Grow the Victims, Silence is Golden, Crimson Snow*

**Lindsey Davis** writes mysteries set in the Roman Empire in A.D. 70+ and featuring Marcus Didius Falco, Private Informer. Titles: *The Silver Pigs, Shadows in Bronze, Venus in Copper, The Iron Hand of Mars, Poseidon's Gold, Last Act in Palmyra, Time to Depart, A Dying Light in Corduba, Three Hands in the Fountain, Two for the Lions, One Virgin Too Many, Ode to a Banker, A Body in a Bath House, The Jupiter Myth, The Accusers, Scandal Takes a Holiday, See Delphi and Die, Saturnalia*

**Paul C. Doherty** writes numerous series under several names, including the Hugh Corbett Mysteries set in England under Edward I; the Canterbury Tale Mysteries, with various detectives, set in 14th century, England; the Egyptian Mysteries featuring Amerotke, a judge, set in 1479 B.C., Egypt; the Alexander the Great Series, set in 334 B.C., Greece; the Brother Athelstan Mysteries, set in 14th-century, England; and the Mathilde of Westminster Series, set in 1308, England

**Carole Nelson Douglas** writes mysteries set in the Victorian era in various locales featuring Irene Adler, opera singer. Titles: *Good Night, Mr. Holmes, Good Morning, Irene* (apa *The Adventuress*), *Irene at Large* (apa *A Soul of Steel*), *Irene's Last Waltz* (apa *Another Scandal in Bohemia*), *Chapel Noir, Castle Rouge, Femme Fatale, Spider Dance*

**Carola Dunn** writes mysteries set in 1920s England featuring Daisy Dalrymple, journalist, and Alec Fletcher, Scotland Yard Inspector. Titles: *Death at Wentwater Court, The Winter Garden Mystery, Requiem for a Mezzo, Murder on the Flying Scotsman, Damsel in Distress, Dead in the Water, Styx and Stones, Rattle His Bones, To Davy Jones Below, The Case of the Murdered Muckraker, Mistletoe and Murder, Die Laughing, A Mourning Wedding, Fall of a Philanderer, Gunpowder Plot, The Bloody Tower*

**P.N. Elrod** writes mysteries set in 1930s Chicago featuring Jack Fleming, vampire and part-time P.I. Titles: *Bloodlist, Lifeblood, Bloodcircle, Art*

in the Blood, Fire in the Blood, Blood on the Water, A Chill in the Blood, The Dark Sleep, Lady Crymsyn, Cold Streets, A Song in the Dark

**Clayton Emery** writes short stories in two series, the Joseph Fisher Colonial American Mysteries and the Robin & Marian Mysteries. Several available to read at www.claytonemery.com/works.html.

**Kathleen Ernst** writes mysteries for children and young adults with various sleuths. Titles: *Trouble at Fort LaPointe* (1732, pre-statehood Wisconsin), *Whistler in the Dark* (1867, Colorado), *Betrayal at Cross Creek* (1775, North Carolina), *Danger at the Zoo* (1935, Ohio), *Secrets in the Hills* (1826, New Mexico), *Midnight in Lonesome Hollow* (1934, Kentucky)

**Terence Faherty** writes mysteries set in Hollywood, California in the 1940s, '50s and '60s, featuring Scott Elliott, veteran and former actor turned P.I. Titles: *Kill Me Again, Come Back Dead, Raise the Devil, In a Teapot*

**Jane Finnis** writes mysteries set in Roman Britain in A.D. 91 and featuring Aurelia Marcella, an innkeeper. Titles: *Get Out or Die, A Bitter Chill*

**Margaret Frazer** writes mysteries set in England in 1431+ and featuring Dame Frevisse, a nun. Titles: *The Novice's Tale, The Servant's Tale, The Outlaw's Tale, The Bishop's Tale, The Boy's Tale, The Murderer's Tale, The Prioress's Tale, The Maiden's Tale, The Reeve's Tale, The Squire's Tale, The Clerk's Tale, The Bastard's Tale, The Hunter's Tale, The Widow's Tale, The Sempster's Tale, The Traitor's Tale.* A second series set in 15th-century England features Joliffe, a traveling player. Titles: *A Play of Isaac, A Play of Dux Moraud, A Play of Knaves*

**Dale Furutani** writes the Samurai Mystery Trilogy, set in 1603 Japan and featuring Matsuyama Kaze, a warrior. Titles: *Death at the Crossroads, Jade Palace Vendetta, Kill the Shogun*

**Roberta Gellis** writes mysteries set in 1139 England featuring Magdalene la Bâtarde, a brothelkeeper. Titles: *A Mortal Bane, A Personal Devil, Bone of Contention, Chains of Folly.* She has also written a mystery set in Ferrara, Italy in 1502 with Lucrezia Borgia as the sleuth. Title: *Lucrezia Borgia and the Mother of Poisons*

**Hal Glatzer** writes mysteries set in the U.S. in the 1930s and '40s, featuring Katy Green, a musician. Titles: *Too Dead to Swing, A Fugue in Hell's Kitchen, The Last Full Measure*

**Alan Gordon** writes mysteries set in Europe and the Middle East in 1157+ and featuring Theophilos (Feste), a member of the Fool's Guild.

Titles: *Thirteenth Night, Jester Leaps In, A Death in the Venetian Quarter, The Widow of Jerusalem, An Antic Disposition, The Lark's Lament*

**Ed Gorman** writes mysteries set in Black River Falls, Iowa in the late 1950s, featuring Sam McCain, a lawyer and P.I., and Eleanor Whitney, a judge. Titles: *The Day the Music Died, Wake Up Little Susie, Will You Still Love Me Tomorrow?, Save the Last Dance for Me, Everybody's Somebody's Fool, Breaking Up Is Hard to Do, Fools Rush In*

**Kerry Greenwood** writes mysteries set in 1920s Australia, featuring P.I. Phryne Fisher. Titles: *Cocaine Blues, Flying Too High, Murder on the Ballarat Train, Death at Victoria Dock, The Green Mill Murder, Blood and Circuses, Ruddy Gore, Urn Burial, Raisins and Almonds, Death Before Wicket, Away with the Fairies, Murder in Montparnasse, The Castlemaine Murders, Queen of the Flowers, Death by Water*

**Carolyn Haines** writes stand-alone mysteries with various sleuths. Titles: *Blood Nimbus* (1944, Louisiana), *Penumbra* (1952, Mississippi), *Summer of the Redeemers* (1963, Mississippi), *Touched* (1926, Mississippi)

**Barbara Hambly** writes mysteries set in 1830s New Orleans and featuring Benjamin January, a free man of color. Titles: *A Free Man of Color, Fever Season, Graveyard Dust, Sold Down the River, Die Upon a Kiss, Wet Grave, Days of the Dead, Dead Water.* Another series is set in England and Europe in 1907 and features James Asher, former spy. Titles: *Those Who Hunt the Night, Traveling with the Dead*

**Lauren Haney** writes mysteries set c. 1463 B.C. on the Egyptian frontier, featuring Lt. Bak, Medjay police. Titles: *Right Hand of Amon, A Face Turned Backward, A Vile Justice, A Curse of Silence, A Place of Darkness, A Cruel Deceit, Flesh of the God, A Path of Shadows*

**Karen Harper** writes mysteries set in England in 1558+ and featuring Queen Elizabeth I. Titles: *The Poyson Garden, The Tidal Poole, The Twylight Tower, The Queene's Cure, The Thorne Maze, The Queene's Christmas, The Fyre Mirror, The Fatal Fashione, The Hooded Hawke*

**Peter Heck** writes mysteries set in the U.S. in the 1890s and featuring author Mark Twain. Titles: *Death on the Mississippi, A Connecticut Yankee in Criminal Court, The Prince and the Prosecutor, The Guilty Abroad, The Mysterious Strangler, Tom's Lawyer*

**Edward D. Hoch** writes short stories set in Connecticut in the 1920s, '30s, and '40s, featuring Dr. Sam Hawthorne. Some have been collected in *Diagnosis: Impossible: The Casebook of Dr. Sam Hawthorne* and *More Things Impossible: The Second Casebook of Dr. Sam Hawthorne*

**Maureen Jennings** writes mysteries set in 1895 Toronto and featuring William Murdoch, a police detective. Titles: *Except the Dying, Under the Dragon's Tail, Poor Tom Is Cold, Let Loose the Dogs, Night's Child, Vices of My Blood, A Journeyman to Grief*

**Laurie R. King** writes mysteries set in England and elsewhere in 1914+ and featuring Mary Russell and Sherlock Holmes. Titles: *The Beekeeper's Apprentice, A Monstrous Regiment of Women, A Letter of Mary, The Moor, O Jerusalem, Justice Hall, The Game, Locked Rooms*

**Simon Levack** writes mysteries set in Mexico in 1517+ and featuring Yaotl, slave to Montezuma's Chief Minister. Titles: *Demon of the Air, Shadow of the Lords, City of Spies*

**Gillian Linscott** writes mysteries set in pre–World War I England, featuring Nell Bray, a suffragette. Titles: *Sister Beneath the Sheet, Hanging on the Wire, Stage Fright, An Easy Day for a Lady, Crown Witness, Dead Man's Sweetheart, Dance on Blood, Absent Friends, The Perfect Daughter, Dead Man Riding, Blood on the Wood*

**David Liss** writes mysteries set in London in 1719–1722 and featuring Benjamin Weaver, pugilist turned P.I. Titles: *A Conspiracy of Paper, A Spectacle of Corruption*

**Jeffrey Marks** writes mysteries featuring General Ulysses S. Grant and set in the U.S. after the Civil War but before his presidency. Titles: *The Ambush of My Name, A Good Soldier*

**Edward Marston** writes several series in various time periods, including the Domesday Mysteries (11th-century England, featuring Ralph Delchard, soldier and Gervase Bret, lawyer); the Elizabethan Theater Mysteries, featuring Nicholas Bracewell, book holder; the Restoration England Mysteries (1688+ and featuring Christopher Redmayne, architect, and Jonathan Bale, constable); and the Railway Mysteries (1851 England, featuring Inspector Robert Colbeck)

**Miriam Grace Monfredo** writes mysteries set in Seneca Falls, New York in the 1840s, '50s, and '60s and featuring Glynis Tryon, a librarian. Titles: *Seneca Falls Inheritance, North Star Conspiracy, Blackwater Spirits, Through a Gold Eagle, The Stalking Horse, Must the Maiden Die*. A connected series, set in various locales during the Civil War, features Glynis's niece, Bronwyn Lyr, a treasury agent. Titles: *Sisters of Cain, Brothers of Cain, Children of Cain*

**Walter Mosley** writes mysteries set in Southern California between 1948 and the 1960s and featuring Easy Rawlins, World War II veteran and

P.I. Titles: *Devil in a Blue Dress, Red Death, White Butterfly, Black Betty, A Little Yellow Dog, Gone Fishin', Bad Boy Brawly Brown, Little Scarlet, Cinnamon Kiss*

**Beverle Graves Myers** writes mysteries set in 1730s Venice, featuring Tito Amato, a castrato opera singer. Titles: *Interrupted Aria, Painted Veil, Cruel Music*

**Kris Nelscott** writes mysteries set in the U.S. in the 1960s, featuring Billy "Smokey" Dalton, an unlicensed P.I. Titles: *A Dangerous Road, Smoke-Filled Rooms, Thin Walls, Stone Cribs, War at Home, Days of Rage*

**Sharan Newman** writes mysteries set in France and elsewhere in 1139+ and featuring Catherine LeVendeur. Titles: *Death Comes as Epiphany, The Devil's Door, The Wandering Arm, Strong as Death, Cursed in the Blood, The Difficult Saint, To Wear the White Cloak, Heresy, The Outcast Dove* (featuring Catherine's cousin Solomon as sleuth), *The Witch in the Well*

**Robin Paige** writes mysteries set in England in the late 19th and early 20th centuries, featuring Kate Ardleigh, a writer, and Charles Sheridan, a scientist and nobleman. Titles: *Death at Bishop's Keep, Death at Gallow's Green, Death at Daisy's Folly, Death at Devil's Bridge, Death at Rotting-dean, Death at Whitechapel, Death at Epsom Downs, Death at Dartmoor, Death at Glamis Castle, Death in Hyde Park, Death at Blenheim Palace, Death on the Lizard*

**Ann Parker** writes mysteries set in Leadville, Colorado in 1879–80 and featuring Inez Stannert, a saloonkeeper. Titles: *Silver Lies, Iron Ties*

**I.J. Parker** writes mysteries set in 11th-century Japan, featuring Sugawara no Akitada of the Ministry of Justice. Titles: *Rashomon Gate, The Hell Screen, The Dragon Scroll, Black Arrow*

**Anne Perry** writes the Thomas and Charlotte Pitt series (1881+ London), the William Monk series (1856+ England), and the WWI Quintet.

**Elizabeth Peters** writes mysteries set in late 19th-and early 20th-century Egypt, featuring Amelia Peabody Emerson, archaeologist. Titles: *Crocodile on the Sandbank, The Curse of the Pharoahs, The Mummy Case, Lion in the Valley, The Deeds of the Disturber, The Last Camel Died at Noon, The Snake, the Crocodile, and the Dog, The Hippopotamus Pool, Seeing a Large Cat, The Ape Who Guards the Balance, The Falcon at the Portal, Thunder in the Sky, The Lord of the Silent, The Golden One, Children of the Storm, Guardian of the Horizon, The Serpent on the Crown, Tomb of the Golden Bird*

**Ellis Peters** wrote the Brother Cadfael (herbalist) mysteries in novels and short stories set from 1137–1145 in England and Wales. Titles: *A Morbid Taste for Bones, One Corpse Too Many, Monk's Hood, St. Peter's Fair, The Leper of St. Giles, The Virgin in the Ice, The Sanctuary Sparrow, The Devil's Novice, Dead Man's Ransom, The Pilgrim of Hate, An Excellent Mystery, The Raven in the Foregate, The Rose Rent, The Hermit of Eyton Forest, The Confession of Brother Haluin, The Heretic's Apprentice, The Potter's Field, The Summer of the Danes, The Holy Thief, Brother Cadfael's Penance, A Rare Benedictine* (short stories)

**Amanda Quick** writes mysteries set in Regency England, featuring Lavinia Lake and Tobias March, P.I.s. Titles: *Slightly Shady, Don't Look Back, Late for the Wedding*

**S.S. Rafferty** wrote short stories about Colonial America in the 1750s, featuring Captain Jeremy Cork, a gentleman adventurer. They are collected as *Cork of the Colonies* (apa *Fatal Flourishes*)

**Mary Reed and Eric Mayer** write mysteries set in Byzantium in A.D. 525+, featuring John the Eunuch, Lord Chamberlain to the Emperor Justinian. Titles: *One for Sorrow, Two for Joy, Three for a Letter, Four for a Boy, Five for Silver, Six for Gold*

**Candace Robb** writes mysteries set in England in 1363+ and featuring Owen Archer, agent for the Archbishop of York, and his wife Lucie. Titles: *The Apothecary Rose, The Lady Chapel, The Nun's Tale, The King's Bishop, The Riddle of St. Leonard's, A Gift of Sanctuary, A Spy for the Redeemer, The Cross-Legged Knight.* A second series, featuring Dame Margaret Kerr, is set in Scotland in 1297. Titles: *A Trust Betrayed, The Fire in the Flint, A Cruel Courtship*

**David Roberts** writes mysteries set in 1930s England, featuring Lord Edward Corinth and Verity Browne, journalist. Titles: *Sweet Poison, The Bones of the Buried, Hollow Crown, Dangerous Sea, The More Deceived, A Grave Man, The Quality of Mercy*

**Lynda S. Robinson** writes mysteries set in 1329 B.C., Egypt, featuring Lord Meren, "Eyes and Ears of Pharaoh." Titles: *Murder at the Place of Anubis, Murder at the God's Gate, Murder at the Feast of Rejoicing, Eater of Souls, Drinker of Blood, Slayer of Gods*

**Caroline Roe** writes mysteries set in 14th-century Spain, featuring physician Isaac of Girona. Titles: *Remedy for Treason, Cure for a Charlatan, An Antidote for Avarice, Solace for a Sinner, A Potion for a Widow, A Draught for a Dead Man, A Poultice for a Healer, Consolation for an Exile*

**Roberta Rogow** writes mysteries set in 1880s England and featuring Rev. Charles Dodgson and Sir Arthur Conan Doyle. Titles: *The Problem of the Missing Miss, The Problem of the Missing Hoyden, The Problem of the Spiteful Spiritualist, The Problem of the Evil Editor, The Problem of the Surly Servant*

**Kate Ross** wrote four mysteries set in Regency England, featuring Julian Kestrel, a dandy. Titles: *Cut to the Quick, A Broken Vessel, Whom the Gods Love, The Devil in Music*

**Laura Joh Rowland** writes mysteries set in 17th-century Japan, featuring Sano Ichiro, "Most Honorable Investigator of Events, Situations, and People" and his wife, Reiko. Titles: *Shinju, Bundori, The Way of the Traitor, The Concubine's Tattoo, The Samurai's Wife, Black Lotus, The Pillow Book of Lady Wisteria, The Dragon King's Palace, The Perfumed Sleeve, The Assassin's Touch, The Red Crysanthemum, The Snow Empress*

**Steven Saylor** writes mysteries set in 1st century B.C. Rome, featuring Gordianus the Finder, a P.I. Titles: *Roman Blood, Arms of Nemesis, Catilina's Riddle, The Venus Throw, A Murder on the Appian Way, The House of the Vestals* (short stories), *Rubicon, Last Seen in Massilia, A Mist of Prophecies, The Judgment of Caesar, A Gladiator Dies Only Once* (short stories)

**Troy Soos** writes mysteries set from 1912 into the 1920s in various U.S. cities and featuring Mickey Rawlings, baseball player. Titles: *Murder at Fenway Park, Murder at Ebbets Field, Murder at Wrigley Field, Hunting a Detroit Tiger, The Cincinnati Red Stalkings, Hanging Curve*

**Daniel Stashower** writes mysteries set in 1897–8 New York and featuring magician Harry Houdini and his brother, Dash Hardeen. Titles: *The Dime Museum Murders, The Floating Lady Murder, The Houdini Specter*

**Marianne Wilski Strong** writes short stories that have appeared in *Alfred Hitchcock's Mystery Magazine* and *Ellery Queen's Mystery Magazine*, featuring Kleides of Athens. Recent titles include "Death at Delphi," "Death at the Theatre," and "Death at the Port"

**Victoria Thompson** writes mysteries set in 1890s New York City, featuring Sarah Brandt, a midwife, and Frank Malloy, a police detective. Titles: *Murder on Astor Place, Murder on St. Mark's Place, Murder on Gramercy Park, Murder on Washington Square, Murder on Mulberry Bend, Murder on Marble Row, Murder on Lenox Hill, Murder in Little Italy, Murder in Chinatown*

**Peter Tremayne** writes mysteries set in 7th-century Ireland, featuring Sister Fidelma, nun and dalaigh. Titles: *Absolution by Murder, Shroud for* the Archbishop, *Suffer Little Children*, *The Subtle Serpent*, *The Spider's Web*, *Valley of the Shadows*, *The Monk Who Vanished*, *Act of Mercy*, *Hemlock at Vespers* (short stories), *Our Lady of Darkness*, *Smoke in the Wind*, *The Haunted Abbot*, *Badger's Moon*, *Whispers of the Dead* (short stories), *The Leper's Bell*, *Master of Souls*

**Patricia Wynn** writes mysteries set in 1715 England, featuring Blue Satan, a highwayman, and Hester Kean. Titles: *The Birth of Blue Satan*, *The Spider's Touch*, *The Motive from the Deed*

# Selected Bibliography

## Books

Browne, Ray B. and Lawrence A. Kreiser, Jr., eds., *The Detective as Historian: History and Art in Historical Crime Fiction* (Bowling Green, OH: Bowling Green State University Popular Press, 2000)

Burgess, Michael and Jill H. Vassilakos, eds., *Murder in Retrospect: A Selective Guide to Historical Mystery Fiction* (Westport CT: Libraries Unlimited, 2005)

Grape, Jan, Dean James and Ellen Nehr, eds., *Deadly Women: The Woman Mystery Reader's Indispensable Companion* (NY: Carroll & Graf Publishers Inc., 1998)

Hodge, Jane Aiken, *The Private World of Georgette Heyer* (London: Arrow Books, 2006)

Thrall, William Flint and Addison Hibbard, *A Handbook to Literature*, Revised and Enlarged by C. Hugh Holman (NY: The Odyssey Press, 1960)

## Print Articles, Essays, and Interviews

Blos, Joan W., "The Overstuffed Sentence and Other Means for Assessing Historical Fiction for Children," *School Library Journal*, November 1985, pp. 38–39

Brainard, Dulcy, "PW Interviews: Barbara Michaels/Elizabeth Peters," *Publishers Weekly*, October 23, 1987, pp. 39–40

Coulter, Lynn, "Sky Writing: Lady of Turquoise," *Sky*, May 2003 (offprint)

Cuthbertson, Sarah, "The Fascination for Sister Fidelma" (interview with Peter Tremayne), *Solander: The Magazine of the Historical Novel Society*, v. 8, no.1 (May 2004), pp. 2–6

Cuthbertson, Sarah, "Toiling in the Trenches" (interview with Steven Saylor), *Solander: The Magazine of the Historical Novel Society*, v. 4, no. 2 (Autumn, 1998); online at www.historicalnovelsociety.org/solander

Feder, Sue, "Edith Pargeter aka Ellis Peters," Malice Domestic XVII Program Book, pp. 10–12

Gladwell, Malcolm, "Something Borrowed," *The New Yorker*, November 22, 2004; online at http://www.newyorker.com

Herbert, Rosemary, "PW Interviews: Ellis Peters," *Publishers Weekly*, August 9, 1991, pp. 40–41

Linscott, Gillian, "The View from Back There," *Mystery Readers Journal*, v. 9, n. 3, pp. 24–26

Lovesey, Peter, "Have You Tried Murder," in Sylvia Burack, ed., *Writing Mystery and Crime Fiction* (Boston: The Writer, Inc., 1985) pp. 98–102

Newman, Sharan, "Who Cares if It Really Happened?" *Mystery Readers Journal*, v. 9, n. 3, pp.30–32

Saylor, Steven, "All Roads Lead to Rome," *Mystery Readers Journal*, v. 9, n. 2, pp. 33–34

Shankland, Michael, "The Horrible Fascination" (interview with Paul Doherty), *Solander: The Magazine of the Historical Novel Society*, v. 14, n. 2 (Autumn, 2003); online at http://www.historicalnovelsociety.org/solander

Vink, Renée, "Interview with Steven Saylor," *Murder: Past Tense*, July–December 2002, pp. 18–19

## Online Articles and Interviews (used with permission)

Doherty, Paul, "The History Mystery," www.shotsmag.co.uk

Douglas, Carole Nelson, "At Home Online: Anne Perry," www.mysteryreaders.org

Lewis, Steve, "An Interview with Edward Hoch," www.mysteryfile.com/Hoch.html

Mayer, Eric, "Writing the Historical Mystery," www.myshelf.com/haveyouheard/05/writingthehistoricalmystery_article.htm (October, 2005)

Miller, Ron, "Dale Furutani's Samurai Mystery Trilogy Plumbs His Ancestry," www.thecolumnists.com/miller/miller62.htm (September 21, 2000)

Perry, Anne, "At Home Online: Peter Lovesey," www.mysteryreaders.org

Stabenow, Dana, "At Home Online: Laurie King," www.mysteryreaders.org

## Print Reviews

Adler, Dick, "Bodies Piling up in England," *Chicago Tribune*, December 25, 2005

Stasio, Marilyn, "Ghost Writers," *The New York Times*, February 5, 2006

Vicarel, Jo Ann, "Mystery," *Library Journal*, February 1, 2006

Webb, Betty, "Small Press," *Mystery Scene*, no. 93 (Winter 2006)

## Tapes and CD-ROMs

"Interview with Troy Soos," Recorded Books, 2000 (included in Recorded Books edition of *Hanging Curve*)

CD-ROM of Malice Domestic 2004 (panel on "Past Crimes in Not So Modern Times," quote from Michael Kilian)

CD-ROM of Malice Domestic 2006 (panel on "Writing the Historical Mystery," comments by Terence Faherty)

## Websites

(Quotes and other information from the following are used with permission of the owner of the domain)

http://members.aol.com/dfurutani/trilogy.html

www.carriebebris.com

www.crimethrutime.com

www.lindseydavis.co.uk

www.mysteryreaders.org

www.paulcdoherty.com

www.phrynefisher.com

www.sff.net/people/peter.heck/twain.htm

www.sharannewman.com

www.simonlevack.com

# Index

*Glamour Shots*

### About the Author

Kathy Lynn Emerson is the author of fourteen historical mysteries in two series, a collection of historical mystery short stories, three novels of historical romantic suspense, and three contemporary mysteries. She has also written assorted nonfiction, romance novels, and children's fiction. She has taught creative writing at the college level and frequently conducts workshops on "painless research" and other writing-related topics.

Emerson lives in rural Maine with her husband, and welcomes visitors and e-mail at www.KathyLynnEmerson.com.

# MORE MYSTERIES
## FROM PERSEVERANCE PRESS
☠ *For the New Golden Age* ☠

**JON L. BREEN**
**Eye of God**
ISBN 978-1-880284-89-6

**TAFFY CANNON**
ROXANNE PRESCOTT SERIES
**Guns and Roses**
*Agatha and Macavity Award
nominee, Best Novel*
ISBN 978-1-880284-34-6

**Blood Matters**
ISBN 978-1-880284-86-5

**Open Season on Lawyers**
ISBN 978-1-880284-51-3

**Paradise Lost**
ISBN 978-1-880284-80-3

**LAURA CRUM**
GAIL MCCARTHY SERIES
**Moonblind**
ISBN 978-1-880284-90-2
**Chasing Cans**
ISBN 978-1-880284-94-0

**JEANNE M. DAMS**
HILDA JOHANSSON SERIES
**Crimson Snow**
ISBN 978-1-880284-79-7
**Indigo Christmas** *(forthcoming)*
ISBN 978-1-880284-95-7

**KATHY LYNN EMERSON**
LADY APPLETON SERIES
**Face Down Below
the Banqueting House**
ISBN 978-1-880284-71-1

**Face Down Beside
St. Anne's Well**
ISBN 978-1-880284-82-7

**Face Down O'er the Border**
ISBN 978-1-880284-91-9

**ELAINE FLINN**
MOLLY DOYLE SERIES
**Deadly Vintage**
ISBN 978-1-880284-87-2
**Done to Death** *(forthcoming)*
ISBN 978-1-880284-88-9

**HAL GLATZER**
KATY GREEN SERIES
**Too Dead To Swing**
ISBN 978-1-880284-53-7

**A Fugue in Hell's Kitchen**
ISBN 978-1-880284-70-4

**The Last Full Measure**
ISBN 978-1-880284-84-1

**PATRICIA GUIVER**
DELILAH DOOLITTLE PET
DETECTIVE SERIES
**The Beastly Bloodline**
ISBN 978-1-880284-69-8

**NANCY BAKER JACOBS**
**Flash Point**
ISBN 978-1-880284-56-8

**JANET LAPIERRE**
PORT SILVA SERIES
**Baby Mine**
ISBN 978-1-880284-32-2

**Keepers**
*Shamus Award nominee,
Best Paperback Original*
ISBN 978-1-880284-44-5

**Death Duties**
ISBN 978-1-880284-74-2

**Family Business**
ISBN 978-1-880284-85-8

VALERIE S. MALMONT
TORI MIRACLE SERIES
**Death, Bones, and Stately Homes**
ISBN 978-1-880284-65-0

DENISE OSBORNE
FENG SHUI SERIES
**Evil Intentions**
ISBN 978-1-880284-77-3

LEV RAPHAEL
NICK HOFFMAN SERIES
**Tropic of Murder**
ISBN 978-1-880284-68-1

**Hot Rocks**
ISBN 978-1-880284-83-4

LORA ROBERTS
BRIDGET MONTROSE SERIES
**Another Fine Mess**
ISBN 978-1-880284-54-4

SHERLOCK HOLMES SERIES
**The Affair of the Incognito Tenant**
ISBN 978-1-880284-67-4

REBECCA ROTHENBERG
BOTANICAL SERIES
**The Tumbleweed Murders**
(completed by Taffy Cannon)
ISBN 978-1-880284-43-8

SHELLEY SINGER
JAKE SAMSON & ROSIE VICENTE SERIES
**Royal Flush**
ISBN 978-1-880284-33-9

NANCY TESLER
BIOFEEDBACK SERIES
**Slippery Slopes and Other Deadly Things**
ISBN 978-1-880284-58-2

PENNY WARNER
CONNOR WESTPHAL SERIES
**Blind Side**
ISBN 978-1-880284-42-1

**Silence Is Golden**
ISBN 978-1-880284-66-7

ERIC WRIGHT
JOE BARLEY SERIES
**The Kidnapping of Rosie Dawn**
*Barry Award, Best Paperback Original. Edgar, Ellis, and Anthony Award nominee*
ISBN 978-1-880284-40-7

*REFERENCE/ MYSTERY WRITING*

KATHY LYNN EMERSON
**How To Write Killer Historical Mysteries: The Art and Adventure of Sleuthing Through the Past**
ISBN 978-1-880284-92-6

CAROLYN WHEAT
**How To Write Killer Fiction: The Funhouse of Mystery & the Roller Coaster of Suspense**
ISBN 978-1-880284-62-9

**Available from your local bookstore or from Perseverance Press/John Daniel & Co. at (800) 662-8351 or www.danielpublishing.com/perseverance.**